SIGNAL 2018

The Third International Conference on Advances in Signal, Image and Video Processing

May 20 - 24, 2018

Nice, France

SIGNAL 2018 Editors

Antonio José Ribeiro Neves, University of Aveiro, Portugal
Laurent Fesquet, Associate Professor, TIMA laboratory, Grenoble, France
Alina Trifan, University of Aveiro, Portugal
Wilfried Uhring, Université de Strasbourg, France I

Printed from e-media with permission by:

Curran Associates, Inc.
57 Morehouse Lane
Red Hook, NY 12571

Some format issues inherent in the e-media version may also appear in this print version.

Printed by Curran Associates, Inc. (2018)

International Academy, Research, and Industry Association (IARIA)
412 Derby Way
Wilmington, DE 19810

Phone: (408) 893-6407
Fax: (408) 527-6351

petre@iaria.org

Additional copies of this publication are available from:

Curran Associates, Inc.
57 Morehouse Lane
Red Hook, NY 12571 USA
Phone: 845-758-0400
Fax: 845-758-2633
Email: curran@proceedings.com
Web: www.proceedings.com

Table of Contents

SIGNAL 2018

Foreword

The Third International Conference on Advances in Signal, Image and Video Processing (SIGNAL 2018), held between May 20 - 24, 2018 - Nice, France, continued the inaugural event considering the challenges mentioned above. Having these motivations in mind, the goal of this conference was to bring together researchers and industry and form a forum for fruitful discussions, networking, and ideas.

Signal, video and image processing constitutes the basis of communications systems. With the proliferation of portable/implantable devices, embedded signal processing became widely used, despite that most of the common users are not aware of this issue. New signal, image and video processing algorithms and methods, in the context of a growing-wide range of domains (communications, medicine, finance, education, etc.) have been proposed, developed and deployed. Moreover, since the implementation platforms experience an exponential growth in terms of their performance, many signal processing techniques are reconsidered and adapted in the framework of new applications. Having these motivations in mind, the goal of this conference was to bring together researchers and industry and form a forum for fruitful discussions, networking, and ideas.

We take here the opportunity to warmly thank all the members of the SIGNAL 2018 Technical Program Committee, as well as the numerous reviewers. The creation of such a high quality conference program would not have been possible without their involvement. We also kindly thank all the authors who dedicated much of their time and efforts to contribute to SIGNAL 2018. We truly believe that, thanks to all these efforts, the final conference program consisted of top quality contributions.

Also, this event could not have been a reality without the support of many individuals, organizations, and sponsors. We are grateful to the members of the SIGNAL 2018 organizing committee for their help in handling the logistics and for their work to make this professional meeting a success.

We hope that SIGNAL 2018 was a successful international forum for the exchange of ideas and results between academia and industry and for the promotion of progress in the field of signal processing.

We are convinced that the participants found the event useful and communications very open. We also hope that Nice provided a pleasant environment during the conference and everyone saved some time for exploring this beautiful city.

SIGNAL 2018 Chairs:

SIGNAL Steering Committee

Wilfried Uhring, Université de Strasbourg, France
G. Sahoo, BIT Mesra, Ranchi, India
Malka N. Halgamuge, University of Melbourne, Australia
Laurent Fesquet, TIMA / CNRS-Grenoble INP-UGA, France
Jérôme Gilles, San Diego State University, USA
Constantin Paleologu, Polytechnic University of Bucharest, Romania
Zhongyuan Zhao, Beijing University of Posts and Telecommunications, China
Demetrios Sampson, Curtin University, Australia
Andrea Kutics, International Christian University, Japan
Pavel Loskot, Swansea University, UK

SIGNAL 2018

Committee

SIGNAL Steering Committee

Wilfried Uhring, Université de Strasbourg, France
G. Sahoo, BIT Mesra, Ranchi, India
Malka N. Halgamuge, University of Melbourne, Australia
Laurent Fesquet, TIMA / CNRS-Grenoble INP-UGA, France
Jérôme Gilles, San Diego State University, USA
Constantin Paleologu, Polytechnic University of Bucharest, Romania
Zhongyuan Zhao, Beijing University of Posts and Telecommunications, China
Demetrios Sampson, Curtin University, Australia
Andrea Kutics, International Christian University, Japan
Pavel Loskot, Swansea University, UK

SIGNAL Industry/Research Advisory Committee

Sergey Y. Yurish, Excelera, S. L. | IFSA, Spain
Filippo Vella, National Research Council of Italy, Italy
Jai Gopal Pandey, CSIR-CEERI (Gov. of India), India
Tudor-Catalin Zorila, Toshiba Cambridge Research Laboratory, UK

SIGNAL 2018 Technical Program Committee

Waleed H. Abdulla, The University of Auckland, New Zealand
Afaq Ahmad, Sultan Qaboos University, Oman
Kiril Alexiev, Institute for Information and Communication Technologies -Bulgarian Academy of Sciences, Bulgaria
Hamada Alshaer, University of Edinburgh, UK
Cristian Anghel, Politehnica University of Bucharest, Romania / Pentalog, France
Vijayan K. Asari, University of Dayton, USA
Abdourrahmane M. Atto, University Savoie Mont Blanc, France
Nadia Baaziz, Université du Québec en Outaouais, Canada
Junaid Baber, Asian Institute of Technology, Thailand
Vesh Raj Sharma Banjade, Intel Coporation, USA
Denis Beautemps, CNRS | GIPSA-lab, France
Haithem Ben Chikha, Tunisia Polytechnic School, Tunisia
Wassim Ben Chikha, Tunisia Polytechnic School, Tunisia
Stefano Berretti, University of Florence, Italy
Silvia Biasotti, CNR - IMATI, Italy
Jacques Blanc-Talon, DGA, France
Larbi Boubchir, LIASD - University of Paris 8, France
Abdel-Ouahab Boudraa, Ecole Navale/Arts & Métiers ParisTech, France
Samia Boukir, Bordeaux INP (Bordeaux Institute of Technology), France
Salah Bourennane, Ecole Centrale de Marseille/Institut Fresnel, France
Rafael F. S. Caldeirinha, Polytechnic Institute of Leiria, Portugal

Li Liu, University Grenoble Alpes | CNRS, France
Xin Liu, University of Oulu, Finland
Yanjun Liu, Feng Chia University, Taiwan
Pavel Loskot, Swansea University, UK
Lisandro Lovisolo, Universidade do Estado do Rio de Janeiro (UERJ), Brazil
Khoa Luu, Carnegie Mellon University (CMU), USA
Baptiste Magnier, Ecole des Mines d'Alès, France
Nouri Masmoudi, National Engineering School of Sfax, Tunisia
Sylvain Meignen, University of Grenoble, France
Mahmoud Mejdoub, Sfax University, Tunisia
Karie Nickson Menza, Kabarak University, Kenya
Lyudmila Mihaylova, University of Sheffield, UK
Mario Mustra, University of Zagreb, Croatia
Mohammad Mahdi Naghsh, Isfahan University of Technology, Iran
Antal Nagy, University of Szeged, Hungary
Kianoush Nazarpour, Newcastle University, UK
Antonio J. R. Neves, University of Aveiro, Portugal
L. Gustavo Nonato, University of Sao Paulo - Sao Carlos, Brazil
Wesley Nunes Gonçalves, Federal University of Mato Grosso do Sul, Brazil
Antonio Orsino, Tampere University of Technology, Finland
Tim O'Shea, Virginia Tech University / DeepSig Inc, USA
M. Tankut Özgen, Anadolu University, Eskisehir, Turkey
Constantin Paleologu, Polytechnic University of Bucharest, Romania
Giuseppe Palestra, University of Bari, Italy
Jai Gopal Pandey, CSIR-CEERI (Gov. of India), India
Giuseppe Patane', CNR-IMATI, Italy
Danilo Pelusi, University of Teramo, Italy
Pascal Picart, Université du Maine, France
Zsolt Polgar, Technical University of Cluj Napoca, Romania
Joy Prabhakaran, International Institute of Information Technology - Bangalore, India
Surya Prakash, Indian Institute of Technology Indore, India
J. K. Rai, Amity University Uttar Pradesh, Noida, India
Mehul S. Raval,Ahmedabad University - School of Engineering and Applied Science, India
Grzegorz Redlarski, Gdansk University of Technology, Poland
Abdallah Rhattoy, Moulay Ismail University - Higher School of Technology, Morocco
Carlos Ribeiro, Instituto de Telecomunicações | Instituto Politecnico de Leiria, Portugal
Yves Rozenholc, Université Paris Descartes, France
Diego P. Ruiz-Padillo, University of Granada, Spain
G. Sahoo, BIT Mesra, Ranchi, India
Serrano Salvatore, Università di Messina, Italy
Ramiro Sámano Robles, CISTER Research Centre | ISEP - Instituto Superior de Engenharia do Porto, Portugal
Demetrios Sampson, Curtin University, Australia
Antonio José Sánchez Salmerón, Instituto de Automática e Informática Industrial | Universidad Politécnica de Valencia, Spain
Lorenzo Seidenari, University of Florence, Italy
Giuseppe Serra, University of Udine, Italy
Lakesh K. Sharma, University of Maine Cooperativ

Copyright Information

GPU-accelerated Signal Processing for Search of Pulsars

Stanislav Klimenko(1), Kira Konich(2), Igor Nikitin(3), Lialia Nikitina(3), Sergey Tyul'bashev(4)

(1) Institute of Computing for Physics and Technology,
Moscow Institute for Physics and Technology (State University), Protvino, Russia

(2) Bauhaus University, Weimar, Germany

(3) Fraunhofer Institute for Algorithms and Scientific Computing, Sankt Augustin, Germany

(4) Pushchino Radio Astronomy Observatory, Lebedev Physical Institute, Pushchino, Russia

email: stanislav.klimenko@gmail.com, kira.konycheva@uni-weimar.de,
igor.nikitin@scai.fraunhofer.de, lialia.nikitina@scai.fraunhofer.de, serg@prao.ru

***Abstract*—This short paper describes the accelerated signal processing for the search of radio pulsars recorded by Big Scanning Antenna telescope at Pushchino Radio Astronomy Observatory. Acceleration is achieved by parallelization of computations on multiprocessor systems and, especially, on Graphics Processing Units. Parallelization provides computational speeds sufficient for signal processing and pulsar detection in the observations in real-time.**

Keywords–Statistical signal processing; Big data analysis; Monitoring and control systems; Radio astronomy applications.

I. INTRODUCTION

Big Scanning Antenna (BSA) is a unique instrument used at Pushchino Radio Astronomy Observatory of Lebedev Physical Institute. This radio telescope has the structure of a phased array of size 187 m x 384 m (10 football fields, see Figure 1). It has no moving parts, consists of 16,384 half-wave dipoles located in a grid of 64 dipoles in 256 lines. The telescope performs simultaneous measurements along the meridian plane and uses the rotation of the Earth to scan the celestial sphere. The telescope has a working frequency band of 109-113 MHz. It is one of the most sensitive telescopes in the world in this frequency range. The telescope is used in a number of projects: in studying pulsars, dynamic processes in near solar and interplanetary plasma, analyzing the structure of compact radio sources, studying active galactic nuclei [1]–[3].

The signal of the radio telescope consists of 1536 channels, representing simultaneous measurements in 48 spatial directions (beams) and 32 frequency bands. Each measurement represents a stream of 32-bit numbers taken at a frequency of about 80 Hz, so the total density of the data stream from the telescope is about 4 Mbps.

A typical one-hour observation is shown in Figure 2. The image is similar to a snapshot of a night sky from an ordinary optical telescope, the difference is that here the signal is recorded in the radio range and only the sources of periodic signals are reconstructed. The typical signal level is so small that it is usually not visible directly in the observation data and is extracted from noise only by special processing algorithms.

The telescope simultaneously detects the signal in 32 frequency bands, in which the signal manifests a phase shift. The reason for this shift is the dispersion in the interstellar medium, i.e., the propagation velocity of radio waves deviates from the speed of light in a vacuum and begins to depend on the frequency. As a result, the signals in different frequency bands arrive at different time. The shift is proportional to the total propagation time of the signal, i.e., the distance to the source. Thus, the phase shift of the signal in frequency bands allows to measure the distance to the source.

Similar effects appear in Search for Extraterrestrial Intelligence (SETI), [4]–[6]. When looking for narrow band radio signals from deep space, one needs to account for Doppler drift due to the relative motion of the telescope and the signal source. Doppler drift is time dependent, since the Earth is rotating together with the telescope fixed on its surface. Also, the source of the signal is presumably located on the surface of a planet or orbits around a planet. The both effects, frequency dependent time shift in the search of pulsars and time dependent frequency shift for SETI, lead to the signal smearing over the exposition time, like shaking the camera smears the snapshot. To increase the sensitivity of detection, the both type of effects should be compensated on processing stage.

In [7] [8], we described a method of statistical accumulation, specially developed for the search for pulsar signals. The method consists in computing the integral of the form

$$corr(T, a, b) = \int df\,dt\,s(t, f)\,\Delta((t - (a + bf))/T), \quad (1)$$

where $s(t, f)$ is the signal depending on time and frequency, $\Delta()$ is the periodic delta function, T is the period, $a+bf$ is the phase shift, linearly depending on frequency. The integral over the frequency-time plane defines the functional scalar product of the measured signal with the expected waveform, i.e., periodically repeating pulses with the phase shift proportional to frequency variation. When the signal is normalized to unity, the integral represents a correlator of the signal with the expected shape. The method consists in finding the signal parameters (T, a, b) maximizing this correlator.

The reconstructed signal parameters: the period T, the common phase a and the frequency shift b represent individual characteristics of the pulsar. The period is determined by the rotation speed of the pulsar, the phase describes the profile of the pulse, the shift can be used to determine the distance to the source.

This paper is devoted to the acceleration of the processing of signals of this kind. The processing is computationally expensive and requires massive parallelization. For acceleration we use multiple Central Processing Units (CPUs), Graphics Processing Units (GPUs) and compare their performance in application to the search of pulsars.

Figure 1. BSA telescope at Pushchino Radio Astronomy Observatory. On the left: satellite view. On the right: phased array structure.

Figure 2. A typical one-hour observation. The window $21^\circ \times 15^\circ$ of the celestial sphere is shown, grayscale represents the intensity of the signal in the interval 0...15 dB. Intensity spots correspond to the sources of periodic signals, pulsars.

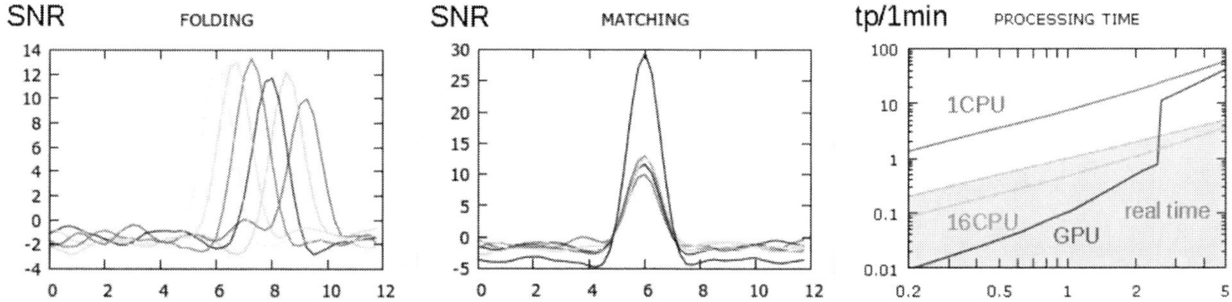

Figure 3. Signal processing algorithms. On the left: the result of folding algorithm, peaks in six frequency bands arrive at different times due to dispersion on the interstellar medium. In the center: matching algorithm collects peaks together and increases the resulting intensity. The horizontal axis represents the elapsed time, measured in data points. The vertical axis represents signal-to-noise ratio. On the right: processing time tp as a function of processing window size tw. Real time zone is marked by gray color.

Algorithm folding(T,x,y):

```
// T - probe period, x - input signal,
// y - output
// consts: np - num.datapoints,
// nf - num.freq.bands

{ int nT=(int)(np/T), nphase=(int)T;
  // loop over phase
  for(int j=0;j<nphase;j++){
    // loop over periods
    for(int i=0,n=0;i<nT;i++){
      float t=T*(i+(float)j/nphase);
      if(t<np-1){ int i0=(int)t; n++;
        // loop over freq.bands
        for(int f=0;f<nf;f++)
              y[f+nf*j]+=x[f+nf*i0];
      }
    }
// normalization
    if(n>0)for(int f=0;f<nf;f++)
              y[f+nf*j]/=sqrt(n);
  }
}
```

Algorithm matching(dp,yt,s):

```
// dp - probe dispersion parameter
// yt - input (transposed array from the prev.alg.)
// s - output signal
// max_sum, phase_max - output signal metric

{ int nphase=(int)T;
  // loop over freq.bands
  for(int f=0;f<nf;f++){
    int d0=dp*(nf-1-f),d1=nphase*f;
    int i0=d0%nphase+d1,i1=(nf*nphase-d0)%nphase;
    // loop over phase, with a jump at j=i1
    for(int j=0,k=i0;j<i1;j++,k++)s[j]+=yt[k];
    for(int j=i1,k=d1;j<nphase;j++,k++)s[j]+=yt[k];
  }
  // normalization
  for(int j=0;j<nphase;j++){ s[j]/=sqrt(nf);
    // metric evaluation
    if(s[j]>max_sum){ max_sum=s[j]; phase_max=j; }
  }
}
```

Figure 4. Signal processing algorithms.

Recently, multiprocessor architectures and GPUs have been used to accelerate the processing of astrophysical signals, also, for the search of pulsars. In particular, [9] [10] describe the implementation of Fourier Domain Acceleration Search Method, using GPU acceleration for the search of pulsars with Square Kilometre Array telescope. In [11] GPU acceleration is applied for pulsar signal processing on Goldstone Apple Valley radio telescope. In the present paper, we concentrate on the usage of multiple CPUs and GPUs for acceleration of signal processing from BSA radio telescope.

In Section II, we describe general computational aspects of signal processing algorithms used for the search of pulsars. In Section III, we present the acceleration of computation using multiprocessor systems. The obtained results are summarized in Section IV.

II. Signal Processing Algorithms

Calculating in (1) the integral over the time dt, it can be converted to the sum of the signal over the periods T, i.e., the signal folding over the trial period in each frequency band. The integral over the frequency df then corresponds to the matching of the signals in different frequency bands, taking into account the shift between the bands. The principle of the reconstruction methods is shown in Figure 3, the prototype algorithms are shown in Figure 4.

The processing is a multiple summation of data segments in different combinations, requiring extremely intensive computations. The estimates of [7], [8] show the computational complexity of the order $O(N_f N_b N_p^2 \log(T_1/T_0))$, where N_f is the number of frequency bands, N_b is the number of observation beams, N_p is the number of data points taken in the analysis, $T_{0,1}$ is the search limits for the period. Previously, to process one-hour observation in less than one hour, the coarser, shortened data consisting of 6 frequency bands with a time resolution of 0.1 sec have been considered. In this paper, we investigate the possibility of processing complete data in real time, which requires additional acceleration of processing methods. For this purpose, we use a massive parallelization of computations.

III. Acceleration of Signal Processing

At first, the full one-hour data occupying 1.8 GB are cut into segments, containing observations in every beam in a given time window tw, which we consider as a parameter in our study. In order not to loose the signals spreaded across the cut borders, we use an additional collocated segmentation, shifted by $tw/2$. This doubles the total processing time, but guarantees the reconstruction of all signals. The optimal value for tw is related with the size of the beam and constitutes 3-5min. Reducing the window size is possible, but leads to sensitivity loss, i.e., reducing tw by factor k reduces the sensitivity by factor $k^{1/2}$. An important aspect is a capability of the algorithms to perform in real-time, i.e., to have processing time not more than the time of data capture.

After the data splitting, each segment is processed in parallel, using the maximum number of available processors. We have experimented with Intel 3GHz CPUs vs 0.812TFLOPS Nvidia Quadro K620 GPU. The processing time tp as a function of window size tw is shown on Figure 3 right. Real time zone corresponds to $tp \leq tw$ and is displayed on this figure in gray. One CPU cannot reach the real time zone for all values of tw. When using 16 CPUs, the required real-time reconstruction speed is achieved for all tw. For the variant with collocated segmentation, 32 CPUs should be used.

At large tw, processing on GPU brings only insignificant advantage over 1CPU variant and is also located outside the real time zone. At about $tw = 2.5$ min, the data in processing window start to match shared memory of the device, bringing performance boost by a factor 15. Then, GPU outperforms 16CPU variant and is located completely in real time zone.

IV. Conclusion and Future Work

The accelerated signal processing for the search of radio pulsars recorded by Big Scanning Antenna telescope at Pushchino Radio Astronomy Observatory has been presented. For this purpose the parallelization of computations on multiprocessor systems has been implemented. Typically, 16 CPU systems are sufficient for real-time processing of raw data from the radio telescope. The best results are achieved with GPU processing, which ensures the maximum degree of parallelization of computations. Here, below the threshold $tw < 2.5$ min, the data in processing window match shared memory of the device, providing a significant 15x performance boost. This allows to reach the computational speed, sufficient with a margin to process the signal from the radio telescope and to reconstruct pulsars from the observations in real-time.

Our further plans include the development of efficient algorithms, separating near Earth Radio Frequency Interference (RFI) from deep space signals. Interference from terrestrial and near-Earth radio sources poses a serious problem for detection of weak radio signals. In practice, the telescope receives high gain signal from the main beam and low gain signals from all possible directions. Low gain signals are not correlated with the position of the main beam and penetrate the telescope through the side lobes. On the other hand, the near-Earth RFI has a significantly higher intensity than the deep space signals. Therefore, at the output of the telescope, near-Earth RFI can overexpose the intensity of the sought-for signals. The main idea for filtering algorithms is to use correlation between different beams to select those signals highly localized on celestial sphere, i.e., deep space signals.

REFERENCES

[1] V. M. Malofeev, "Measurements of the pulse energy of weak pulsars at frequencies of 61 and 102 MHz", Astronomy Letters, vol. 19, 1993, pp. 138-142.

[2] V. M. Malofeev and O. I. Malov, "Detection of Geminga as a radiopulsar", Nature, vol. 389, 1997, pp. 697-699.

[3] S. A. Tyul'bashev, "A study of radio sources using interplanetary scintillations at 111 MHz: core-dominated sources", Astronomy Reports, vol. 53, 2009, pp. 19-29.

[4] J. Welch et al., "The Allen Telescope Array: The First Widefield, Panchromatic, Snapshot Radio Camera for Radio Astronomy and SETI", Proceedings of the IEEE, vol. 97/8, 2009, pp. 1438-1447.

[5] A. P. V. Siemion et al., "A 1.1 to 1.9 GHz SETI Survey of the Kepler Field: I. A Search for Narrow-band Emission from Select Targets", The Astrophysical Journal, vol. 767, 2013, pp. 94-107.

[6] A. P. V. Siemion et al., "Searching for Extraterrestrial Intelligence with the Square Kilometre Array", Proceedings of Science AASKA14, 2015, p. 116.

[7] K. Konich, I. Nikitin, S. Klimenko, V. Malofeev, S. Tyulbashev, "Radio Astronomical Monitoring in Virtual Environment", Procedia Computer Science, vol. 66, 2015, pp. 592-601.

[8] S. Klimenko et al., "Methods of registration of weak radio signals", Lecture Notes in Computer Science, vol. 10220, 2017, pp. 47-63.

[9] S. Dimoudi, W. Armour, "Pulsar Acceleration Searches on the GPU for the Square Kilometre Array", 2015, arXiv:1511.07343.

[10] K. Adamek, S. Dimoudi, M. Giles, W. Armour, "Improved Acceleration of the GPU Fourier Domain Acceleration Search Algorithm", 2017, arXiv:1711.10855.

[11] G. Jones, R. Shannon, "A Joint Radio Gamma-ray Variability Study of the Crab Pulsar", in: High-Energy Emission from Pulsars and their Systems, Proceedings of the Asrophysics and Space Science, Springer 2011, pp. 213-217.

An End-to-End Traffic Vision and Counting System Using Computer Vision and Machine Learning: The Challenges in Real-Time Processing

Haiyan Wang, Mehran Mazari, Mohammad Pourhomayoun
Computer Science Department
California State University Los Angeles
Los Angeles, USA
Email: mpourho@calstatela.edu

Hunter Owens
Data Science Federation
City of Los Angeles
Los Angeles, USA
Email: hunter.owens@lacity.org

Janna Smith
Department of Transportation
City of Los Angeles
Los Angeles, USA
Email: janna.smith@lacity.org

William Chernicoff
Toyota Mobility Foundation
Washington DC, USA
Email: william.chernicoff@toyota.com

Abstract— **The goal of this research is to design and develop an end-to-end system based on computer vision and machine learning to monitor, count, and manage traffic. The end goal of this study is to make our urban transportation safer for our people, especially for pedestrians and bicyclists, who are the most vulnerable components of traffic collisions. Several methods have been proposed for traffic vision, particularly for pedestrian recognition. However, when we want to implement it in real-time in the scale of a large city like Los Angles, and on live video streams captured by regular traffic cameras, we have to deal with many challenges. This paper introduces the main challenges in traffic vision in practice, and proposes an effective end-to-end system for traffic vision, detection, tracking, and counting to address the challenges.**

Keywords - Computer Vision; Machine Learning; Kalman Filter; Object Detection.

I. Introduction and Motivation

More than 50% of the world's population now live in urban areas. By 2050, 66% of the world's population is projected to be urban [1][2]. As urban populations rise, it is essential for city planners and designers to focus more on designing smart cities and addressing the main challenges such as traffic issues, and the impacts of increased vehicle use.

According to the U.S. Department of Transportation (USDOT), the number of traffic fatalities has increased by nearly 6% in 2016 [3]. The city of Los Angeles has one of the highest rates of traffic death among large U.S. cities. Every year, more than 200 people die in traffic accidents only in the city of Los Angeles. The most vulnerable components of the traffic collisions are pedestrians and bicyclists (accounted for almost half of the fatalities). Thus, it is essential to develop intelligent transportation systems, and human-centered traffic approaches to protect our pedestrians and bicyclists and ensure that they can travel safely, efficiently, and comfortably to their destinations.

The goal of this study is to design and develop an end-to-end system based on computer vision and machine learning to monitor, track, count, and manage traffic, particularly to monitor and count pedestrians and bicyclists in real-time.

Traffic monitoring has become a very popular and important field of research and study in the past couple of years. Several methods have been proposed for traffic vision, particularly for pedestrian detection [4][5]. However, when we want to do it in practice, in real-time on video streams captured by regular traffic cameras, and when we want to implement it in the scale of a large city, it will be very different from lab settings and we have to deal with many challenges.

This paper particularly introduces the main practical challenges in traffic vision, and proposes an effective end-to-end system for traffic vision, detection, tracking, and counting, and addresses the main challenges in this field.

II. Practical Challenges in Traffic Vision

Here are some of the main challenges and difficulties that a traffic vision system may face:

- Poor quality of videos because of camera low resolution, light conditions, dirty or unadjusted lens, or weather conditions.
- Dealing with stretched, convex, or squeezed videos collected by traffic cameras and wide-angle lenses.
- Undesired angle, location, and direction of the camera.
- Camera vibration and shake because of wind or the cars passing by.
- Light distortion at night by passing cars.
- Inconsistent light change during the day time and shadow effect.
- Moving or stationary objects that may block the target view.

Figure 1 illustrates some examples of difficult situations. In Figure 1-(a), the pedestrian is partially visible. The view is blocked by the wall. In Figure 1-(b) the light condition is poor and inconsistent, it is even difficult to detect the pedestrian with human eye. The video is stretched and convex (as we see, the curb line in the left is completely converted to a curve). In Figure 1-(c), the pedestrian is hardly visible because of extreme shadow and inconsistent light.

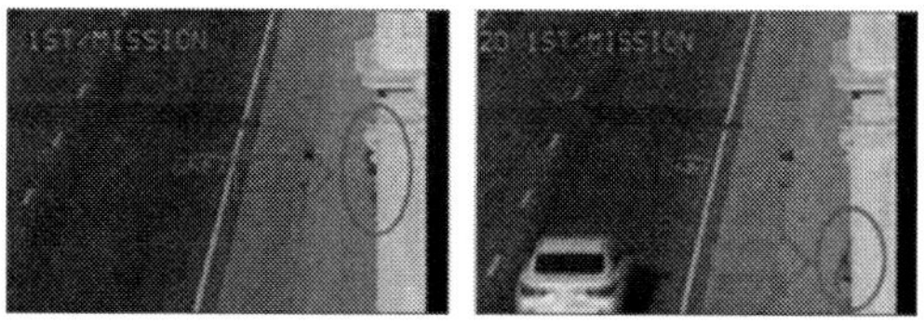

(a)

(b)

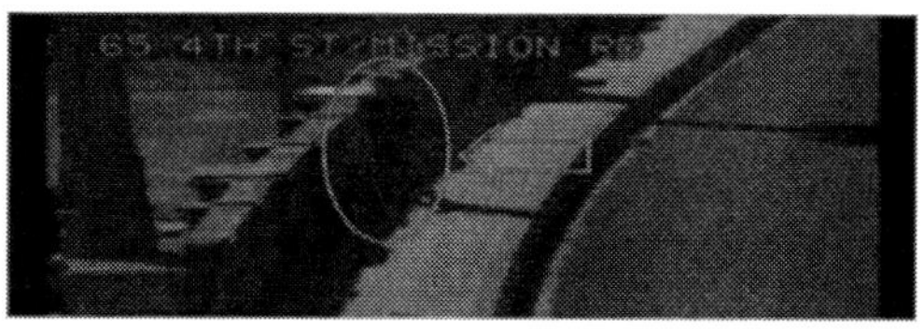

(c)

Figure 1. Examples of difficult situations: (a) Undesired location and direction of camera, and also camera vibration; (b) Light condition is poor and inconsistent, also the video is stretched and convex; (c) Extreme shadow, light change during the day time, inconsistent lighting.

III. System Architecture and Method

We have developed an end-to-end system including a series of image/video processing, computer vision algorithms, Machine Learning, and optimal state estimator algorithms that receive video streams in real-time, and monitor, recognize, track, and count pedestrians and cyclists in the video. The next sections describe the 3 main parts of the system: 1) raw video processing, 2) feature engineering and Machine Learning for object detection, and 3) trajectory prediction for traffic tracking and counting.

A. Video Processing

Figure 2 shows the system architecture. The first step in an end-to-end traffic vision system is raw video preprocessing, which includes a series of standard algorithms for quality enhancement, and brightness and contrast adjustment. In the case of wide-angle lenses that may make the image convex, we can also use correction algorithms to convert the video back to more natural view.

The next step in our system is background estimation and subtraction (we can also call it foreground detection or moving object detection). In this concept, any moving object is considered as foreground, and any stationary object in a period of time (i.e., an object with fixed location in a number of sequential frames) is considered as background. We have tried several effective algorithms for background estimation/subtraction including frame differencing, mean filter, running Gaussian average, and mixture of Gaussian modeling (MOG) [6][7]. It turned out that mixture of Gaussian modeling (MOG), and also mean filtering achieved the best results for background subtraction. Figure 3 shows the results of background subtraction (i.e., moving object detection) based on mean filtering.

It is important to notice that the background continuously changes during the day-time because the sunlight direction and intensity changes. Figure 4 shows the estimated background of a video captured by a traffic camera at 7:06AM and another time at 7:19AM. As we see, the background has significantly changed in only 13 minutes. Thus, we need to continuously estimate and update the

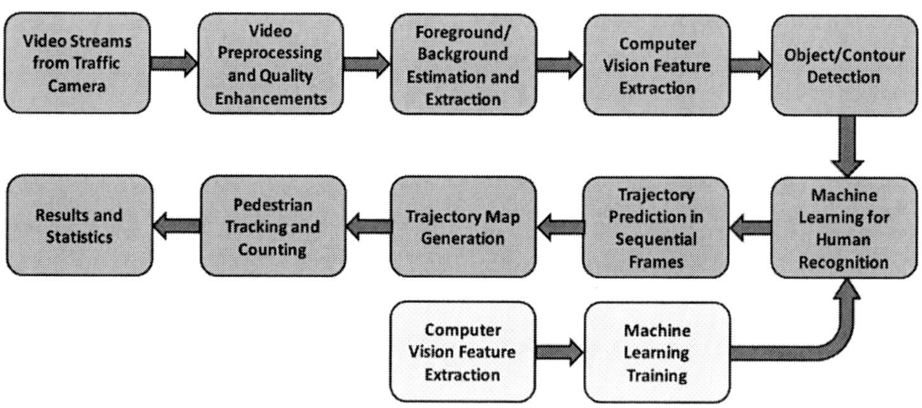

Figure 2. End-to-end system architecture.

background to always have the best background subtraction performance.

We have to notice that background removal not only improves the performance and accuracy of object recognition algorithm (i.e., the next step, which is machine learning algorithm), but also significantly reduces the computational load of the object recognition algorithm by reducing the size of the area of interest. This will be even more important when we want to use computationally expensive machine learning algorithms such as Convolutional Neural Networks (ConvNet also known as CNN) [13].

(a)

(b)

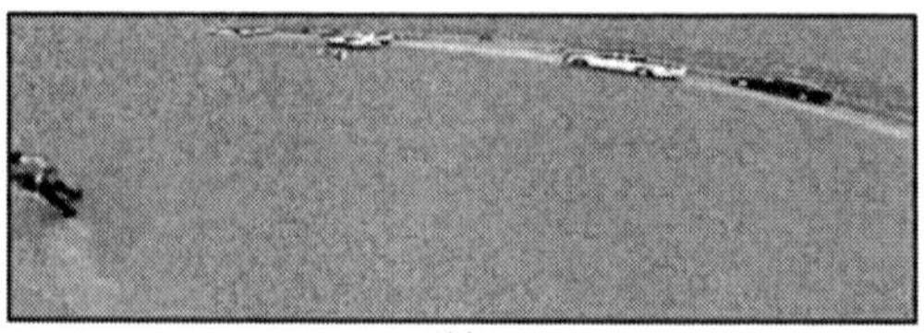

(c)

Figure 3. Background subtraction: (a) Original video frame, (b) Estimated background, (c) Moving objects after background subtraction.

Figure 4. Background change in only 13 minutes.

B. *Machine Learning for Object Detection*

The next step is to extract and select the best set of computer vision features that can be used in machine learning algorithms for object detection. Depending on the type of machine learning algorithm, this step may include feature extraction, feature selection, and/or dimensionality reduction. We have tried many different types of features and machine learning algorithms for object recognition.

One of the most effective and popular features are Histogram of Oriented Gradient (HOG) features [8] that along with SVM classifier can form an effective method for pedestrian recognition [8]. HOG is a feature descriptor that counts occurrences of gradient orientation in localized portions of an image [8]. It has been proven to be one of the most effective hand-made features that can be used for object recognition.

We have also tried deep learning methods, particularly the Convolutional Neural Networks (ConvNet) including R-CNN (Region-based Convolutional Network), and YOLO (You Only Look Once) algorithms [9][10][11]. A big advantage of ConvNet methods compared to other classic machine learning algorithms is that there is no need to generate and use hand-made features for ConvNet. The algorithm automatically learns to generate the best set of convolutional features that can best represent the image. However, ConvNet is computationally expensive and sometimes very difficult to run in real-time on high-frame-rate videos. In addition, when the training dataset is not large enough, it is usually hard to train a deep neural network. In this case, *Transfer Learning* methods that take advantage of a pre-trained neural network model on another dataset can be very helpful to ease and expedite the training stage.

Figure 5-(a) shows our pedestrian detection results using HOG features and SVM classifier. Figure 5-(b) shows our results using YOLO algorithm.

(a)

(b)

Figure 5. Pedestrian detection using machine learning algorithms. (a) using HOG features and SVM classifier, (b) using YOLO.

C. Trajectory Prediction for Traffic Tracking and Counting

After detecting a target object (e.g., a pedestrian or bicyclist) in several sequential frames, we use *Optimal State Estimator* to estimate the *Trajectory* of each target object. Since several objects may exist in each frame at a time (e.g., several pedestrians walking together in same direction or different directions), it is essential to estimate the trajectory of each object individually.

To this end, we use Kalman Filter [12] as an optimal state estimator to predict the next location of the object and estimate the trajectory of the object over time. This allows us to track each object individually during the video. For example, suppose that we want to track a pedestrian. We use Kalman filter to predict the next location of the pedestrian in next frame based on its previous locations and walking pace. Then, after receiving the next frame, we compare our prediction with the actual pedestrian detected in next frame. This comparison tells us if this pedestrian was the same person in previous frame, or it is a new one. If the predicted location and actual location match, we consider this pedestrian as previous one, and continue completing the trajectory of this pedestrian (see Figure 6). Using this approach, we can build a trajectory map including individual trajectories for all pedestrians in the video, and then track each pedestrian from the first frame he enters until the last frame when he moves out.

Every time we detect a pedestrian whose location does not match to any of the previously predicted locations (i.e., it does not locate on any of the existing estimated trajectories), we consider that person as a new pedestrian and consequently, increment the pedestrian counter. This will allow us to track and count each pedestrian everywhere in the video, and avoid double counting them in sequential frames.

Figure 6. Location prediction and Trajectory estimation.

IV. CONCLUSION

The city of Los Angeles has one of the highest rates of traffic death among large U.S. cities. Fortunately, the city has launched the *Vision Zero* initiative as a strategy and commitment to reduce traffic fatalities. The main goal of LA's Vision Zero is to eliminate all traffic fatalities by 2025. Since the most vulnerable components of traffic accidents are pedestrians and bicyclists, it is essential to develop intelligent transportation systems, and human-centered traffic approaches to protect pedestrians and bicyclists. This paper introduced an effective end-to-end system based on computer vision and machine learning to detect, monitor, track, and count pedestrians and bicyclists in real-time. This approach particularly enables us to recognize and monitor busy intersections that are prone to traffic accidents, and allows us to control and manage traffic in those intersections to protect our pedestrians and bicyclists.

The California State University Los Angeles in partnership with the Los Angeles Department of Transportation (LADOT), the City of Los Angeles' Data Science Federation, and Toyota Mobility Foundation has developed this effective and scalable system to detect, monitor, track, and count pedestrians and bicyclists in real-time. This system is potentially scalable to the 56,000 miles of streets in Los Angeles. Despite of many practical challenges (mentioned in Section II), the developed system works very well with the existing regular traffic cameras and therefore, there is no need to install any special or new cameras for this purpose. This system will help to increase safety and traffic flow through better traffic management and planning. This would be transferrable to other cities and municipalities as well. Figure 7 shows some of the results for pedestrian and bicyclist detection, tracking, and counting on real video streams captured by traffic cameras in Los Angeles.

(a) (b)

Figure 7. System results on real-time traffic video streams: (a) Bicyclist tracking and counting, (b) Pedestrian tracking and counting.

ACKNOWLEDGMENT

The authors would like to appreciate Toyota Mobility Foundation for supporting this research. The authors would like to appreciate LADOT, City of LA, and ITA Data Science Federation for valuable help and support.

REFERENCES

[1] World Urbanization Prospects, UN-Department of Economic and Social Affairs.

[2] Unicef, Urban World, www.unicef.org/sowc2012/urbanmap.

[3] USDOT, https://www.nhtsa.gov/press-releases/usdot-releases-2016-fatal-traffic-crash-data.

[4] P. Dollar, C. Wojek, B. Schiele, and P. Perona, "Pedestrian Detection: An Evaluation of the State of the Art," in IEEE Trans. on Pattern Analysis and Machine Intelligence, 2012.

[5] Benenson R., et al. "Ten Years of Pedestrian Detection, What Have We Learned?" ECCV, Springer, 2015.

[6] M. Piccardi, "Background subtraction techniques: a review", IEEE Int. Conf. on Systems, Man and Cybernetics, 2004.

[7] T. Bouwmans, F. El Baf, and B. Vachon, "Background Modeling using Mixture of Gaussians for Foreground Detection – A Survey". Recent Patents on Computer Science, 2008.

[8] N. Dalal and B. Triggs, "Histograms of oriented gradients for human detection," IEEE Computer Society Conference on Computer Vision and Pattern Recognition, 2005.

[9] R. Girshick, "Fast R-CNN," IEEE International Conference on Computer Vision (ICCV), 2015.

[10] S. Ren, et al., "Faster R-CNN: Towards Real-Time Object Detection with Region Proposal Networks," IEEE Trans. on Pattern Analysis and Machine Intelligence, 2017.

[11] J. Redmon, S. Divvala, R. Girshick, and A. Farhadi, "You Only Look Once: Unified, Real-Time Object Detection," IEEE Conf. on Computer Vision and Pattern Recognition, 2016.

[12] P. Zarchan and H. Musoff, "Fundamentals of Kalman Filtering: A Practical Approach", ISBN 978-1-56347-455-2, 2000.

[13] Alex Krizhevsky, Ilya Sutskever, and Geoffrey E. Hinton, "ImageNet Classification with Deep Convolutional Neural Networks", NIPS 2012.

FPGA Based Disparity Value Estimation

Celal GÜVENDİK
Vestel Elektronik San. ve Tic. A.Ş.
R&D Department
Manisa, Turkey
email:ceguvendik@hotmail.com

Özgür TAMER
Electrical and Electronics Eng. Dept.
Dokuz Eylul University
Izmir, Turkey
email:ozgur.tamer@deu.edu.tr

Abstract- **Depth map of an image provides information about the distance of the objects in the image to the stereoscopic camera. This information is widely employed in three dimensional visualization of stereoscopic images. Depth map of an image can be evaluated by calculating the disparity values of objects in the image. Disparity is the planar difference between corresponding points in an image pair, captured by a stereoscopic camera. In this work, we propose a fast and accurate method for evaluating the disparity values of images captured by a digital stereoscopic camera system. The stereovision system, evaluating the disparity values, runs on a field programmable gate array chip and uses an off the shelf stereo camera module to capture stereo images. The disparity values, evaluated by the system, show good match with the theoretical values.**

***Keywords:** Computer stereovision; stereoscopic camera; disparity; depth map; image segmentation; FPGA.*

I. INTRODUCTION

The ability of the human eye to see in three dimensions and judge the distance of an object is called depth perception [1]. Creating a virtual depth perception by using stereoscopic images has been studied even in the first years of photography. Digital images captured by a stereo camera system can be used to estimate the corresponding depths of objects in the images. This process is called depth map generation and it has become a popular research area in recent years with the development of computers capable of processing digital images in real time [2]. The application areas of evaluating depth information from a stereoscopic image cover a wide range, from movie industry to smart surveillance systems, even smart robots and the video games. Depth maps help us to identify the distance of any point in the image to the camera.

Several methods have been proposed to acquire the depth information of an image including stereo with two or more cameras, triangulating light stripers, millimeter wavelength radar, and scanning and flash Light Detection And Ranging (LIDAR). Radar and Lidar use the time of flight information of an electromagnetic pulse or a laser pulse to estimate the distance of an object to the observation point. Generally, they are used in combination with a camera to evaluate a depth map of an image. Triangulating light stripers project laser or visible light stripes on objects and the shape and the distance of the object is estimated according to the deformation of the stripe [3].

Most widely used method for depth map generation is to employ stereo camera pairs. A stereo camera pair consists of two identical cameras in a line. Construction of depth map using a stereo camera is based on finding pixels corresponding to the identical objects in the images captured by both cameras and evaluating the distance based on the difference of the location of the objects. This difference is called the disparity and it is given in more detail in Section 2.

An automatic depth map estimation technique from a single input image has been proposed by Battiato [2]. Their method is based on first classifying digital images as indoor, outdoor with geometric elements or outdoor without geometric elements and estimating the depth map. They first detect vanishing lines in an image and characterize the depth gradients, which are assigned according to these lines. Holzzman and Hochgatterer presented a solution for mobile devices with a single camera [4]. They use multiple images and the inertial sensors of the phone to generate the depth map. Aldavert and colleagues presented a stereo camera based method to align obstacle maps and matches between features in the stereo image pairs [5]. They use Gauss-Newton algorithm to evaluate the relation and the geometry of the corresponding map. Fua proposed a parallel algorithm for stereoscopic depth map generation [6]. His technique used correlation to calculate the sparse disparity values of pixels. Then these values are interpolated and a dense depth map is evaluated. The performance of the algorithm is significant. A super resolution depth map generation technique assisted by a stereo vision system has been proposed by Yang et. al. [7]. They use a low-resolution depth map as input, we recover a high-resolution depth map and color stereo image pair to evaluate a high-resolution depth map for the corresponding image. A Kinect® sensor and a stereo camera based depth map estimation system is proposed by the same research group [8]. In this method, they employed a kinect sensor instead of a low resolution depth map to acquire a high resolution depth map. The system proposed by Meier et al. produces disparity maps and optical flow field at 127 fps and 376x240 pixels resolution based on block matching [9]. Their system focuses on evaluating the velocity of Micro Aerial Vehicles (MAVs) for a robust operation of navigation control loops which makes estimation speed a critical parameter. Another method using FPGA is proposed by Wang et. al. [10]. Their system gives the user to adjust the system according to the image resolution, disparity range and parallelism degree for optimization of the performance. Results are superior according to the comparison tables presented in the article.

In this paper, an FPGA based stereovision technique is employed to evaluate the disparity value of an object in a scene. While evaluating the disparity value, the geometrical and computational parameters of a stereovision system are also examined. The most appropriate disparity values are chosen from possible disparities. By employing the camera system parameters with these disparit values, all the objects at a certain distance in a scene can be segmented. The proposed stereo vision system works on the Digilent's Genesys® board which includes a Virtex® 5 FPGA by Xilinx corporation. The Digilent® Vmod® Cam is used as the stereo camera while the display is a generic computer screen with an HDMI interface.

This paper is organized as follows. A brief introduction about disparity techniques is presented in Section II and FPGA implementation of the proposed method is introduced in Section III. Experimental results of the implemented hardware on the built testbed are presented in Section VI and the results are concluded in Section V.

II. MATERIALS AND METHODS

Disparity can be determined as the dissimilarity of the right and left images that are acquired by a stereo camera system [11]. Each camera of the stereo system captures the same view from a different angle of view as presented in Figure 1. Parameters x and x' in Figure 1 are the distance between points in image plane corresponding to the same scene point three dimensional and their camera center. B is the baseline of the stereo camera and f is the focal length of camera [11]. Disparity is defined as;

$$d = x - x' = \frac{Bf}{Z} \qquad (1)$$

Here, d is the disparity, B is the baseline, f is the focal length and the Z is the distance from camera to object captured. Thus, the disparity of a point in a scene is inversely proportional to the difference in distance of corresponding image points and their camera centers. By using this information, the depth of all pixels in a stereoscopic image can be found.

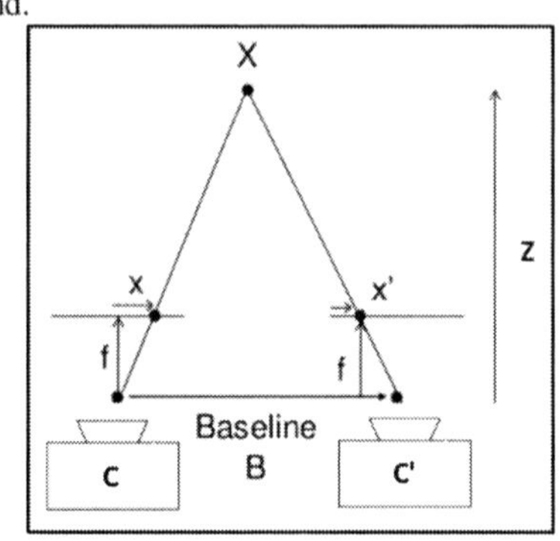

Figure 1. The relation between disparity (x-x'), baseline (B), focal length (f) and the distance (Z) between camera and the object "X"

The scene can be segmented according to the depth information by using stereo cameras. Objects with similar distances with the camera will be segmented separately from the rest of the image.

A. *FPGA Implementation*

The hardware is implemented using Verilog HDL on Xilinx® ISE 14.5 and implemented on Xilinx® Virtex-5® XC5VLX50T FPGA chip. The FPGA development board is GenesysTM and the stereo camera board is VmodCAMTM. Both of them have the Digilent brand [12] and [13].

In Figure 2, the general structure of the implemented hardware is given as a block diagram. The first block is the camera driver block. The camera board has two independent cameras that are integrated. The frames from left and the right cameras are buffered in the block RAMs.

The second block is the Disparity Map calculator block. In this block, the frames are stored as the left and the right images in the block RAMs. The first block is used to generate the disparity map with the disparity value that is given externally. The generated disparity map is buffered in the block RAM. The third block is the clock generator, which generates necessary clocks for the other blocks by using the 100 MHz system clock [14].

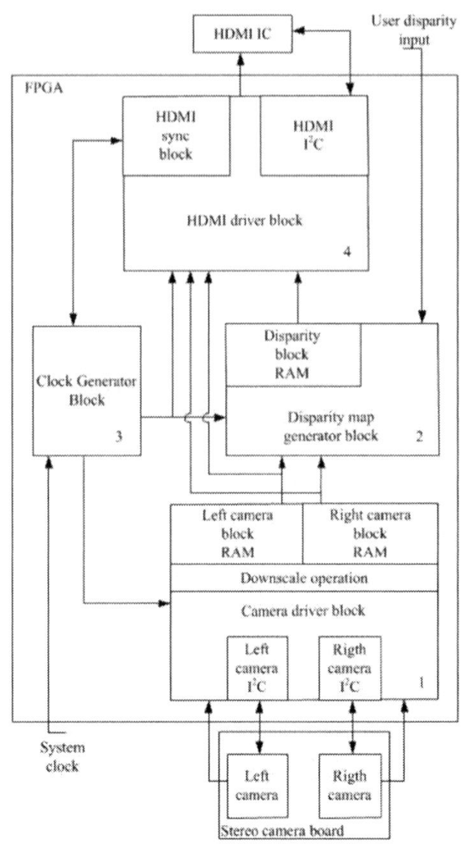

Figure 2. General Structure of hardware

The last block works as the HDMI driver. This block initializes the HDMI transmitter IC and sends the contents of left camera data, right camera data and the disparity map to the HDMI IC. This block also has a pixel clock and digital video synchronous signal generator to drive the HDMI chip. With the help of this block instant test results are viewed.

B. *Disparity Map Generator Block*

The aim in this block is to provide that the objects in different distance from cameras can be segmented by using stereovision with the disparity information.

The disparity map is generated by keeping one of the frames constant, and shifting the other as much as the given value horizontally. After the shifting operation, the images are subtracted from each other and these subtraction values are stored. This difference frame is the disparity map of the scene for the given disparity value. To calculate the disparities, right image frame is shifted vertically as the value of the disparity register in hardware.

C. *Disparity Value EvaluatiOn*

To evaluate the disparity value of an object located at a certain distance a test bed is built and some standard test objects are manufactured. Figure 3(a) and 3(b) shows the test bed and the test objects, respectively (in B, the ruler is 30 cm). Here, background of the test bed is made up of white fabric to make the objects visible.

In Figure 4(a),(b), the test setup is shown;

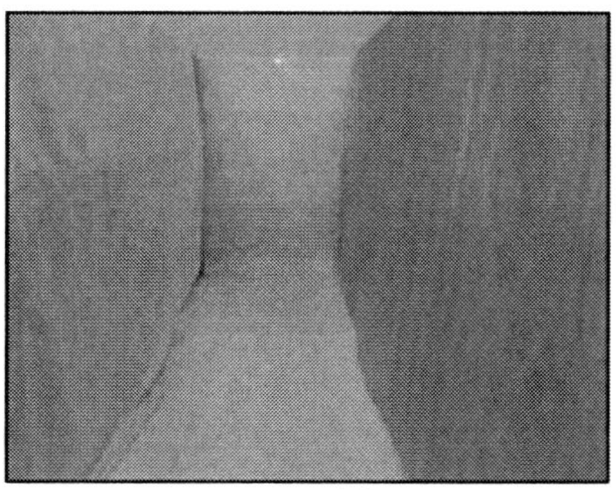

(a)

(b)

Figure 3. The test bed(a) and the test objects (b)

During the tests, these objects are positioned at several distances (only result for one meter is presented in this work) from the cameras. Another variable to be evaluated during the experiment is the disparity value, which is entered manually during calibration process. Several experiments were performed with different disparity values at a fixed distance to validate the disparity value. The results are displayed on the LCD screen located at the side of the testbed.

(a)

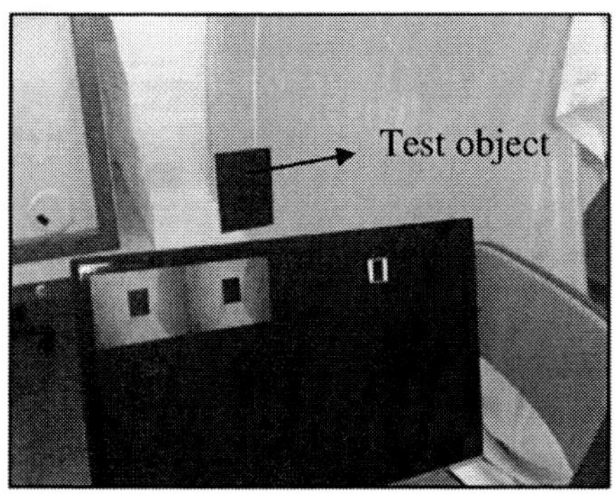

(b)

Figure 4. Stereo camera and FPGA development board in (a), and disparity demonstration in (b)

The rectangular object is positioned at 1 meter from the stereo camera. Firstly, the registers for the disparity is zero so; the result stream is not at the correct disparity level. This case can be observed in Figure 5(a) by observing the white pixels around the rectangular object on the screen. Each white pixel means that the corresponding pixels do not match and difference is high.

The next operation is to find the correct disparity level of the object at one meter from the cameras. By using equation (1), it can be calculated that the disparity value of (0010110)2=(22)10 is the appropriate value for one meter distance. In Figure 6, it can be seen that the slide switch values are set to the appropriate disparity value evaluated theoretically.

As seen in Figure 6, if the disparity value is set to the correct value for the object distance, the left and the right images of the object almost overlap totally in the disparity map and the white surrounding around the rectangular image almost disappears. This means that, the adjusted disparity value is true? In order to validate the result, the disparity values (0010111)2=(21)10 and (0010101)2=(23)10 are also tested as shown in Figure 7 and Figure 8, respectively. It can be observed that when these disparity levels are entered to the switch, white surrounding around the rectangle object starts to appear.

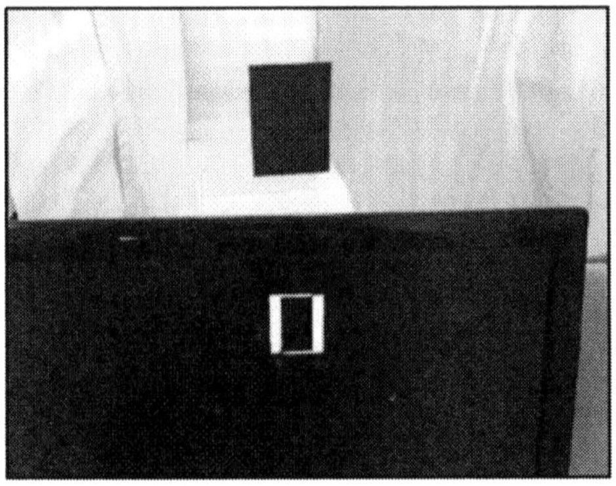

Figure 5. The disparity map for a zero disparity level at 1 meter distance. from the cameras

As a result for the 1 meter test, we are able to determine the correct disparity value by finding the one with minimum number of white pixels around any object.

Figure 6. The appropriate disparity value of (0010110)2=(22)10 for one meter distance from the cameras

Figure 7. Disparity map for (0010101)2=(21)10 disparity level at one meter from the cameras

Figure 8. Disparity map for (0010111)2=(23)10 disparity level at one meter from the cameras

III. RESULTS

This setup is tested from 25 cm to 3 m by 25 cm steps and the appropriate disparity levels are observed and compared with the calculated disparity levels. For each distance disparity values from 0 to 127 are entered as the disparity value are entered to the system and the one with minimum number of white pixels is determined as the correct disparity value for the corresponding distance.

The theoretical value of the disparity values are also evaluated by using the disparity formula given in equation (1). Here, the cameras has 3.81 mm lens (f in equation (1)) and distance between cameras is 6.3 cm (similar to human eyes). The formula gives the disparity result in cm when the other parameters are in cm. These disparity values are changed to pixel value by dividing them to pixel width of the image sensor. The image sensors are 2.2 μm x 2.2 μm and the pixels were downscaled because of the limited amount of memory inside the FPGA chip. Thus, the pixel width is assumed here, 4 times of real value ($2.2\times4=8.8$ μm) because of the 1/16 representation of pixels.

As it can be seen from Figure 9 and Table 1, the observed and the calculated disparity values have no difference bigger than 8 pixels. This situation can be named as the system tolerance (max. 4 pixels from right and 4 pixels from left image).

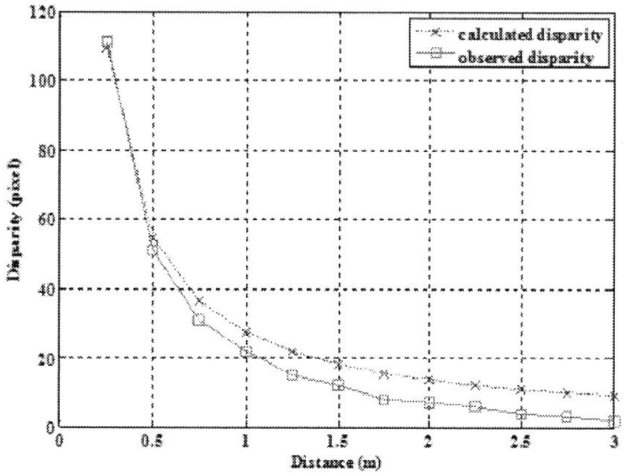

Figure 9. Comparison of the observed and calculated disparity values

TABLE I. VALUES OF THE GRAPH IN FIGURE 12

Distance from cameras (m)	Calculated Disparity (pixels)	Observed Disparity (pixels)
0.25	109	111
0.50	54	51
0.75	36	31
1.00	27	22
1.25	22	15
1.50	18	12
1.75	15	8
2.00	13	7
2.25	12	6
2.50	11	4
2.75	10	3
3.00	9	2

The differences are almost stable after 0.5 m from the cameras, in the near zone (in 0.25 m and 0.5 m) they are smaller than the others.

IV. CONCLUSION

In this paper, the relationship between disparity and the distance of an object in a scene is examined experimentally and the images are segmented according to the depth information. The stereovision technique is used to obtain the disparity values.

The system is implemented on an FPGA and the relation between the disparity and the distance of an object from the cameras is measured in a test bed and the test object is segmented according to the distance.

The results in the near zone seems better than the results in the far zone depending on the inverse ratio between the disparity and the distance. In the near zones the disparity values are bigger which brings out that the distances are represented with more pixels than they are represented in far zones from the cameras. Thus, the disparity values shows better match with theoretical values in the near zones than they are in the far zones. On the other hand, it must be noted that the observed values depend on the observer and they can vary only a few pixels.

One remarkable property of this implementation is that, no external components rather than the FPGA chip are used. This makes it a tiny application and applicable to any Virtex 5 board independent of the board design while it can still be applied to other FPGA chips with minor changes in the code.

A. *Future Work*

Most remarkable future work is to adapt the system for an automatic depth map generation of a scene. This could be accomplished by first segmenting the objects visually and acquiring the disparity values automatically from the proposed system. This would be a promising solution for real time depth map generation on a streaming video file.

The design can also be developed to process more complex task and big images by using onboard DRAMs or FPGA chips with larger resources with an appropriate hardware design.

REFERENCES

[1] I. P. Howard and B. J. Rogers, *Seeing in Depth: Depth perception*. I. Porteous, 2002.

[2] S. Battiato, S. Curti, M. Cascia, E. Scordato, "Depth-Map Generation by Image Classification," in *Proceedings of SPIE*, 2004, pp. 95--104.

[3] A. Klette, Reinhard Schluns, Karsten Koschan, *Computer Vision*. Springer, 1998.

[4] C. Holzmann and M. Hochgatterer, "Measuring Distance with Mobile Phones Using Single-Camera Stereo Vision.," in *ICDCS Workshops*, 2012, pp. 88–93.

[5] D. Aldavert, A. Ramisa, R. Toledo, and L. Ramon, "Obstacle Detection and Alignment Using an Stereo Camera Pair," Technical report, Artificial Intelligence research institute, Spain, 2008.

[6] P. Fua, "A parallel stereo algorithm that produces dense depth maps and preserves image features," *Mach. Vis. Appl.*, vol. 6, no. 1, pp. 35–49, 1993.

[7] Y. Yang, M. Gao, J. Zhang, Z. Zha, and Z. Wang, "Depth map super-resolution using stereo-vision-assisted model," *Neurocomputing*, vol. 149, pp. 1396–1406, 2015.

[8] S. Zhang, C. Wang, and S. C. Chan, "A New High Resolution Depth Map Estimation System Using Stereo Vision and Kinect Depth Sensing," *J. Signal Process. Syst.*, vol. 79, no. 1, pp. 19–31, 2015.

[9] D. Honegger, P. Greisen, L. Meier, P. Tanskanen, and M. Pollefeys, "Real-time velocity estimation based on optical flow and disparity matching," in *Intelligent Robots and Systems (IROS), 2012 IEEE/RSJ International Conference on*, 2012, pp. 5177–5182.

[10] W. Wang, J. Yan, N. Xu, Y. Wang, and F.-H. Hsu, "Real-time high-quality stereo vision system in fpga," *IEEE Trans. Circuits Syst. Video Technol.*, vol. 25, no. 10, pp. 1696–1708, 2015.

[11] S. Mattoccia, "Stereo vision: algorithms and applications," 2011.

[12] "Digilent, VmodCAM Reference Manual." 2011.

[13] "Digilent, Genesy Board Reference Manual." 2013.

[14] "Xilinx Virtex-5 Libraries Guide for HDL Design." 2009.

HELD1: Home Equipment Laboratory Dataset for Non-Intrusive Load Monitoring

Pirmin Held, Steffen Mauch, Alaa Saleh, Dirk Benyoucef
Furtwangen University, Germany
Mechanical and Medical Engineering
Email: {pirmin.held, steffen.mauch, alaa.saleh, dirk.benyoucef}@hs-furtwangen.de

Djaffar Ould Abdeslam
Université de Haute-Alsace, France
IUT de Mulhouse
Email: djaffar.ould-abdeslam@uha.fr

***Abstract*—Non-Intrusive Load Monitoring (NILM) can be split into event detection, classification and energy tracking. Different algorithms have already been proposed for the respective tasks. Each algorithm has been verified based on publicly available data sets to assess its performance. The two types of data sets that currently exist can be distinguished into two types: laboratory measurements and data sets from real world environment. In general, the available laboratory measurements provide data of individual devices; these are only of limited use for overall benchmark tests. Measurements, in which several devices have been active simultaneously, only exist in real scenario datasets. Nevertheless, the assignment of reference data in real scenarios is somehow problematic: issues are, for example, the synchronization between reference data and measured data, absence or excess of events and the number of on and off cycles of each device respectively. Furthermore, the probability distribution of the devices, as well as long measurement cycles with correspondingly large amounts of data, but low number of events, are challenging. Therefore, it is very difficult to compare the current NILM algorithms. Home Equipment Laboratory Dataset (HELD1) has multiple switching on and off events of several devices acting individually and/or simultaneously. Since the individual devices can be controlled separately, the reference data is available in a very high quality. Thus, high number of events can be generated within a short measuring time. In addition, the dataset contains different complex scenarios of various numbers of appliances. The objective of this data set is to offer a better basis to enhance the comparability between the individual NILM approaches.**

Keywords–NILM dataset; feature extraction; feed forward neural net; supervised classification.

I. Introduction

In the past years, Non-Intrusive Load Monitoring (NILM) has gained more and more attention. The initial idea of Non-Intrusive Load Monitoring (NILM) has been to determine the consumption of individual devices. The visualization of the amount of power that is consumed by individual devices [1] should raise the consumers consciousness. NILM in the Ambient Assisted Living (AAL) context focuses on analyzing the behavior of persons in need of care to detect critical situations [2]. NILM can be split into the following aspects: event detection, classification, and tracking. Depending on the application, the complexity of the task is quite different. In the AAL context, a classification of the devices is necessary. To measure the power consumption of each single device, which was the primary idea of NILM, it is necessary to track the power consumption of the individual devices additionally.

Thus, the requirements for data sets vary from task to task. Apart from fundamental aspects, such as resolution, sampling rate, and waveform capturing, the reference data are of utmost importance. The reference data are needed for a successful training and the evaluation of the algorithms results. It is extremely important that the reference data are reliable, otherwise the training of the algorithms will be incorrect. For example a supervised classifier needs information about the device and the position of the event. During the evaluation of the tests, the results will be compared with the reference data. Inconsistent reference data leads to an unreliable assessment of the tested algorithms.

Most of the public data sets, e.g., Blued [3], Redd [4] or UK-Dale [5] have been recorded in real scenarios. In Table I several public data sets have been compared. The advantage of such an approach is that the different modalities for the use of appliances are realistic. However, the use of real scenarios has drawbacks, too: extremely long periods of time have to be measured in order to obtain sufficient switching-on and switching-off cycles for each consumer. And, if the measuring period is to short, the risk persists that some consumers have not been switched on or off. Such a situation is particularly problematic with respect to classification. In the case of measuring over a very long period like months or years, the danger, that errors will occur during the generation of reference data rises. Having measurement campaigns where data have been sampled at a high rate, the amount of data being generated over a period of years is enormous. Additional difficulties in the generation of reference data, rises from complex devices such as washing machines or dishwashers. It is difficult to map the reference data of the internal consumers of complex devices. Therefore, in general, events of these devices are not marked in the data sets.

Other data sets, such as PLAID [6], WHITED [7] and COOLL [8]) have been recorded under laboratory conditions. Here, individual loads are measured independent of each other. In these data sets, there are no scenarios prevalent where several devices are operated simultaneously. Nevertheless, the advantage of these data sets is that many on / off cycles are available in a short period of time. These data sets enable a good examination of device-specific properties, especially since a very high sampling rate of up to 100 kHz has been applied. However, these data sets are far removed from real conditions, since only one load was activated at the same time. Due to fluctuations in the grid and also phase shifts, it is not possible to simply combine the individual measurements by superpositioning. Thus, there is no straight forward method to simulate multiple consumers being active at the same time.

Due to the afore mentioned aspects, our goal has been to generate a new data set based on real measurements from real consumers, which are switched on and off randomly by a personal computer. In the proposed experimental setup, up to ten different consumers can be active at the same time. The advantage of this laboratory setup is that the appliances are switched on and off at a higher frequency than in an ordinary utilization. Additionally, it is possible to adjust the frequency distribution of the switch-on and switch-off cycles of the individual consumers individually. Combinations of devices with different power consumption and scenarios, combined with various numbers of appliances being active at the same time, were recorded.

TABLE I. COMPARISON OF NILM DATASETS

dataset	samplerate aggregate measurement	samplerate ground truth	duration	single/ multiple devices/ laboratory data set
REDD [4]	1sec / 15kHz	3sec	3 to 19 days	-/yes/no
BLUED [3]	12kHz	event based	8 days	-/yes/no
PLAID [6]	30kHz	-	5sec	yes/no/yes
WHITED [7]	44kHz	-	5sec	yes/no/yes
COOLL [8]	100kHz	-	6sec	yes/no/yes
UK-DALE [5]	16kHz	6sec	3-17 months	-/yes/no
ECO [9]	1sec	1sec	8 months	-/yes/no
SustData [10]	50Hz	50Hz	5 years	-/yes/no
HELD1	4kHz	event based	scenario	yes/yes/yes

Since the new data set HELD1 has been recorded under laboratory conditions, the reference data are available in very high quality. Current and voltage data are available, along with reference data consisting of on and off events of the corresponding device ID. The data set is hosted public and free to use for anyone; it is hosted at [11].

The paper is structured as follows: The dataset including the measurement system and scenarios is described in Sec. II. Feature extraction is presented in Sec. III followed by the classification in Sec. IV, which introduces a feedforward neural net. Sec. V presents the results followed by the conclusion in Sec. VI.

II. HELD1 Dataset

This section describes the measurement system, and the different measurement scenarios of the HELD1 dataset. In addition, the power distribution of the existing consumers in the record is presented.

A. *Measurement system*

The measuring system, see Fig. 1, has already been described in detail in [12]. The sampling rate for current and voltage is 4 kHz. To avoid aliasing, a low-pass filter with a cutoff frequency of 1.3 kHz is applied before sampling. The analog-digital converter operates with 16 bits which corresponds to a theoretical resolution of $\sqrt{2} \cdot 63\,\mathrm{A}/2^{16} = 0.961\,\mathrm{mA}$ being equal to $0.61\,\mathrm{W}$. In reality, current and voltage measurements have a noise of $\approx 16\,\mathrm{mA}$ and $\approx \pm 2\,\mathrm{V}$ when the inputs shorted to ground. This corresponds to $\pm 8\,\mathrm{mA} \cdot 230\,\mathrm{V} = \pm 1.84\,\mathrm{W}$.

In the HELD1 data set, up to 18 different consumers are used. Their characteristics are given in Table II. The appliances are selected simple consumers, which do not have any major internal load switching.

Some appliances did not work reliably during the measurement campaign, thus, their measurements were excluded from the dataset. Therefore, the numbering of the devices in Table II is not continuous.

Some of the used devices are shown in Fig. 2.

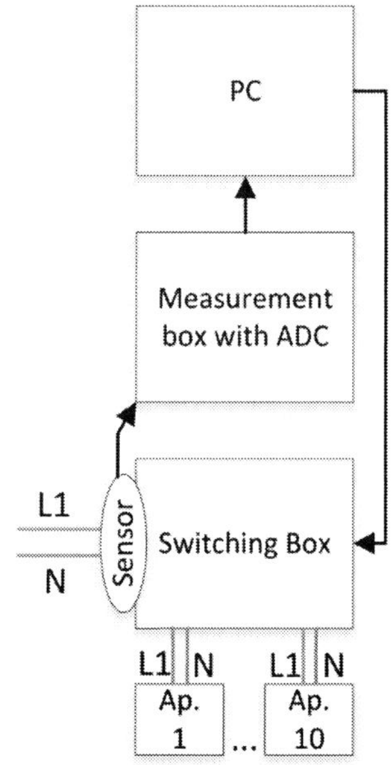

Figure 1. Block diagram of the measurement system; ADC means analog digital converter, Ap. appliance, L1 phase 1, N neutral line, PC personal computer

TABLE II. DEVICE LIST

ID	Name	P(W)
001	Toaster	998
002	Hairdryer (setting 2)	1155
003	Radio	6.2
005	Vacuum Cleaner (red)	424
007	Hair Straightener	56
009	Heat Gun (setting 1)	820
010	Router	9.2
011	Desk Lamp	20
013	Refrigerator (white)	170
014	Refrigerator (blue)	190
015	Fluorescent Lamp	40
016	Light Bulb Box	20
017	Kettle	2100
019	Hairdryer (setting 1)	500
020	Heat Gun (setting 2)	1603
021	Fan	22
022	Multifunction Tool (Dremel ®)	30
023	LED lamp	1

B. *Measurement scenarios*

The data set is divided into four consecutive measurements:

- Training data (consisting of individual measurements, 100 on / off events per device)
- Test measurement one (max. one device being active at the same time)
- Test measurement two (up to four active devices being active at the same time)
- Test measurement three (up to six devices being active at the same time)

In test measurements, each device was turned on and off in total 20 times. Additionally during the test measurements, the devices were randomly switched on and off under consideration of the corresponding scenario. For all scenarios, the minimum time distance between two events is three seconds.

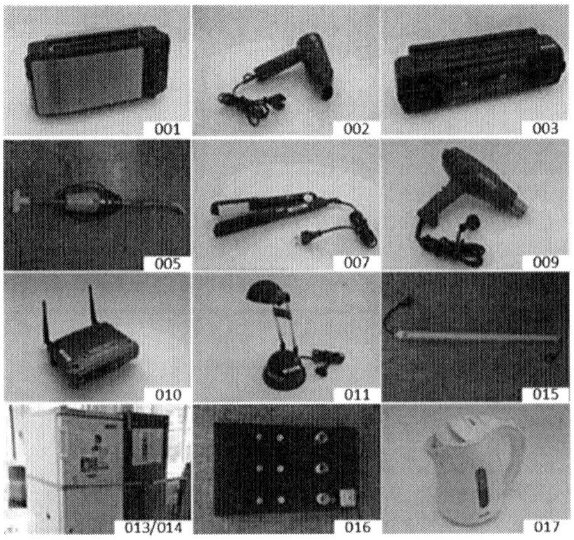

Figure 2. Illustration of random selected individual appliances with corresponding device ID

C. *Power distribution of the appliances*

In Fig. 3, different power distributions of the consumers are shown. A few individual consumers (e.g., refrigerator or kettle) have two different clusters of power distribution. The reason can be found in a different power consumption between the switching on and the switching off steady state in these appliances. Fig. 4 shows a zoomed extract of Fig. 3 in the lower power range, due to better visalization. Figures 3 and 4 result from the training data record, where only one device is active at the same time. If several devices are active simultaneously, the overall noise level is increased. This results in larger clusters of the individual appliances which leads to a higher probability of overlapping clusters in test dataset two and three.

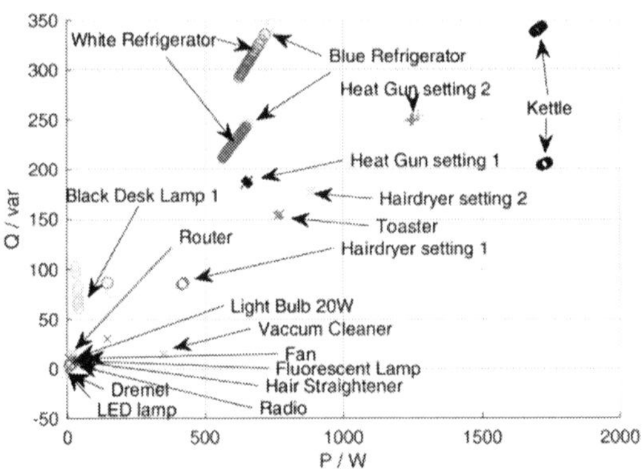

Figure 3. Power distribution of the individual consumers

Most devices can already be separated by P and Q (see Fig. 3 and 4). However, some clusters show overlapping data, e.g., the clusters of the hair straightener, multifunction tool (Dremel®, radio, LED lamp or the two refrigerators. The idea is that the distinctiveness of these devices can be improved by adding the harmonics to the feature space of P and Q.

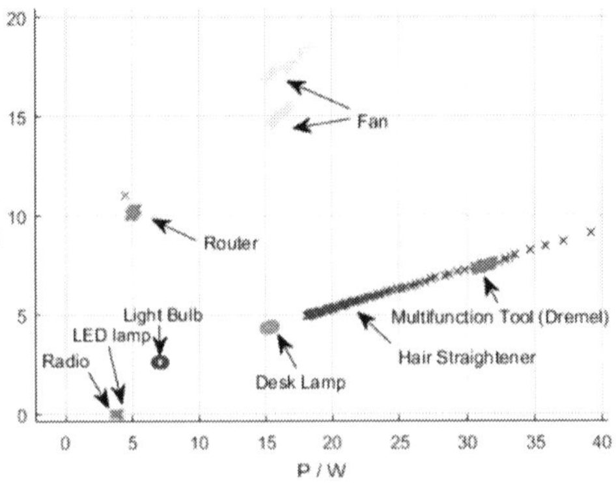

Figure 4. Detailed illustration of the active and reactive power of the different devices in the lower power range shown in Fig. 3

III. Feature Extraction

Before performing a classification, it is necessary to extract the different features out of the given data. Most frequently, active power P and the reactive power Q has been used as features in context of NILM. Harmonics are used as additional features to reduce the probability of overlapping features. Moreover, the use of harmonics benefits from the high frequency sampling. The harmonics $H \in \mathbb{R}^7$ are calculated for each device D as shown in Equ. (1).

$$H_D(\omega) = \int_{-\infty}^{+\infty} s(t)e^{-j\omega t} \Bigg|\ \omega = 50, 100, \ldots, 350\,\text{Hz} \quad (1)$$

Since more than one load can be switched on at the same time, the difference between the signal (P, Q, H) before and after the event is calculated. This principle is visualized in Fig. 5 with a real power signal. Two windows including 4000 sampling points are used. The 8000 sampling points before and after the event are not considered. The switching on and

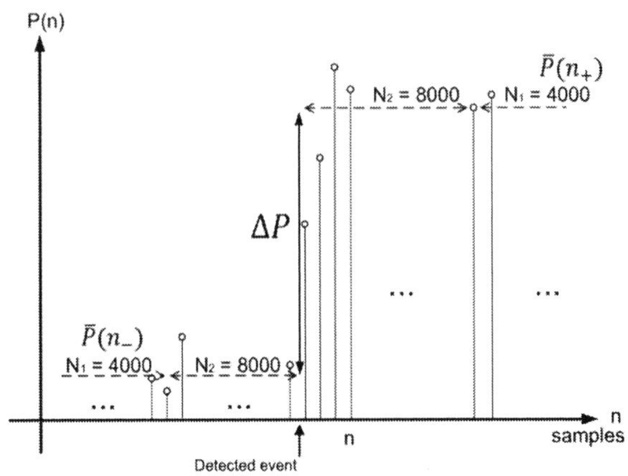

Figure 5. Representation of the feature extraction based on the real power

off events are handled as two independent features. The result is a doubling of the clusters in the feature space. In general, on and off events usually differ only in the sign. This utilization increases the feature space but does not result in a disadvantage during the classification, because switching on and off events can easily be distinguished.

$$P(n_-) = \frac{1}{N_1}\sum_{l=1}^{N_1}(P(n-l-N_2)) \quad (2)$$

$$P(n_+) = \frac{1}{N_1}\sum_{l=1}^{N_1}(P(n+l+N_2)) \quad (3)$$

$$\Delta P = P(n_+) - P(n_-) \quad (4)$$

The calculation of Q and H is analogous to the calculation of P which is given in Equ. (2), (3) and (4). The normalization of the signals is as follows:

$$\tilde{P}_D = \Delta P_D - \min(\Delta P_D) \quad (5)$$

$$\tilde{Q}_D = \Delta Q_D - \min(\Delta Q_D) \quad (6)$$

$$\tilde{H}_D(\omega) = \Delta H_D - \min(\Delta H_D(\omega)) \quad (7)$$

$$\Big| \quad \omega = 50, 100, ..., 350$$

The individual waveforms $\tilde{P}$, $\tilde{Q}$, $\tilde{S}$ are combined into the matrix

$$X = \begin{pmatrix} \tilde{P}_1 & \tilde{Q}_1 & \tilde{S}_1 \\ \vdots & \vdots & \vdots \\ \tilde{P}_{18} & \tilde{Q}_{18} & \tilde{S}_{18} \end{pmatrix}. \quad (8)$$

The last step in the normalization procedure is as follows:

$$Y = \begin{pmatrix} \frac{1}{\max(X(\cdot,1))} & 0 & \cdots & 0 \\ \vdots & \ddots & & \vdots \\ 0 & 0 & \cdots & \frac{1}{\max(X(\cdot,9))} \end{pmatrix} \quad (9)$$

$$Z = X \cdot Y \quad (10)$$

Every column m of X is divided by the maximum of the m-th column of X (Equ. (9) and (10)). $X(\cdot, m)$ means that the m-th column of the matrix X is used. By multiplication of X and Y, the matrix Z is calculated.

IV. CLASSIFICATION

In order to generate a reference value for the classification of HELD1, the individual measurements were used as training values. The features have been chosen as described in Sec. III. As classification method, a feedforward net, as shown in Fig. 6, is applied. During the training phase, the values for weights w and bias b have been determined. For the training, scaled conjugate gradient back-propagation [13] has been chosen.

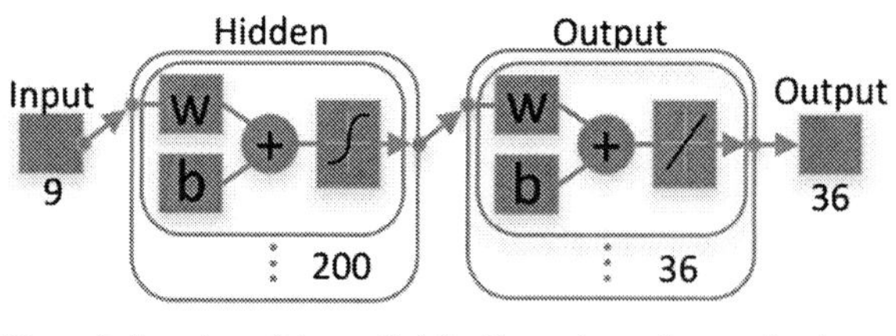

Figure 6. Overview of the applied feedforward neural network, whereas weights are depicted with w and bias with b.

ΔP, ΔQ and the first seven harmonics are used as input of the neural network. Thus, the total input is nine dimensions. The number of consumers to be distinguished defines the corresponding number of dimensions of the output. Additionally, as on and off events are treated as separate events, the number of outputs is doubled. In order to find the required size of the neural network, the number of hidden layers has been varied between one and 500. The accuracy of the achieved result is visualized in Fig. 7. The results were obtained by application of the test measurements '0003', '0116' and '0201'. In order to determine the lower, upper, and average values of the results for the corresponding number of hidden layers, each neural net has been trained in total 100 times.

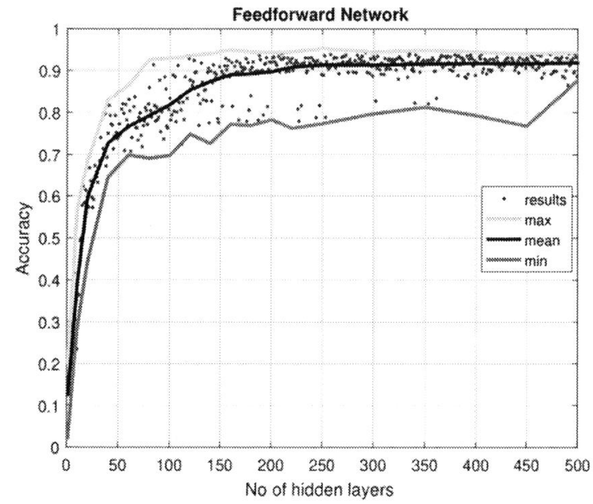

Figure 7. Result of the classification according to different numbers of hidden layers

An accuracy of $\approx 90\,\%$ can be achieved with about 200 hidden layers (Fig. 7). A further enlargement of the net has no positive effect on the achieved accuracy and the result of classification. The variance of results can be explained by the random initialization of each neural net for every new initiated training. The optimization problem is not convex, therefore local minima prevail.

V. RESULTS

The individual classification result of each measurement file is listed in Table III to VII. Table III shows the results of test measurement two, where only one device was active at one time. The overall recognition rate is $\approx 93.15\,\%$. In order to identify the occurring errors, the results of measurement '0076' are exemplified in Table IV. Target values are plotted in the columns, whereas the actual values are given in corresponding row. Each device in this measurement had in total 40 events. For ID nine, there are only 39 events, since the last event was immediately before the end of the recorded measurement; thus no feature could be calculated. In this measurement, six different consumers were used. The devices with ID 3, 11 and 21 were detected incorrectly. These devices were not included in the measurement file '0076' but the neural net had been trained with all available devices.

Since both refrigerators (ID 13 and 14) are showing almost similar consumption characteristics, these devices have been randomly mixed, which leads to an increase of wrong

TABLE III. CLASSIFICATION PERFORMANCE OF TEST MEASUREMENT ONE

Measurement File	No. of Events	Accuracy
0076	240	88.285%
0077	240	87.342%
0078	240	86.611%
0079	240	89.121%
0080	240	87.029%
0117	400	91.729%
0118	400	90.727%
0119	400	88.446%
0120	400	88.722%
0202	400	98.496%
0203	400	97.744%
0204	400	99.499%
0205	400	99.749%

TABLE IV. CONVERSION MATRIX OF THE CLASSIFICATION RESULTS OF MEASUREMENT '0076'

Dev. ID set \ actual	3	5	9	11	13	14	16	17	19	21
3	0	0	0	0	0	0	0	0	0	0
5	0	39	0	0	0	0	1	0	0	0
9	0	0	39	0	0	0	0	0	0	0
11	0	0	0	0	0	0	0	0	0	0
13	0	0	0	1	33	3	0	0	0	3
14	0	0	0	0	17	23	0	0	0	0
16	0	0	0	0	0	0	0	0	0	0
17	0	0	0	0	0	0	0	39	0	1
19	1	0	0	0	0	0	0	0	38	1
21	0	0	0	0	0	0	0	0	0	0

assignments. All other devices have been identified correctly with an accuracy of $\approx 97\,\%$ in measurement '0076'.

TABLE V. CLASSIFICATION PERFORMANCE OF TEST MEASUREMENT TWO

Measurement File	No. of Events	Accuracy
0005	400	57.789%
0008	400	52.393%
0009	400	57.868%
0011	400	55.138%
0171	400	59.25%
0172	400	62.907%
0173	400	56.391%
0175	400	59.649%
0192	400	59.649%
0193	400	61.905%
0194	400	66.165%
0195	400	64.16%
0206	400	73.434%
0207	400	68.672%
0208	400	45.614%
0209	400	67.92%
0210	400	66.667%

Table V contains scenario test measurement two with up to four devices active at the same time. The total recognition rate is $60.92\,\%$. Table VI shows the results of measurement '0194' exemplarily. Again, the two refrigerators are the major source of error. The detection rate for the nine remaining devices in measurement '0194' is $72\,\%$. As several devices are operated simultaneously, the probability of mis-detection increased, especially for small consumers.

Table VII presents the results of scenario test measurement three with up to six devices active at the same time. The overall recognition rate reveals $58.85\,\%$.

TABLE VI. CONVERSION MATRIX OF THE CLASSIFICATION RESULTS OF MEASUREMENT '0194'

Dev. ID set \ actual	3	5	7	9	10	11	13	14	15	16	17	19	21	23
3	20	0	1	0	0	1	1	0	0	0	0	0	3	14
5	0	36	0	0	0	0	3	1	0	0	0	0	0	0
7	0	0	33	0	0	5	1	0	0	0	0	0	1	0
9	2	0	0	29	0	0	1	0	0	4	0	0	4	0
10	1	0	0	0	25	2	7	0	0	1	0	0	0	4
11	1	0	2	0	0	28	1	0	0	4	0	0	1	3
13	0	0	0	0	0	0	0	0	0	0	0	0	0	0
14	0	0	0	0	0	6	22	6	1	0	0	0	4	1
15	0	0	0	0	0	0	0	0	0	0	0	0	0	0
16	0	0	0	0	0	1	1	0	0	29	0	0	0	9
17	0	0	1	0	0	4	1	0	0	0	32	0	2	0
19	3	0	0	0	0	0	0	0	0	4	0	26	6	0
21	0	0	0	0	0	0	0	0	0	0	0	0	0	0
23	0	0	0	0	0	0	0	0	0	0	0	0	0	0

TABLE VII. CLASSIFICATION PERFORMANCE OF TEST MEASUREMENT THREE

Measurement File	No. of Events	Accuracy
0241	400	58.897%
0242	400	58.145%
0243	400	61.654%
0244	400	58.647%
0245	400	56.892%

VI. CONCLUSION

This paper presents HELD1 as a data set for NILM which has been recorded under laboratory conditions. The primary advantage of this data set is the reliable reference data. Further advantages are the identical probability distribution for all consumers as well as a high density of events within the recorded data. This reduces the size of measurement data and the calculation effort. To the knowledge of the authors, this is the first data set being published in context of NILM, that provides measurements under laboratory conditions with several consumers being active at the same time. Therefore, the dataset reflects realistic scenarios. For supervised learning, individual measurements with 100 switch-on and switch-off cycles are available. A classification procedure using neural networks for the allocation of first reference values is presented. In the future, the data set will be supplemented with further measurements to offer even more different scenarios.

ACKNOWLEDGMENT

We would like to thank Steven Kyle Johnson and Fabian Suske for carrying out the measurements. This work was created as part of the iMon project (funding number 03FH001IX4).

REFERENCES

[1] G. Hart, "Residential energy monitoring and computerized surveillance via utility power flows," vol. 8, no. 2, pp. 12–16.

[2] P. Klein, "Non-intrusive information sources for activity analysis in ambient assisted living scenarios." [Online]. Available: https://tel.archives-ouvertes.fr/tel-01526695/

[3] K. Anderson, A. Ocneanu, D. Benitez, A. Rowe, and M. Berges, "BLUED: A fully labeled public dataset for event-based non-intrusive load monitoring research," in Proceedings of the 2nd KDD Workshop on Data Mining Applications in Sustainability (SustKDD). [Online]. Available: http://inferlab.org/wp-content/uploads/2012/08/2012_anderson_SustKDD.pdf

[4] J. Z. Kolter and M. J. Johnson, "REDD: A public data set for energy disaggregation research," in Workshop on Data Mining Applications in Sustainability (SIGKDD), San Diego, CA, vol. 25. Citeseer, pp. 59–62, 00406. [Online]. Available: http://citeseerx.ist.psu.edu/viewdoc/download?doi=10.1.1.454.5796&rep=rep1&type=pdf

[5] J. Kelly and W. Knottenbelt, "The UK-DALE dataset, domestic appliance-level electricity demand and whole-house demand from five UK homes," vol. 2, p. 150007, 00034.

[6] J. Gao, S. Giri, E. C. Kara, and M. Bergés, "PLAID: a public dataset of high-resoultion electrical appliance measurements for load identification research: demo abstract." ACM Press, pp. 198–199, 00002.

[7] M. Kahl, A. U. Haq, T. Kriechbaumer, and H.-A. Jacobsen, "WHITED- a worldwide household and industry transient energy data set," 00000. [Online]. Available: http://nilmworkshop.org/2016/proceedings/Poster_ID18.pdf

[8] T. Picon, M. N. Meziane, P. Ravier, G. Lamarque, C. Novello, J.-C. L. Bunetel, and Y. Raingeaud, "COOLL: Controlled on/off loads library, a public dataset of high-sampled electrical signals for appliance identification," 00001. [Online]. Available: https://arxiv.org/abs/1611.05803

[9] C. Beckel, W. Kleiminger, R. Cicchetti, T. Staake, and S. Santini, "The ECO data set and the performance of non-intrusive load monitoring algorithms." ACM Press, pp. 80–89, 00049. [Online]. Available: http://dl.acm.org/citation.cfm?doid=2674061.2674064

[10] L. Pereira, F. Quintal, R. Gonçalves, and N. J. Nunes, "SustData: A public dataset for ICT4s electric energy research." in ICT4S, 00012. [Online]. Available: http://www.atlantis-press.com/php/download_paper.php?id=13462

[11] P. Held, S. Mauch, A. Saleh, D. Ould Abdeslam, and D. Benyoucef, "Home equipment laboratory dataset (HELD1)." [Online]. Available: http://141.28.27.61/

[12] T. Bier, D. Benyoucef, D. Abdeslam Ould, J. Merckle, and P. Klein, "Smart meter systems measurements for the verification of the detection & classification algorithms," 00003.

[13] F. M. Møller, "A scaled conjugate gradient algorithm for fast supervised learning," 00000.

Comparative Study of Different Pre-processing Methods for Discriminating Live Fish Based on Hyperspectral Imagery

Mohammadmehdi Saberioon, Petr Císař, Pavel Souček
University of South Bohemia in České Budějovice, Faculty of Fisheries and Protection of Waters, South Bohemian Research Centre of Aquaculture and Biodiversity of Hydrocenoses, Nové Hrady, Czech Republic
e-mail: {msaberioon; cisar; psoucek}@frov.jcu.cz

Laurent Labbé, Pablo Pelissier
INRA, UE 0937 PEIMA (Pisciculture Expérimentale INRA des Monts d'Arrée), Sizun, France
e-mail: {laurent.labbe; pablo.pelissier}@inra.fr

***Abstract*—The main aim of this study was to compare the performance of different pre-processing algorithms when coupled with Support vector machine as the classifier to differentiate live fish based on their diet received during cultivation using hyperspectral imagery system. Rainbow trout (*Oncorhynchus mykiss*) were fed either a fish meal-based diet or a 100 % plant-based diet. Hyperspectral images were made using a push-broom hyperspectral imaging system in the spectral region of 394-1009 nm. Six spectral pre-treatment methods were used, including Savitzky-Golay, First Derivative, Second Derivative, Standard Normal Variate and Multiplicative Scatter Correction were employed to improve the robustness and performance of the classifier. According to the criteria of correct classification rate and Kappa coefficient, the support vector machine with linear kernel when coupled with Savitzky-Golay pre-processing was determined as the best method for classifying live fish due to their diet.**

Keywords-Hyperspectral; Pre-processing algorithms; classification; Support vector machine; Fish diet.

I. INTRODUCTION

Researchers have used different optical sensors for measuring and determining light interaction with fish skin. Several studies used colorimeters to determine skin color, which usually provides readings in XYZ, RGB and CIE Lab color space [1]. These instruments allow accurate and reproducible measurements of the color with no influence by the observed or surroundings [2]. For instance, Yi et al. [3] used portable Minolta Chroma meter to show the effect of astaxanthin and xanthophylls as carotenoid sources on growth and skin color of large yellow croaker. Some also used visible and Near Infrared (Vis/NIR) spectroscopy to document the color changes on the fish skin. Lin et al. [4] showed a satisfactory application of Vis/NIR spectroscopy to detect bruises in Pacific pink salmon (*Oncorhynchus gorbuscha*) through the skin. Costa et al. [5] used Vis/NIR spectroscopy of skin to differentiate the sea bass (*Dicentrarchus labrax*) with 87% accuracy at 48hr post-mortem quality cultured in the tank from sea cage. Although fish skin color described with proximal sensors is accurate, their use has been criticized due to the small area measured by the machine, and that aspect of the overall colors are lost [6]. Also, for accurate measurement, the surface color should be quite uniform or homogenous and that may many points on the sample must be measured to obtain the representative color profile, which sometimes is destructive [7].

Researchers also used consumer grade cameras as a non-invasive tool for measuring skin color parameters. Digital images from consumer-grade cameras can overcome the deficiencies of visual and instrumental techniques and offer an objective measurement of color and other physical factors [8]. Wallat et al. [9] demonstrated how a compact true color camera could be employed for objective measurement of the skin color of live goldfish (*Carassius auratus*). Zatkova et al. [10] utilized a digital camera to estimate changes in skin color of wels catfish (*Silurus glanis*). They showed the feasibility of digital cameras for monitoring skin color changes due to diet alteration. Colihueque et al. [11] developed a method for estimating skin color, spottiness and darkness using consumer digital camera and digital image analysis for categorizing cultured rainbow trout (*Oncorhynchus mykiss*). Costa et al. [12] used a digital camera to analyze skin color to discriminate the effects of seabass fed organic or commercial diet. Segade et al. [13] also showed the effect of diet on seahorse (*Hippocampus hippocampus*) body color using images obtained from consumer-grade digital cameras. Consumer-grade cameras provide the capability to rapidly scan both larger areas, as well as smaller details but can only study color in Visible (Vis) bands. Furthermore, all above-mentioned studies have not described the interaction of light in Near Infrared (NIR) bands to show the chromatic changes on the fish skin.

Hyperspectral Imagery (HSI) is an emerging technology that integrates both spectroscopy and imaging in a single system; it has potential to capture the subtle spectral difference under different physiological and pathological conditions. HSI is enabling simultaneous acquisition of spatial and spectral information from an object. The system has the ability to image the same scene in hundreds of contiguous narrow wavebands, from the visible to the short-wave infrared region of electromagnetic spectrum (400-2500 nm). In other words, HSI has higher spatial resolution than the multispectral image, which is obtained by consumer grade digital cameras.

The main challenge limiting the application of hyperspectral for fish discrimination is finding suitable data pre-processing and classification strategy. Choosing the most robust technique can help to achieve a more reliable classification model. In order to remove inappropriate information, which cannot be handled correctly by the classifier, pre-processing approaches are used. Usually, these approaches aim to decrease the noise and enhance possible spectral features. The most widely used spectral pre-processing methods can be commonly divided into three groups, namely smoothing, baseline removal, and scaling [14]. The first category is smoothing such as Savitzky-Golay (SG), which is used for noise reduction; the second category is baseline removal, such as the First Derivative (FD) and Second Derivative (SD), which is used for correcting background signals or baseline that is far away from zero level. Multiplicative Scatter Correction (MSC) is also another popular transformation method used to remove the scatter effects on spectral data. Another group is range scaling, this method is applicable when the total intensity in the spectra is sample-dependent, and samples need to be scaled in such a way that intensities can be compared. Standard Normal Variate (SNV) is one of the popular pre-processing methods, which centering and scaling each individual spectrum for correcting the multiplicative interferences of light scatter [15]. To the best of our knowledge, comparison of different pre-processing methods has not yet been commonly used as a forensic method to determine live fish diets based on their skin. The main aim of this study was to compare the performance of different pre-processing algorithms when coupled with Support vector machine as a classifier to differentiate live fish based on their diet received during cultivation using hyperspectral imagery system. In section 2, Materials and methods will be described. Afterward, results and discussion will be provided in section 3. Finally, the conclusion will be presented in section 4.

II. Materials and Methods

A. *Fish and Cultural Condition*

The fish species were produced at INRA-PEIMA (Sizun, France). Experiments were designed in a split-block design with three replications for each diet; therefore, 80 fish were fed a commercial based diet (3 tanks) and 80 were fed a plant-based diet (3 tanks). After three weeks, all fish were used for hyperspectral image acquisition.

B. *Diets and Feeding Controls*

Diets were manufactured at the INRA NUMEA facility of Donzacq (France). The Fish meal-based diet contained fishmeal and fish oil as protein and lipid source respectively. Plant based diet (PBD) is contained a mixture of wheat gluten, extruded peas, corn gluten meal, soybean meal and white lupin as protein sources; and the combination of palm seed, rapeseed and linseed oil, rich in saturated, mono-unsaturated and n-3 poly-unsaturated fatty acids, respectively, as the lipid source. A mineral and a vitamin premix equally were added to both diets.

C. *Image Acquisition*

A push-broom, line-scanning reflectance hyperspectral imaging system was used to acquire the hyperspectral images of rainbow trout in a dark room to avoid the interference due to stray light and to get pure spectral reflectance. This system includes a high-performance CCD camera (Photonfocus 1312 CL) along with focus lens, a spectrograph (Specim V10E, Spectral Imaging Ltd., Oulu, Finland) attached to the camera acquire hyperspectral images in the wavelength range of 393-1009 nm, an illumination source (150 W halogen lamp attached to a fiber optic line light positioned at an angle of 45 degree to the moving table to reduce the shadowing effects), a moving table and a computer system equipped with an image acquisition software (SpectralScanner, DV optics).

To acquire the spectral and spatial information, each rainbow trout was placed on the sample loading device and they conveyed to the camera field of view (FoV) of the camera with adjusted speed (1.6 mm/s) and exposure time (10 s) to be scanned line by line. The procedure was controlled and implemented by image acquisition software (Specim Lumo software, Spectral Imaging Ltd., Oulu, Finland). The raw hyperspectral image for each sample consisted of several congruent images representing intensities at 784 wavelength bands from 393 to 1009 nm. Due to the low signal-to-noise rate at the two ends of the spectral ranges, only the wavelength ranging from 400 to1000 nm wavelength was used. Totally, 160 hyperspectral images were created, recorded and stored in raw format before being processed. Before measurement, each fish mildly anesthetized with Benzocaine to reduce the movement and minimize the stress. The surface of each rainbow trout also was wiped with piece of tissue paper to remove extra water from skin before data acquisition.

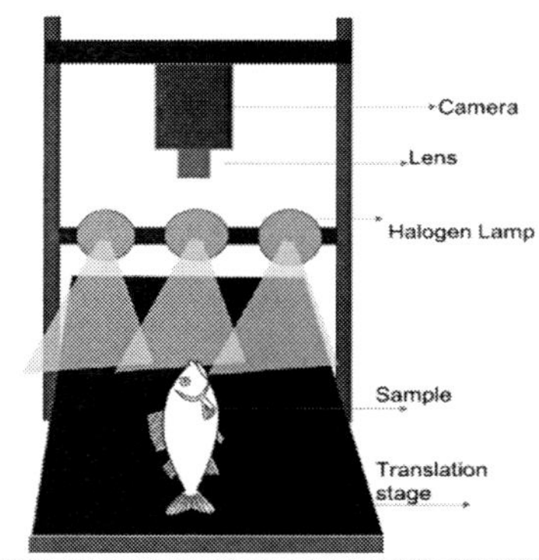

Figure 1. Schematic demonstration of the main components of the used hyperspectral imaging system

D. *Hyperspectral Image Calibration*

The acquired hyperspectral images were corrected using (1).

$$I_i = (R_i - D_i) / (W_i - D_i) \quad (1)$$

where I is the corrected hyperspectral image, R is the raw hyperspectral image, W is the white reference image and D is the dark reference image, as well as i is the pixel index. Afterward, the reflectance spectrum from the region of interest (ROI) was computed by averaging the spectral value of all pixels in the ROI for each sample using the Environment for Visualizing Images software (ENVI 5.3, Harris geospatial solutions, FL, USA).

E. *Spectral Pre-processing*

Six forms of spectra pre-processing were used in this study to remove the non-constituent-related effects in spectra data and to develop optimal classifier model. The six forms were SG smoothing with second order polynomial fit and 11 smoothing points, the FD and SD transformation, MSC and SNV.

F. *Classifier*

After pre-treatment, Support vector machine (SVM) with the linear kernel as a classifier was employed to develop the classification models for discriminating two different diets. The dataset from 160 hyperspectral for rainbow trout was divided into training set (80% of total samples) used to develop the classifier models and a validation set (20% of total samples) used to assess the prediction accuracy of each model. Further details can be found in Vapnik [16]. R package Caret [17] used for SVM classification model.

G. *Evaluation of Classification*

The classifier was evaluated through the analysis of correct classification rate (CCR, %) and Cohen's Kappa coefficient in the validation set. CCR can be calculated using (2).

$$CCR = (N_1 / N_0) \times 100 \quad (2)$$

where N1 is number of correct estimation of samples and N0 is the total number of samples. Kappa coefficient (K) also calculated using (3).

$$K = (Pr(a) - Pr(e)) / (1 - Pr(e)) \quad (3)$$

where Pr(a) is observed agreement and Pr(e) is probability of random agreement.

III. RESULTS AND DISCUSSION

The raw spectra of the two diets were shown in Figure 1. Also, different pre-processing algorithms for all samples were displayed in Figure 2.

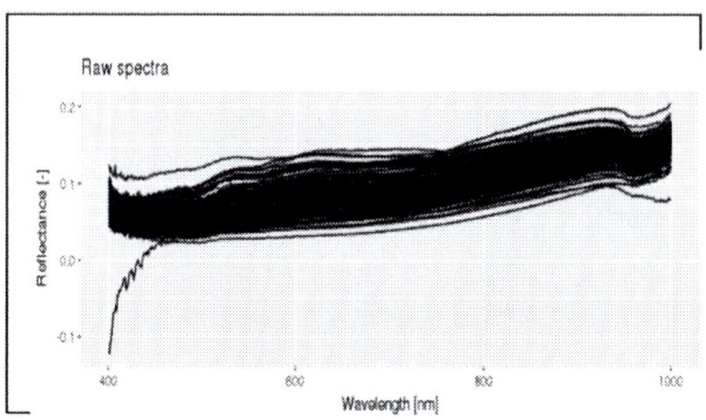

Figure 2. representative Vis/NIR Spectra of fish skin raw.

Table 1 shows the average CCRs for testing set with six spectral pre-processing techniques based on the whole spectral range. When the raw and pre-processed spectra were used to build the classification models, CCRs ranged between 0.740 and 0.871. After application of SD, classification accuracy decreased compare to classification using spectra without pre-processing, however, application of SG, FD, SNV and MSC improved the classification compared to raw spectra. Thus, spectral pre-processing of SD was not helpful and to some extend reduced the accuracy of classification, but other pre-processing treatments improved the performance of classifier for the full range of wavelengths.

TABLE I. MODEL PERFORMANCE FOR IDENTIFICATION OF DIFFERENT DIET ON VALIDATION SET

Method	CCR	Kappa
Raw- SVM	0.741	0.485
SG-SVM	0.871	0.741
FD-SVM	0.806	0.612
SD-SVM	0.730	0.483
SNV-SVM	0.774	0.548
MSC-SVM	0.838	0.676

The best performance for classification with the highest CCR of 0.871 and Kappa coefficient of 0.740 achieved when smoothing solely used as a pre-processing method for full wavelength.

IV. CONCLUSION

The present study provided an alternative tool for the classification of live fish based on their information acquired from skin using hyperspectral images. Overall, classification models established showed good performance when SG used as pre-treatment of spectra. Further studies should be carried out to not only improve the classification accuracy using different machine learning algorithms but also increasing classification power for online evaluation of fish skin at industrial scale.

ACKNOWLEDGMENT

This work was funded by projects CENAKVA [CZ.1.05/2.1.00/01.0024] and CENAKVA II (the results of the project LO1205 were obtained with a financial support from the MEYS of the CR under the NPU I program); The CENAKVA Centre Development [No. CZ.1.05/2.1.00/19.0380]; and the European Union's Horizon 2020 research and innovation program under grant agreement No. 652831" (Aquauexcel2020).

REFERENCES

[1] M. Saberioon, A. Gholizadeh, P. Cisar, A. Pautsina, and J. Urban, "Application of machine vision systems in aquaculture with emphasis on fish: state-of-the-art and key issues," Reviews in Aquaculture, vol. 9, no 4, pp. 369-387, 2016.

[2] F. Clydesdale and E. Ahmed, "Colorimetry — methodology and applications∗," C R C Critical Reviews in Food Science and Nutrition, vol. 10, no. 3, pp. 243–301, 1978.

[3] X. Yi et al., "Effects of dietary astaxanthin and xanthophylls on the growth and skin pigmentation of large yellow croaker Larimichthys croceus," Aquaculture, vol. 433, pp. 377, 2014.

[4] M. Lin et al., "Bruise Detection in Pacific Pink Salmon (Oncorhynchus gorbuscha) by Visible and Short-Wavelength Near-Infrared (SW-NIR) Spectroscopy (600–1100 nm)," Journal of Agricultural and Food Chemistry, vol. 51, no. 22, pp. 6404–6408, 2003.

[5] C. Costa, S. D'Andrea, R. Russo, F. Antonucci, F. Pallottino, and P. Menesatti, "Application of non-invasive techniques to differentiate sea bass (Dicentrarchus labrax, L. 1758) quality cultured under different conditions," Aquaculture International, vol. 19, no. 4, pp. 765-778, 2011.

[6] F. Mendoza and J. Aguilera, "Application of image analysis for classification of ripening bananas," Journal of Food Science, vol. 69, no. 9, pp. E471–E477, 2004.

[7] K. Yam and S. Papadakis, "A simple digital imaging method for measuring and analyzing color of food surfaces," Journal of Food Engineering, vol. 61, no. 1, pp. 137–142, 2004.

[8] Y.-R. Chen, K. Chao, and M. Kim, "Machine vision technology for agricultural applications," Computers and Electronics in Agriculture, vol. 36, no. 2–3, pp. 173-191, 2002.

[9] G. Wallat, A. Lazur, and F. Chapman, "Carotenoids of Different Types and Concentrations in Commercial Formulated Fish Diets Affect Color and Its Development in the Skin of the Red Oranda Variety of Goldfish," North American Journal of Aquaculture, vol. 67, no. 1, pp. 42-51, 2017.

[10] I. Zaťková, M. Sergejevová, J. Urban, R. Vachta, D. Štys, and J. Masojídek, "Carotenoid-enriched microalgal biomass as feed supplement for freshwater ornamentals: albinic form of wels catfish (Silurus glanis)," Aquaculture Nutrition, vol. 17, no. 3, pp. 278-286, 2009.

[11] N. Colihueque, M. Parraguez, F. Estay, and N. Diaz, "Skin Color Characterization in Rainbow Trout by Use of Computer-Based Image Analysis," North American Journal of Aquaculture, vol. 73, no. 3, pp. 249-258, 2011.

[12] C. Costa, P. Menesatti, E. Rambaldi, L. Argenti, and M. Bianchini, "Preliminary evidences of color differences in European sea bass reared under organic protocols," Aquacultural Engineering, vol. 57, pp. 82-88, 2013.

[13] Á. Segade, L. Robaina, O. Ferrer, G. Romero, and M. Domínguez, "Effects of the diet on seahorse (Hippocampus hippocampus) growth, body color and biochemical composition," Aquaculture Nutrition, vol. 21, no. 6, pp. 1-7, 2014.

[14] A. Gholizadeh, L. Borůvka, M. Saberioon, J. Kozák, R. Vašát, and K. Němeček, "Comparing different data preprocessing methods for monitoring soil heavy metals based on soil spectral features," Soil and Water Research, vol. 10, no. 4, pp. 218-227, 2015.

[15] J. Duckworth, C. Roberts, J. Workman Jr. , and J. Reeves III, "Mathematical Data Preprocessing," vol. agronomymonogra, in Near-infrared Spectroscopy in Agriculture, ASA, CSSA, SSSA, 2004, pp. 115–132.

[16] V. Vapnik, "Statistical learning theory," John Wiley & Sons: Hoboken, NJ, USA, 1998.

[17] M. Kuhn, "Building Predictive Models in R Using the caret Package," Journal of Statistical Software, vol. 28, no. 5, pp. 1-62, 2008.

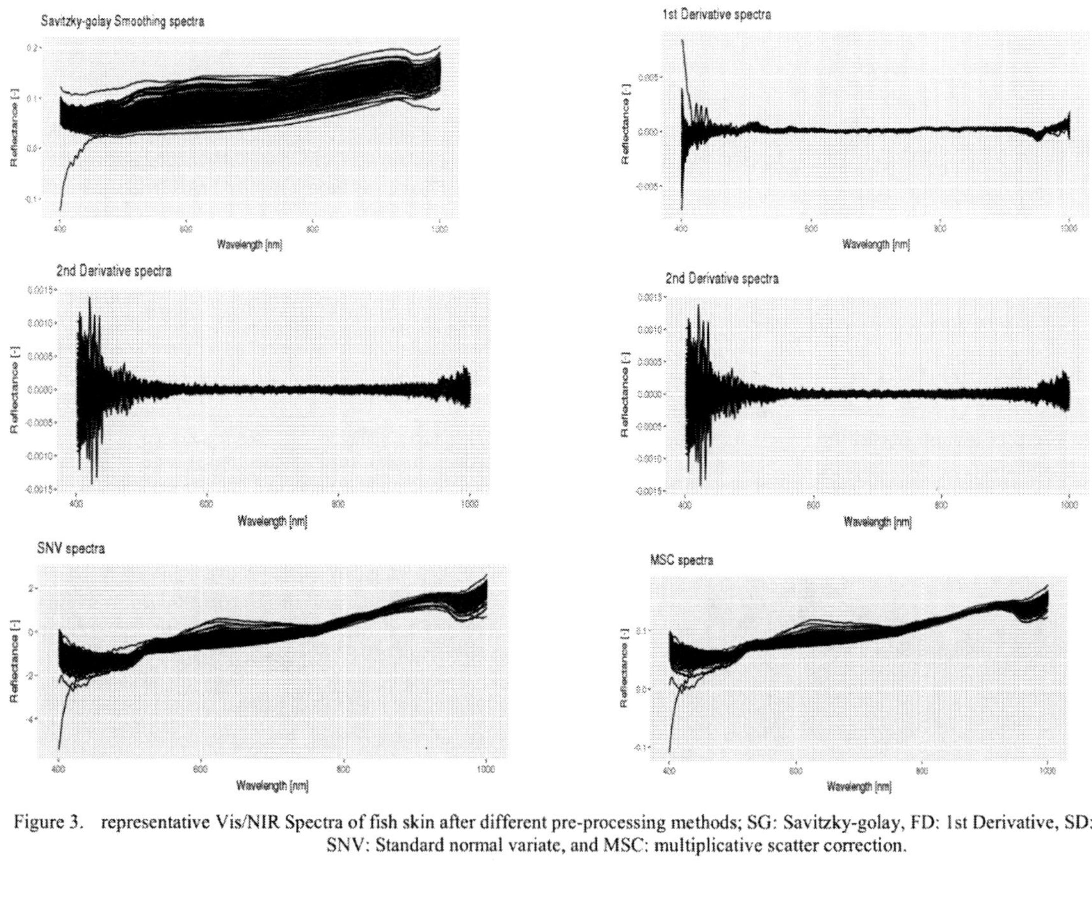

Figure 3. representative Vis/NIR Spectra of fish skin after different pre-processing methods; SG: Savitzky-golay, FD: 1st Derivative, SD: 2nd Derivative, SNV: Standard normal variate, and MSC: multiplicative scatter correction.

Mass Segmentation in Mammograms Using Texture Features and Fuzzy C-means Algorithm

Moustapha Mohamed Saleck*, Abdelmajide El Moutaouakkil
LAROSERI, Dept. of Computer Science,
Chouaib Doukkali University,
El Jadida, Morocco
E-mail* : saleck.moustapha@gmail.com
E-mail : elmsn@hotmaill.fr

***Abstract*— The Fuzzy C-means (FCM) is one of the most efficient algorithms used in various studies, which aims at segmenting the masses in mammogram images, thus to build a Computer Aided Diagnosis (CAD) system capable of helping the physicians for an early diagnosis of the breast cancer. In this paper, we will introduce a new approach using FCM algorithm, in order to extract the mass from Region-of-Interested (ROI). The proposed method aims at avoiding the limitations of cluster number estimation in FCM by selecting as input data, the set of pixels, which are able to provide us the information required to perform the mass segmentation by fixing two clusters only. The Gray Level Occurrence Matrix (GLCM) is used to extract the texture features for getting the optimal threshold, which separate between selected set and the other sets of the pixels that influence on the mass boundary accuracy. The performance of the proposed method is evaluated by specificity, sensitivity, accuracy and overlap. The results obtained from experiments show a good efficiency at the different measures used in this study.**

Keywords- *Mammograms; Mass; Fuzzy C-Means; Segmentation; Texture features.*

I. INTRODUCTION

Breast cancer is one of the most common dangerous diseases in women. According to the World Health Organization, every year, breast cancer kills more than 500,000 women around the world [1]. Although several imaging techniques, such as sonography and magnetic resonance imaging plays important role in breast cancer diagnosis, X-ray mammography is still the most effective screening technique for the early detection of breast cancer [2].

In the last few decades a large amount of researches has been conducted to detect and segment breast cancer in mammograms images. Soares et al. [3] used taxonomic indexes to describe the texture of the regions of interest. Then, a Support Vector Machine (SVM) was proposed to classify the regions as mass and non-mass. Younesi and al. [4] developed a segmentation method for detection of masses in mammogram images using adaptive thresholding method and fuzzy entropy feature. Anitha et al. [5] proposed an automatic method to identify the suspicious mass region by using a Dual Stage Adaptive Thresholding (DuSAT). Cordeiro and al. [4] proposed an adaptive semi-supervised version of the Grow-Cut algorithm to perform mammographic image segmentation. This method is achieved based on automatic selection of internal points using the differential evolution optimization algorithm and modification of cellular automata evolution rules by introducing Gaussian fuzzy membership functions. Nija et al. [5] investigated combining several image enhancement algorithms in order to enhance the performance of masses segmentation. The results of this investigation showed that a particular combination of image enhancing algorithms that includes Contrast - Limited Adaptive Histogram Equalization (CLAHE) and Median Filtering is an effective way to enhance the appearance of the breast region in mammogram images to be further segmented and classified.

Extracting the mass from Region of Interest (ROI) is a difficult task in mammography Computer-Aided Diagnosis (CAD) due to several factors, such as low contrast, density, indistinct borders and ill-defined shapes of the mass. Fuzzy clustering is more efficient than traditional techniques to handle the fuzziness of mammograms. On the other hand, choosing an optimal number of clusters is a big challenge for automating segmentation of masses by clustering.

In this paper, we aim to develop an automated system for mass segmentation in mammograms using FCM algorithm setting two cluster only (C=2). In order to achieve this goal, we select as FCM-input the set of pixels that enable us to get meaningful information from Region of Interest (ROI). This set of pixels is limited by maximum intensity of ROI and an optimal threshold given by a decrement operator, we get this optimal threshold when big changes happen in texture features.

The remainder of this paper is organized as follows : Section 2 presents the materials and methods used in this work. Section 3 describes the experimental results obtained from the evaluation of the proposed methods. Finally, Section 4 presents the conclusion.

II. MATERIAL AND METHODS

The proposed method consists of three main stages: Firstly, median filter and contrast limited adaptive histogram equalization are applied for enhancing the contrast and quality of images. Secondly, a decrement operator L is used to find an appropriate threshold by increasing the number of pixels (FCM-input). At every decrement process, we monitor the changes in texture features levels on the area of mass cluster after applying fuzzy c-means clustering with a fixed number of clusters c = 2, where, the set of input data that is subjected to process of clustering should be within a range limited by maximum of intensity M and a threshold test Ti initialized by $T_0 = M - L$. Finally, we choose the value of threshold test, which makes big changes in texture features levels on the mass area as a suitable threshold Top. Figure 1 describes the evolution of input-data and texture features selection in each step of threshold test decrementation.

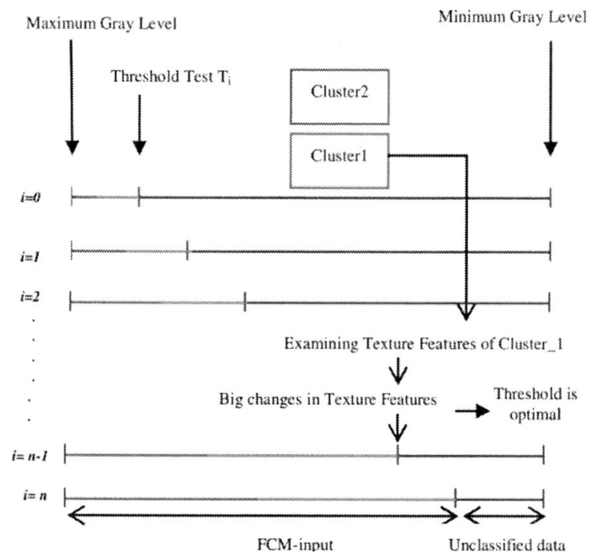

Figure 1. Process of choosing an optimal threshold

A. *Contrast-limited adaptive histogram equalization*

The Contrast Limited Adaptive Histogram Equalization (CLAHE) technique [6] is a special case of Adaptive Histogram Equalization (AHE) [7]. This technique operates on regional areas of pixels in the image called tiles rather than on the entire image. Histograms are calculated from these tiles, producing local histograms. These local histograms are then equalized for getting a uniform distribution. Then, the neighboring tiles are combined based on bilinear interpolation to remove artificially induced boundaries. In this study, we use CLAHE technique to enhance the contrast of image and reduce edge-shadowing effects produced in homogeneous regions and, consequently, improve the accuracy of texture features results.

B. *Fuzzy C-Means (FCM)*

The Fuzzy C-means algorithm was first introduced by Dunn [8] and improved by Bezdek [9]. This algorithm partitions a set of object data X = { *x*1, *x*2, ….., *x*3} into a number of c classes so that items in the same class are as similar as possible, based on minimizing the following quadratic objective function :

$$J = \sum_{k=1}^{c}\sum_{i=1}^{n} u_{ik}^{m} d^2(x_i, v_k) \tag{1}$$

where the fuzzy index m>1 determines the amount of fuzziness of the resulting classification, the membership u_{ik} represents the degree of pixel x_k belonging to cluster k ($1 \leq i \leq n$), and $d_{ik} = \| x_k - c_i \|$ is the distance between pixel x_k and the centroid v

$$u_{ik} = \frac{1}{\sum_{k=1}^{c}\left(\frac{d(x_i, v_k)}{d(x_i, v_i)}\right)^{2(m-1)}} \tag{2}$$

$$v_k = \frac{\sum_{i=1}^{n} u_{ik}^{m} x_i}{\sum_{i=1}^{n} u_{ik}^{m}} \tag{3}$$

The memberships satisfy the constraint that :

$$\sum_{k=1}^{c} u_{ik} = 1, \quad u_{ik} \in [0,1], \quad 0 \prec \sum_{i=1}^{n} u_{ik} \prec n, \tag{4}$$

With this constraint, the objective function reaches a local minimum by updating the fuzzy membership function (2) and cluster centers (3).

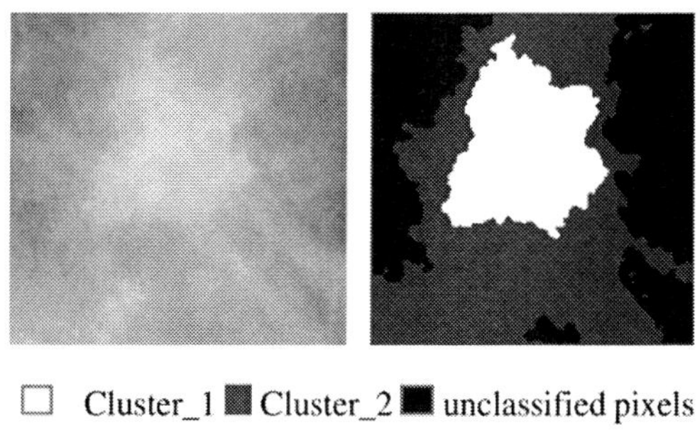

Figure 2. The result of segmentation on image Mdb10.

C. *Texture features*

Statistical texture features have been proven to be useful in classifying masses and normal breast tissues [10][11]. In this work, we examined a set of three texture features (energy, contrast, and homogeneity) from mass area (cluster_1) to identify the most suitable threshold that enables us to extract the boundaries of mass by clustering. The process of texture features selection is achieved using Gray Level Co-occurrence Matrix (GLCM).

D. *Gray-level co-occurrence matrix*

The Gray Level Co-occurrence Matrix (GLCM) is a tabulation of how often different combinations of pixel brightness values (grey levels) occur in an image with the change of distance d (distance to the neighbor pixel: 1, 2, ..

etc) and by varying directions (rotation angle of an offset: 0°, 45°, 90°, 135°) [12]. A number of studies have compared texture feature extraction schemes based on the second-order gray-level statistics, the co-occurrence statistics, gray-level run-length statistics, and Fourier power spectrum. The co-occurrence features were found to be the best of these methods. [13]. In our approach, the GLCM is computed at a distance of d = 1 and for the direction of θ = 0°, 45°, 90 °, 135 ° on cluster_1 area. Based on the authors' database, the smallest masses area is within a 8x8 window. For this reason we use a tile of size 8x8.

III. Experimental Results

For the experiments, the MiniMIAS database was used. It contains 322 mammographic images from left and right breast of 161 patients. The mammograms are digitized at a resolution of 1024 X 1024 pixels and at 8-bit grey scale level.

After many tests, it was found that the best features for distinguishing between masses and normal breast tissues are the features of GLCM constructed at the direction of 0°. At this direction, the GLCM gives a homogeneity value for the masses area in the range [0.9–1], contrast in [0–0.2], and energy in [0.6–1]. Similarly, for normal breast tissue area, the GLCM gives the homogeneity in the range [0.61–0.8], contrast in [0.26–0.71], and energy in [0.14–0.39]. It is observed that the texture features for normal breast tissues and masses area are highly discriminated. In this study, we examined the texture features after the process of clustering in order to find a threshold that allows us to extract the boundaries of tumor with high accuracy. Figure 2 shows the values of texture features during the process of threshold decrementing for image Mdb10.

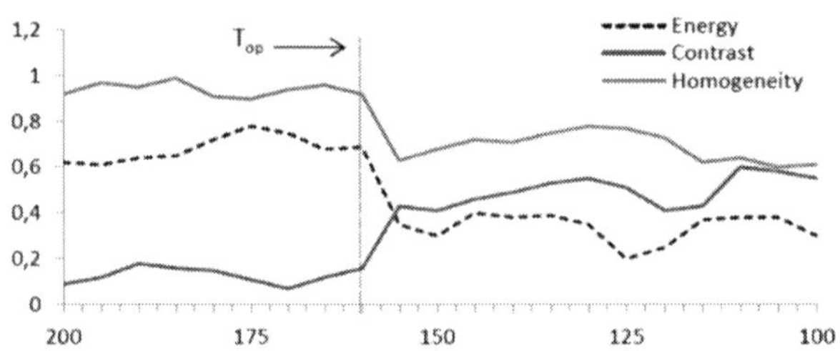

Figure 3. Contrast, Energy and homogeneity values using block size 8 × 8

To evaluate the performance of segmentation all masses are manually marked by radiologist based on the visual criteria.

Assuming that A is the area marked by radiologist and B is the area marked by the system, the area overlap metric (AOM) is given by:

$$AOM(A, B) = Area(A \cap B) / Area(A \cup B) \quad (5)$$

In this work, the test by the measure of overlap (AOM) yielded a mean of 81% for the segmented images.

IV. Conclusions

In this paper, we developed a novel method for automated detection of masses in mammogram images. The proposed work utilizes fuzzy c-means algorithm to extract the tumor from region of interest, where the FCM input data are verified by using the GLCM feature texture in order to automate the process of segmentation.

References

[1] World Health Organization, "WHO Position Paper on Mammography Screening," *WHO Position Pap. Mammogr. Screen.*, p. 78, 2014.

[2] J. Tang, R. M. Rangayyan, J. Xu, I. El Naqa, and Y. Yang, "Computer-aided detection and diagnosis of breast cancer with mammography: recent advances.," *IEEE Trans. Inf. Technol. Biomed.*, vol. 13, no. 2, pp. 236–251, 2009.

[3] F. Soares Sérvulo de Oliveira, A. Oseas de Carvalho Filho, A. Corrêa Silva, A. Cardoso de Paiva, and M. Gattass, "Classification of breast regions as mass and non-mass based on digital mammograms using taxonomic indexes and SVM," *Comput. Biol. Med.*, vol. 57, pp. 42–53, 2014.

[4] F. R. Cordeiro, W. P. Santos, and A. G. Silva-Filho, "A semi-supervised fuzzy GrowCut algorithm to segment and classify regions of interest of mammographic images," *Expert Syst. Appl.*, vol. 65, pp. 116–126, 2016.

[5] N. Al-Najdawi, M. Biltawi, and S. Tedmori, "Mammogram image visual enhancement, mass segmentation and classification," *Appl. Soft Comput. J.*, vol. 35, pp. 175–185, 2015.

[6] K. Zuiderveld, "VIII.5. - Contrast Limited Adaptive Histogram Equalization A2 - Heckbert, Paul S. BT - Graphics Gems," Academic Press, 1994, pp. 474–485.

[7] S. M. Pizer *et al.*, "Adaptive histogram equalization and its variations.," *Comput. vision, Graph. image Process.*, vol. 39, no. 3, pp. 355–368, 1987.

[8] J. C. Dunn, "A Fuzzy Relative of the ISODATA Process and Its Use in Detecting Compact Well-Separated Clusters," *J. Cybern.*, vol. 3, no. 3, pp. 32–57, Jan. 1973.

[9] J. C. Bezdek, *Pattern Recognition with Fuzzy Objective Function Algorithms*, vol. 25, no. 3. 1981.

[10] N. Youssry, F. E. Z. Abou-Chadi, and A. M. El-Sayad, "Early detection of masses in digitized mammograms using texture features and neuro-fuzzy model," in *National Radio Science Conference, NRSC, Proceedings*, 2003, vol. 2003–Janua, pp. K21–K29.

[11] A. M. Khuzi, R. Besar, and W. M. D. W. Zaki, "Texture features selection for masses detection in digital mammogram," in *IFMBE Proceedings*, 2008, vol. 21 IFMBE, no. 1, pp. 629–632.

[12] R. M. Haralick, K. Shanmugam, and I. Dinstein, "Textural Features for Image Classification," *IEEE Trans. Syst. Man. Cybern.*, vol. 3, no. 6, pp. 610–621, 1973.

[13] P. Hiremath and S. Shivashankar, "Texture classification using wavelet packet decomposition," *ICGSTs GVIP J.*, 2006.

A Novel Procedure for Virtual Measurements Generation suitable for Training and Testing in the context of Non Intrusive Load Monitoring

Alaa Saleh, Pirmin Held and Dirk Benyoucef
Furtwangen University, Germany
Mechanical and Medical Engineering
Email:{alaa.saleh, prmin.held, dirk.benyoucef}@hs-furtwangen.de

Djaffar Ould Abdeslam
Universite de Haute-Alsace, France
IUT de Mulhouse
Email: djaffar.ould-abdeslam@uha.fr

***Abstract*— Getting "smarter" Energy by means of advanced electrical and computer engineering tools is the theme of our digital age. This paper presents a new concept for virtual data generation in the context of non-intrusive load monitoring, where the goal is to fill in the gap when aggregate measurements are needed along with individuals ones. We develop a method to generate aggregate measurements starting from single original measurements. The performance of standard NILM tools and algorithms on both original and "virtual" data is compared using own lab measurements.**

Keywords- Smart meters; Non-intrusive load monitoring; Event detection; feature exrtraction; classification; signal processing.

I. INTRODUCTION

Self-healing reliable smart Grids are sought-after all over the world. Non-Intrusive load monitoring is one of the major tools for such ambition; as it delivers detailed information of the energy consumption in a certain facility/building, which can be very useful for various objectives.

Ever since Hart's pioneering work[1] , several approaches were presented over the years [2]; but they were mostly tailored to specific measurements, be it self-collected or from publically available data sets; such measurements were made with a specific application in mind, making them not entirely suitable for extracting and processing of newly adapted features, e.g., harmonical properties in transient states of the current signal [3]. Machine learning algorithms along with advanced signal processing techniques are ready to exploit such features to deliver the best possible identification of electrical appliances.

While several datasets were made publically available in the last decade, they were still not optimal for extracting important features such as harmonical properties. The majority of them were limited to aggregate measurements only or single measurements only, or lacking enough sampling rate in one of them, as shown in Table1.

The question to be addressed in this work is: if only single measurements are available, can we use them for 'synthesizing' whole measurements without actually measure again? it will suffice then for producers to provide interested customers with a list of stand-alone measurements of their device, enabling them to test many scenarios of consumption before actually putting any constellation of devices together,

TABLE I. PUBLIC DATASETS WITH MEASUREMENTS TYPES

Dataset	Type of measurements
REDD	whole-house measurements only [4]
BLUED	whole-house measurements only [5]
PLAID	individual measurements only [6]
UKDALE	whole-house measurements, single measurements with low sampling rate [7]
WHITED	individual measurements only [8]
COOLL	individual measurements only [9]

which is of high importance for big factories and sensitive facilities.

This paper introduces a procedure to generate an approximately identical version of the real whole measurements using single measurements only. The similarity of the resulted signal to the original one will be judged according to the perspective of NILM algorithms.

The remainder of the paper will be organized as follows; In section II, the general data-construction scheme is presented and basic concepts behind it are explained, Section III is devoted to numerical comparisons and tests. Finally, Section IV briefly presents the main conclusions of our study.

II. GENERAL SCHEME AND BASIC CONCEPTS

A flow chart for the proposed procedure is depicted in Figure 1.

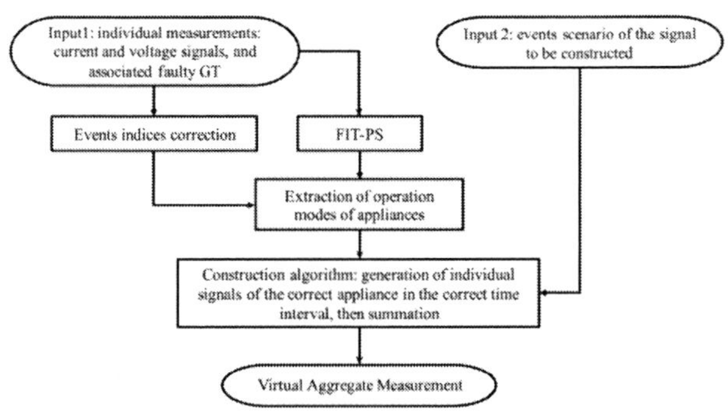

Figure 1. General scheme for virtual aggregation procedure

Figure 1 can be translated to a step-by-step plan for constructing the desired virtual aggregate signal out of real individual measurements:

Step 1. Convert real single measurements to " Frequency Invariant Transformation of Periodic Signals " representation (FIT-PS) [10].

Step 2. Correct event indices.

Step 3. Extract operational modes for each appliance.

Step 4. Generate the targeted current signals according to the desired scenario, adding steady-state periods to meet the desired length, as in Figure 2.

Step 5. Sum the generated current signals according to the desired scenario.

In the following, we will clarify the concepts behind those steps:

A. Phase preserving reconstruction

The general model for reconstructed signal can be written as:

$$I_t = \sum_{i=1}^{N} \delta_i I_i + v \quad (1)$$

where I_t is the aggregate current signal,
N is the number of the appliances,
$I_i, i = 1, \cdots, N$: are the current signals of the individual appliances
$\delta_i, i = 1, \cdots, N$ indicates the state of the corresponding appliance as:

$$\delta_i = \begin{cases} 1, & \text{if the } i^{th} \text{ appliance is 'ON'} \\ 0, & \text{if the } i^{th} \text{ appliance is 'OFF'} \end{cases} \quad (2)$$

v is the additive noise term, which will be assumed to be AWGN with zero mean and appropriate variance.

the loads of the appliances are complex in general, which creates a phase shift between the current signal and the respective voltage signal, this shift can take different values for different appliances.

If we assume the total signal to be composed of two appliances only, and their current signals are given by:

$$I_1 = Ae^{j\theta_1},\ I_2 = Ae^{j\theta_2} \quad (3)$$

Then the total current signal will be obtained as:

$$I = 2Ae^{j\left(\frac{\theta_1+\theta_2}{2}\right)} \cos\left(\frac{\theta_1 - \theta_2}{2}\right) \quad (4)$$

$$|I| = 2A\left|\cos\left(\frac{\theta_1 - \theta_2}{2}\right)\right| \quad (5)$$

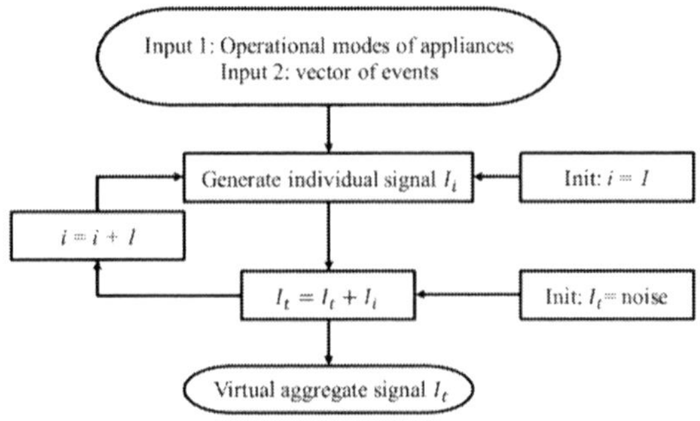

Figure 2. Construction algorithm

Equation (5) shows the dependence of the total signal amplitude on the phase difference between the signals I_1 and I_2, which implies that a simple addition as in (1) will not be correct unless all current signals are added with emphasis on their relative phase.

Fortunately, voltage signal stays almost intact and can be considered a reliable phase reference, so current signals of the individual appliances are converted to FIT-PS representation, which takes the zero-crossing point (from negative to positive) in the voltage signal as a phase reference[10].

B. operational modes extraction

Some appliances have more than one operational mode in general, where we define an operational mode as a distinctive subset of the current signal of a certain device; that can comprise both transient state and part of a steady state. An example is depicted in Figure 3 for a refrigerator.

These operational modes differ from each other and must be taken into account when constructing the virtual aggregate signal. Each operational mode has a different power level in its transient or steady state or both, which can be used to choose the most appropriate one in the construction procedure. Simple structure appliances have only one operational mode in general, e.g., Lamp.

The individual measurements of a certain appliance should be long enough to be able to extract all of their operational modes. The extraction is done as follows:

- For each event, we take a window starting at the event index and containing both transient state and a part of the steady state.
- The power level in the steady state of that window is calculated, then compared with the levels of the previously extracted operational modes of the appliance; it will be added as a new mode if it differs from those previously detected.
- a new sequence number is assigned to the new mode and will be checked again in other occurrences (as the current signal drawn by some appliances will change its operational modes in a sequential manner) .

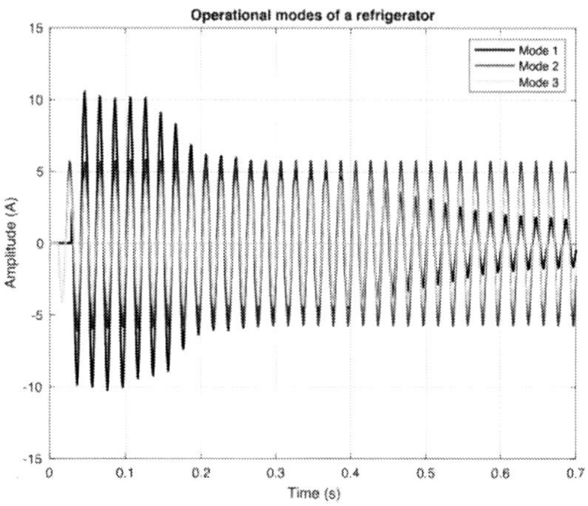

Figure 3. Example of 3 operational modes of a refrigerator

C. *Event indices correction*

Dealing with faulty reference data is an inevitable problem with the vast majority of datasets, so we need to be sure that all events are precise to avoid errors when extracting operational modes.

To correct an event index:

- A window around the possible inaccurate index is taken, it should contain only one event, and be long enough to account for the supposed maximum error (to be set according to training data if possible).
- The event type is checked, if it is an 'off' event, it will be flipped to unify the correction procedure.
- The average between the maximum amplitude of the first few periods in the window and its global maximum is calculated and set as new threshold (yielding better accuracy for low power appliances compared to averaging on the peaks of the last periods in the window).
- The precise event index is the first index in the window where the amplitude exceeds the calculated threshold.

III. Numerical Examples and Tests

In this section, Numerical experiments are to be conducted to test the hypothesis of "suitability of the resulted virtual aggregate signal for training and testing NILM algorithms ".

To do that, the performance of standard NILM algorithms on such generated data will be compared against their performance on an original aggregate signal that has the same scenario of events and appliances. Figure 4 shows a classical chain of processes for typical NILM system.

The comparison will be conducted between the results of standard event detection, feature extraction and classification algorithms on both original aggregate measurements and constructed aggregate measurements. we will use own measurements since the available public datasets are incomplete for our purpose, and to avoid any internal source of error in their reference data.

Figure 4. Typical sequence of processes in NILM system

A. *Collecting single & aggregate measurements*

The measurement system developed previously at our lab [11] was used to collect individual and aggregate measurements; as it enables us to define the set of switching events beforehand. The sampling frequency is set to 4 KHz for both current and voltage signals. Those measurements are part of a public Dataset to be made available in the near future.

Tab. II contains a list of all appliances considered for our tests, this chosen group includes high and low power appliances.

The real measurements were conducted as follows:

- Single measurements for each appliance were taken with 80 pairs of On-Off events, each active cycle was kept running 10 seconds to get transient state and part of the steady state.
- Aggregate measurements, where appliance were switched On and Off randomly, but only 4 appliances can be active on the same time at most.
- A minimum temporal distance of 3 seconds was kept between events.

The virtual aggregate measurements were then generated according to the same scenarios of events followed in the real ones. In Figure 5, an example of those measurements is depicted.

Now that both types of measurements are available, we move to testing NILM tools.

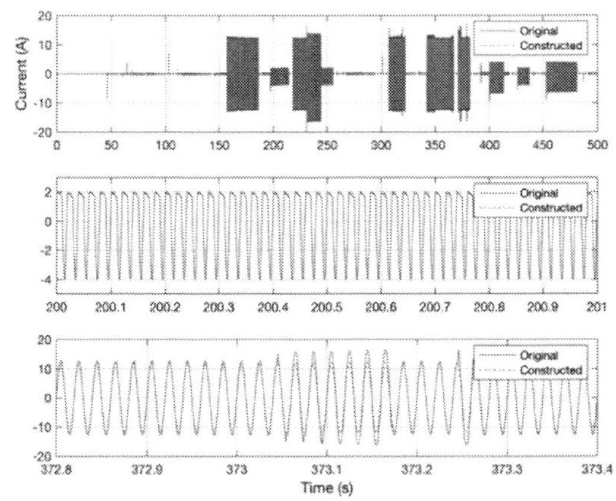

Figure 5. Original and constructed signals together (top), with 2 magnified reigns where they were identical (middle), and most different (bottom)

TABLE II. LIST OF APPLIANCES

ID	NAME	NOMINAL POWER (W)
1	Radio	6
2	Heat gun (setting 1)	820
3	Router	9
4	Black desk lamp	20
5	Light bulb box	20
6	Kettle	2100
7	Black hairdryer (setting 1)	500
8	Fan	22
9	Rotary tool (Dremel)	30
10	LED lamp	1

A. Event Detection

Two different event detectors were used here, the first one is based on the work of Hart [1], while the second is an FBE Event detector [12]. they were applied on the original measurements as well as the constructed ones, and the results are given in the tables III and IV respectively

the following performance metrics were used:

$$P_{recall} = \frac{TP}{FN + TP} \quad , \quad P_{precision} = \frac{TP}{FP + TP} \qquad (6)$$

where *TP* is the number of true detected events,
FN is the number of missed events,
FP is the number of false alarms.

The threshold for Hart Event detector was set to 15W as going below that will result in detecting too many false events due to the high variations of the noise.

Appliances below the chosen threshold were treated as noise in all event-detection tests since the comparison is the main goal here. For FBE detector, several thresholds were chosen and the results are shown in Table IV.

from the tables, both event detectors show a slightly better performance on the constructed measurements (less than 5%).

TABLE III. HART EVENT DETECTOR RESULTS

Signal Type	Thr (W)	Total Event	TP	FN	FP	P_{recall} %	$P_{precision}$ %
Original	1	1600	1411	189	3417	88.19	29.23
Constructed	1	1600	1448	152	5542	90.50	20.72
Original	15	1120	958	162	31	85.54	96.87
Constructed	15	1120	959	161	0	85.62	100

TABLE IV. FBE-BASED EVENT DETECTOR RESULTS

Signal Type	Thr (W)	Total Event	TP	FN	FP	P_{recall} %	$P_{precision}$ %
Original	1	1600	1439	161	135	89.94	91.42
Constructed	1	1600	1480	120	97	92.50	93.85
Original	5	1440	1285	155	53	89.24	96.04
Constructed	5	1440	1322	118	7	91.81	99.47
Original	15	1120	1113	7	37	99.38	96.78
Constructed	15	1120	1090	26	0	97.32	100

B. Feature extraction

we started with a set of steady state features at first, as in most classical NILM literature[2,3], active and reactive powers P and Q were chosen, along with the mean power of the harmonics.

if multiple appliance are active at the same time, a subtraction procedure is done at each event to extract a steady state window suitable for calculating those features of interest, as shown in Figure 6.

while taking the phase and the transient state length into account (assuming that events are well separated which is the case for these measurements).

Apparent, active and reactive powers can then be calculated as:

$$P_A = V_{RMS} * I_{RMS} \qquad (7)$$

$$P = P_A * \cos\theta \qquad (8)$$

$$Q = P_A * \sin\theta \qquad (9)$$

where θ is the phase difference between voltage and current signals.

A band-pass filter is applied on the current signal for each harmonic component $f_{c,n} = nf_0$, where n is the harmonic number, and f_0 is the fundamental frequency. Then the mean harmonic power is given by:

$$P_n = V_{RMS} * I_{n,RMS} \qquad (10)$$

In Figure 6, we compare the selected steady-state features: P_A, P, Q, P_2, P_3, P_4 for two different appliances, a kettle which consumes high power (~ 2 KW), and a Radio that consumes 6 W only, where in each sub-plot, the horizontal axis is for event indices while the vertical is for the power.

while the signals (features) are not identical, yet they are very close to each other, which will be reflected in classification results in the next section.

C. classification

Two standard classifiers [13] were implemented to compare their performance on both types of measurements, the first one is based on a feed-forward neural network (FFNN) while the other one is a support vector machine (SVM) classifier.

both classifiers were trained using extracted features from individual measurements, then tested on the original and constructed virtual measurements respectively.

To simplify the classification process, a power threshold of 25 W was applied to divide the appliances into 2 groups: high power appliances and low power appliances; the features are then fed to the corresponding FFNN subnet (or SVM sub-classifier respectively).

In Table V and VI, results of both classifiers are listed.

Both classifiers delivered slightly better results when applied on constructed measurements, which can be attributed to the higher noise level in the original measurements and the fact that their steady-state features may have more variations and outliers.

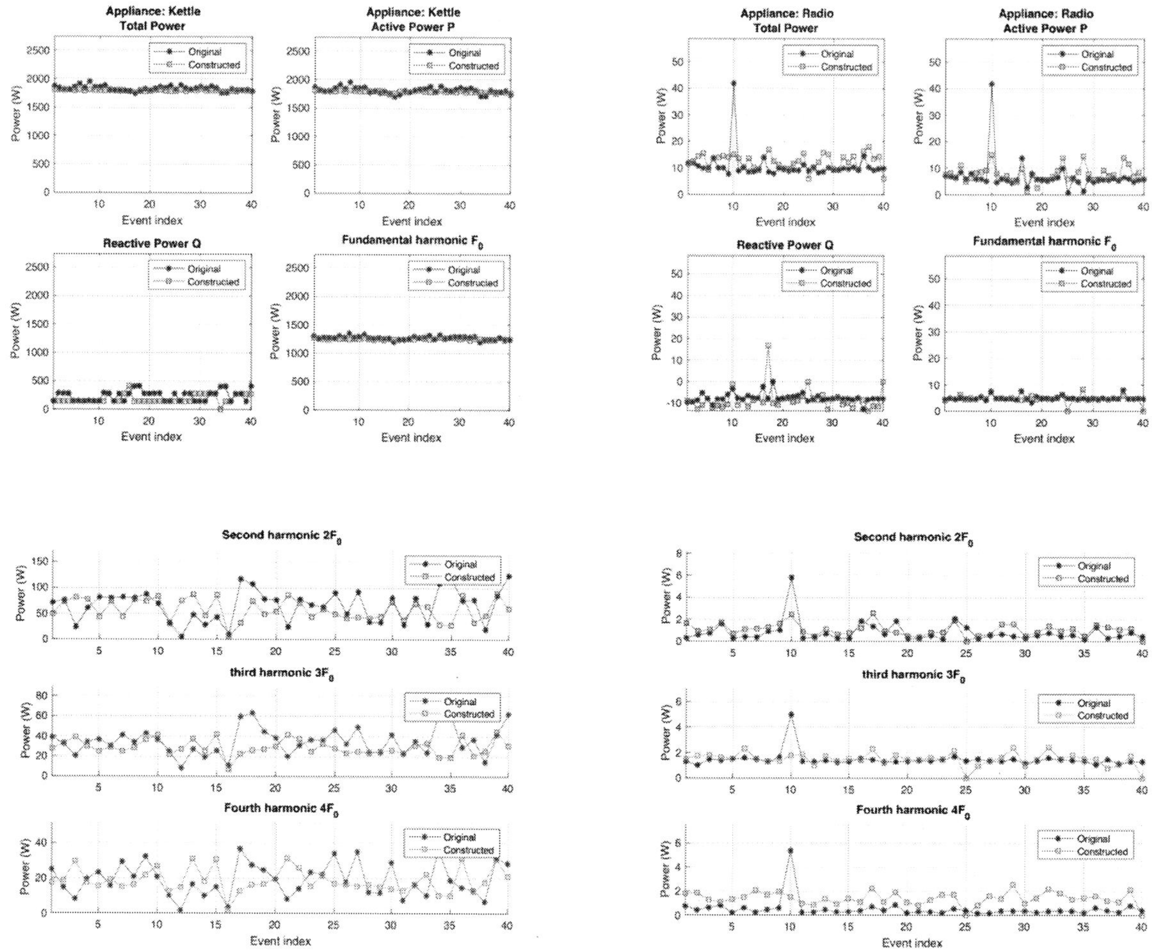

Figure 6. steady state features comparison for : a high power appliance (Kettle, left), a low power appliance (Radio, right)

TABLE V. PERFORMANCE OF FFNN CLASSIFIER

Classifier: FFNN		
%	*High power applinces*	*Low power appliances*
Original	96.9	87.9
Constructed	100	89.6

TABLE VI. PERFORMANCE OF SVM CLASSIFIER

Classifier: SVM						
	High power applinces			*Low power appliances*		
%	*RBF*	*Linear*	*Polynomial*	*RBF*	*Linear*	*Polynomial*
Original	89.7	90.6	96.3	85.4	81.9	86.3
Constructed	99.4	82.2	100	90.6	78.8	90.6

In Figure 7, the detailed confusion matrices for FFNN classifier are also shown, where the two tables on the right side are for constructed measurements, and the tables on the left side are for original measurements.

FFNN correctly classified nearly all of the samples in the test set on both types of measurements in the high power category. Although the overall accuracy rate is very close in low power category, yet a closer look yields differences in misclassification rate among the individual appliances, for example: the Radio (ID=1) was misclassified as Router only once in the original measurements table, while it was misclassified 8 times as Router in the constructed measurements table. This can be attributed to the difference between the modeled additive noise and the real one.

Figure 7. Confusion matrices for FFNN classification results on original measurements (left), and constructed measurements (right)

IV. CONCLUSION AND FUTURE WORK

This paper presents a promising approach for constructing virtual aggregate measurements from original single measurements, enabling better use of available NILM datasets for training and testing Disaggregation algorithms.

Application of standard algorithms for event detection and classification on both types of measurements showed very similar performance. In the future, the noise model will be improved further and virtual single measurements will be tested in a similar manner.

The concept of phase-preserving summation/subtraction will be also used in different disaggregation approaches, e.g., predictive maintenance.

ACKNOWLEDGMENT

This work was created as part of the iMon project (funding number 03FH001IX4).

REFERENCES

[1] G. Hart, "Residential energy monitoring and computerized surveillance via utility power flows," IEEE Technology and Society Magazine, vol. 8,no. 2, Jun. 1989, pp. 12–16.

[2] Hosseini, Sayed Saeed, Kodjo Agbossou, Sousso Kelouwani, and Alben Cardenas, "Non-intrusive load monitoring through home energy management systems: A comprehensive review." Renewable and Sustainable Energy Reviews 79 (2017): 1266-1274.

[3] Du, Yi, Liang Du, Bin Lu, Ronald Harley, and Thomas Habetler, "A review of identification and monitoring methods for electric loads in commercial and residential buildings." In Energy Conversion Congress and Exposition (ECCE), 2010 IEEE, pp. 4527-4533.

[4] J. Kolter, and M. Johnson. "REDD: A public data set for energy disaggregation research, " In Workshop on Data Mining Applications in Sustainability (SIGKDD), 2011

[5] K. Anderson, A. Ocneanu, D. Benitez, A. Rowe, and M. Berges, "BLUED: A fully labeled public dataset for event-based non-intrusive load monitoring research," in Proceedings of the 2nd KDD Workshop on Data Mining Applications in Sustainability (SustKDD), 2011.

[6] J. Gao, S. Gini E. Kara and M. Bergés, "PLAID: a public dataset of high-resoultion electrical appliance measurements for load identification research: demo abstract," in Proceedings of the 1st ACM Conference on Embedded Systems for Energy-Efficient Buildings, 2014.

[7] J. Kelly, W. Knottenbelt, "The UK-DALE dataset domestic appliance-level electricity demand and whole-house demand from five UK homes," Scientific Data, vol. 2, 2015, [online] Available at: https://arxiv.org/abs/1404.0284.

[8] M. Kahl, A. U. Haq, T. Kriechbaumer, and H. A. Jacobsen. "Whited-a worldwide household and industry transient energy data set," In Proceedings of the 3rd International Workshop on Non-Intrusive Load Monitoring (NILM), 2016.

[9] T. Picon, M.N. Meziane, P. Ravier, G. Lamarque, C. Novello, J.C.L. Bunetel, and Y. Raingeaud, "COOLL: Controlled On/Off Loads Library, a Public Dataset of High-Sampled Electrical Signals for Appliance Identification," arXiv preprint arXiv:1611.05803.

[10] P.Held, A. Saleh, D.O. Abdeslam and D. Benyoucef. "Frequency Invariant Transformation of Periodic Signals (FIT-PS) for high frequency Signal Representation in NILM", In BW-CAR| SINCOM, 2016.

[11] T. Bier; D. Ould Abdeslam; J. Merckle; and D. Benyoucef, "Smart meter systems detection & classification using artificial neural networks," 38th Annual Conference on IEEE Industrial Electronics Society, IECON 2012, 2012, pp. 3324 – 3329.

[12] A.Saleh, P. Held, D. Benyoucef, and D. O. Abdeslam. "EMD inspired filtering algorithm for signal analysis in the context of non intrusive load monitoring." In Industrial Electronics Society, IECON 2017-43rd Annual Conference of the IEEE, pp. 3615-3620.

[13] K.Basu,"Classification techniques for non-intrusive load monitoring and prediction of residential loads." PhD diss., Université de Grenoble, 2014.

A Survey on Blind Digital Photographs Forensics Based on Image Analysis

Andreja Samčović
University of Belgrade - Faculty of Transport and Traffic Engineering
Belgrade, Serbia
email: andrej@sf.bg.ac.rs

Abstract— **An increasing number of new publications in the field of multimedia forensics requires thinking about definition of terms in this new research area, as well as relationships with existing disciplines. Some image analysis methods used in forensic discipline are presented in this paper. The focus is on Principal Component Analysis, Error Level Analysis, as well as on Wavelet Transformation. Methods of digital photo forensics, picture formats and formatting, as well as some examples of different forensics tools are presented theoretically and practically on real cases.**

Keywords-multimedia, forensics, digital photos, images, JPEG.

I. Introduction

Blind multimedia forensics is a relatively new research direction in multimedia security [1]. It aims at the detection of altered media content, but does not assume any embedded security scheme. Video footage, scanned images, as well as digital and analog photographs can be the target for manipulations [2]. In this paper, we limit ourselves to digital photographs. From a forensics perspective, several changes in a photograph are widely acceptable. For instance, it is well accepted to improve the image quality, e.g., to enhance the contrast, de-noise an image, or highlight important regions. Forensics investigators search for changes in an image that create a different statement of the image. Thus, an "image forgery" is semantically defined, by considering the information communicated by the original image and the tampered image. The creation of forgeries can be motivated politically, economically, commercially, socially, or individualistically [3].

Digital cameras and video software have made it easier than ever to create high quality pictures and movies. Social Networking Sites, such as MySpace, Google Video, and Flickr make it trivial to distribute pictures, and many are picked up by the mass media. However, there is a problem: how can you tell if a video or picture is real? Is it computer generated or modified? In a world where pictures are more influential than words, being able to distinguish fact from fiction in a systematic way is essential.

Images have power. Whether it is the space shuttle exploding during launch, man walking on the moon, or soldiers raising a flag on *Iwo Jima* during World War II, refuges from Syria, powerful images have influence on the society. The advent of sophisticated digital imaging software and photo-realistic graphics allows artists to strengthen images or convey alternate meanings. Unfortunately, many altered pictures are presented as "real".

Photography lost its innocence many years ago. Only a few decades after *Niepce* created the first photograph in 1814, photographs were already being manipulated. With the advent of high-resolution digital cameras, powerful personal computers and sophisticated photo-editing software, the manipulation of photos is becoming more common. Here, we briefly provide examples of photo tampering throughout history, starting in the middle 1800s. In each case, the original photo is shown on the right and the altered photo is shown on the left.

Figure 1 represents the photograph made by famed photographer *Mathew Brady*, General *Sherman* is seen posing with his generals. General *Francis P. Blair*, shown in the far right, was inserted into this photograph.

Figure 1. General *Sherman* with his generals (1865) [4]

Figure 2 presents the doctored photograph, where *Mao Tse-tung*, shown on the far right, had *Po Ku* removed from the original photograph, after *Po Ku* fell out of favor with *Mao*.

Figure 2. *Mao Tse-tung* (1936) [4]

In the doctored photo, shown in Figure 3, of *Queen Elizabeth* and Canadian Prime Minister in Banff, Alberta, English King *George* VI was removed from the original photograph. This photo was used on an election poster for the Prime Minister. It is hypothesized that the Prime Minister had the photo altered because a photo of just him and the *Queen* painted him in a more powerful light [4].

Figure 3. *Queen Elizabeth*, Canadian Prime Minister and King *George* VI (1939) [4]

The remainder of this paper is organized as follows. Section II presents the image analysis used in digital forensic discipline, such as Principal Component Analysis. Section III describes Error Level Analysis, another method for digital photographs analysis. Some examples carried out by online forensic tool are presented by using this analysis. The wavelet transformation is pointed out in the next section. Finally, we outline some directions for research in the field of digital image forensics

II. IMAGE ANALYSIS TOOLS

The following terms are used throughout this paper:

- **Computer Generated (CG)**. An image created entirely with computer software. For example, every scene from the movie *Toy Story* is computer generated image.
- **Digital photo**. A photograph from a digital camera or scanned image that has not been manipulated.
- **Digitally enhanced photo**. A digital photo that has been manipulated. This includes minor manipulations, such as cropping and red eye reduction, to major re-coloring or digitally combining with other images.
- **Photo-shopping**. Adobe Photoshop is a popular tool that can digitally enhance images. Images that have been modified using Photoshop or similar drawing tools (e.g., Gimp, Corel Draw, MS Paint) are described as being "photo-shopped" or "shopped". The quality of the shopped image depends on both the tool and the artist. Many shopped images are obvious, while others can be very subtle.
- **Principal Component Analysis (PCA)**. An analysis approach based on data clustering.
- **Wavelet Transformations**. An analysis method based on signal decomposition.

Image format analysis can confirm metadata in accuracies and detect the last tool that modified an image [5]. However, format analysis does not evaluate the image itself. Methods, such as principal component analysis, error level analysis, and wavelet transformations permit the identification of specific image manipulations.

A. Principal Component Analysis

The *Joint Photographic Expert Group* (JPEG) image compression standard is currently the most commonly used image format for digital photographs. Most consumer cameras store the picture already in the JPEG format. The main advantages are the simplicity of the format, spatially local compression operations, and the fact that it is an open standard. JPEG compression is lossy, thus every time an image is stored in this format, content is slightly changed. This property has been the starting point for developing forensic algorithms. The information loss enables analysts to distinguish whether an image has been compressed once or multiple times with the JPEG algorithm [6]. Depending on the scenario, an answer to this question can be very useful in practice. For instance, assume that a photographer claims that an image is directly copied from his camera. Thus, the image should be single-compressed. Evidence that the image, or a part of it, is double-compressed can deliver an initial suspicion to a forensic investigator [7].

The image rendered from a JPEG file is not a perfect copy of the original image. Each time a JPEG image is resaved by a graphics editor, the image loses quality – even if the editing tool made no picture changes. This leads to a problem with quantization table analysis: if an image is saved at 75%, loaded into a drawing program, and resaved at 90%, then the quantization tables will reflect 90% while the image quality is 67.5% (90% of 75%).

Errors within a JPEG appear as blocky artifacts and color distortions. The blocky artifacts appear on the 8x8 pixel boundaries used by the JPEG algorithm. In many cases, the JPEG artifacts are too subtle for the human eye to detect. However, PCA tool can identify these JPEG artifacts.

For image analysis, PCA is used to identify the color spectrum within the image. Consider an entire image that is plotted based on the pixel colors (R, G, B) is mapped to (x, y, z), as presented in Figure 4. Most images have a narrow range of colors that appear as a large cluster when plotted. PC1 identifies the widest range across the color set. When two images are spliced to get her from different color sets, they usually end up forming two distinct clusters. With PCA, areas within the picture that come from different clusters will have noticeably different values [8].

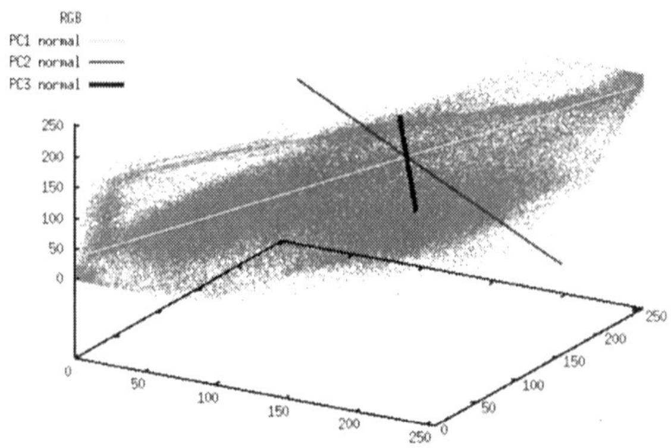

Figure 4. Sample scatter plot of an image and principal components [8]

In 2006, *Andrea Bertaccini* was awarded the "CG Choice Award" from the CG Society for the rendering of *Buzz Aldrin's* famous moon-walk, that is presented in Figure 5. According to the artist, the picture was based the original NASA photo. However, details within the picture suggest additional resources.

Figure 5. Image by *Andrea Bertaccini* and PC1 analysis [8]

The artist stated that the image was created using 3DSMAX and post-processed using Combustion and Photoshop tool. The quantization matrix matches Photoshop's "high (8)" quality, equivalent to a JPEG saved at 89%. However, using the PC1 line shows a significant number of artifacts that resemble a quality around 40%. This suggests that the image was saved multiple times.

III. ERROR LEVEL ANALYSIS

JPEG is a lossy format, but the amount of error introduced by each resave is not linear. A 90% image resaved at 90% is equivalent to a one-time save of 81%. Similarly, saving an image at 75% and then resaving it at 90% (75% to 90%) will generate virtually the same image as 90% to 75%, or saved once at 67.5%. The amount of error is limited to the 8x8 cells used by the JPEG algorithm; after roughly 64 resaves, there is virtually no change. However, when an image is modified, the 8x8 cells containing the modifications are no longer at the same error level as the rest of the unmodified image [8].

Error Level Analysis (ELA) works by intentionally resaving the image at known error rate, such as 95%, and then computing the difference between the images. If there is virtually no change, then the cell has reached its local minima for error at that quality level. However, if there is a large amount of change, then the pixels are not at their local minima and are effectively "original". Figure 6 presents an example of picture manipulation that is used in advertising for "*Old Spice*" company.

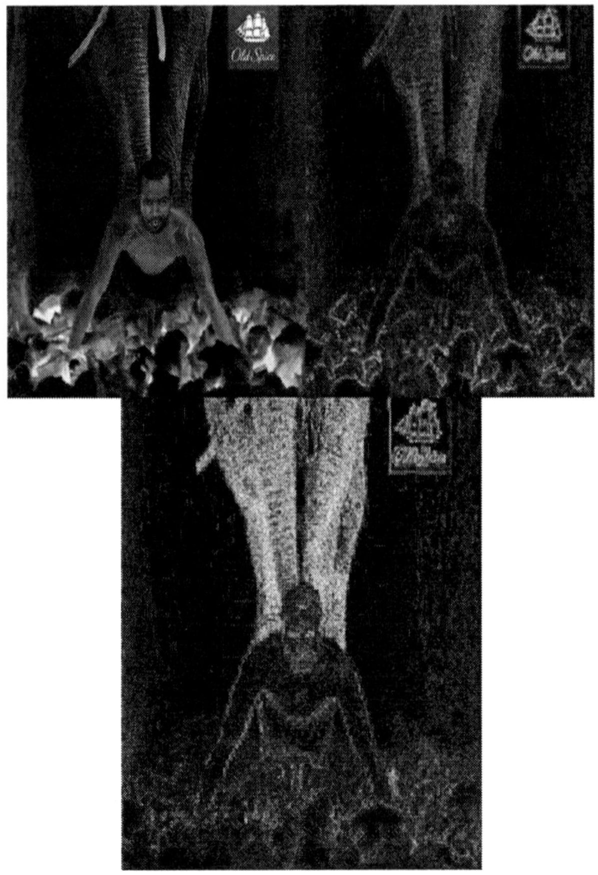

Figure 6. "*Old Spice*" commercial (upper left), 88% of JPEG quality (upper right) and Noise Analysis (lower, online tool "Forensically")

We used Error Level Analysis by online forensic tool "Forensically" and our analysis confirmed that the picture is computer generated and presents a composition of four parts: logo of "*Old Spice*", actor *Isaiah Mustafa*, an elephant and ingle.

IV. Wavelet Transformation

While ELA is useful for identifying recent changes relative to the number of resaves, resaving a picture many times or using a very low quality JPEG can obscure ELA results. However, changes to pictures can still be identified through the use of wavelet transformations.

Wavelets are used for signal decomposition. A single wavelet is a known and well-defined signal. This signal can be scaled and added in order to create more complex signals. Any real signal can be decomposed into a set of wavelets that, when combined, approximate the signal.

Although wavelets can approximate any signal, some signal types are more difficult to approximate. Square waves, or areas with sharp color changes, are difficult to approximate. Although the flat area of the square wave can be approximated quickly, the sharp corners may require many wavelets to properly fit the signal. Similarly, linear transitions are approximated by a series of stepped square waves. In addition, extreme values (black and white) are difficult to approximate. In contrast, wavelets are very good at approximating "natural" colors and noisy images, such as those generated by digital cameras.

Figure 7. Photo-shoped image with *Hillary Clinton*, resolved with 5% of wavelets and ELA

In the case of digital photos, the picture is the signal and wavelets approximate the image. Rendering an 800x600 pixel image requires up to 480,000 wavelets per color channel to perfectly recreate the picture. However, if only a small percentage of the wavelets are used, then the main attributes of the picture become visible, even if they are blurry. As more wavelets are included in the rendering, the image sharpens. And even more wavelets fine - tune the sharpened colors.

This property of wavelets – from blurry to sharp to correct colors – can be used to identify image manipulations [9]. In particular, the entire image should sharpen at the same rate. If the picture components are scaled or merged from different focal lengths, then the components will sharpen at different rates [8].

The left image from Figure 7 was created by "redcard" as part of an image manipulation contest. Rendering the image with 5% of the available wavelets shows a crisp torso and near-crisp arms and legs. However, the face remains fuzzy. The fuzziness ends just below the chin. The wavelet analysis suggests that the head is from a picture of *Hillary Clinton*, the neck and torso comes from a second source, and the arms and legs may be from a third source.

V. Conclusion

Digital photography almost completely replaced analogue pictures. As there are many techniques for counterfeiting digital photography, several tools for multimedia forensics have considered. In image forensics, researchers aim to provide computational tools to support human experts in deciding about the authenticity of an image. The process of detecting image manipulation can be complex, thus there is need for the concentration on the precious details in the picture. The same tool is iteratively applied to observe discrepancies between image regions, as a good forensics tool.

Acknowledgment

This work was partially supported by the Ministry of the Science, Education and Technological Development of the Republic of Serbia (projects TR 32025 and 32048).

References

[1] S. Lian, D. Kanellopoulos, and G. Ruffo, "Recent advances in multimedia information security", Informatica, vol. 33, pp. 3-24, 2009.

[2] R. Bohme, F.C. Freiling, T. Gloe, and M. Kirchner, "Multimedia forensics is not computer forensics", Proceedings 3rd International Workshop on Computational Forensics (IWCF 2009), The Hague, Netherlands, pp. 1-14, 13-14 August 2009.

[3] A. Samčović, "Recent advances in digital image forensics", XXXII Simposium on new technologies in postal and telecommunications traffic (PosTel 2014), Belgrade, Serbia, pp. 299-308, 2-3 December 2014.

[4] H. Farid, "A survey of image forgery detection", IEEE Signal Processing Magazine, vol. 26, No. 2, pp. 16-25, 2009.

[5] W. Ku, „Exploiting "The world is flat" syndrome in digital photo collections for contextual metadata", Proceedings 8th International Symposium on Multimedia (ISM 2006), pp. 1-7, 2006.

[6] Y.Q. Zhao, F.Y. Shih, and Y.Q. Shi, "Passive detection of paint-doctored JPEG images", Proceedings IWDW 2010, Lecture Notes on Computer Science 6526, pp. 1-11, 2011.
[7] A. Samčović, "Review of multimedia passive forensic techniques for image forgery detection", VI Conference on Business Information Security (BISEC 2014), Belgrade, Serbia, pp. 54-60, 18 June 2014.
[8] N. Krawetz, "A picture's worth...digital image analysis and forensics", Texas, United States, Hacker Factory Solutions, pp. 11-16; 52-64, 2007.
[9] Y.J. Ming, "A method of the hiding fingerprint image data based on wavelet coefficients redundancy", Proceedings 3rd International Conference on Computer Science and Information Technology (ICCSIT 2010), Chengdu, China, pp. 441-444, 9-11 July 2010.

Simultaneous Velocity Estimation and Range Compression for High Speed Targets ISAR Imaging Based on the Chirp Fourier Transform

Zibo Zhou, Libing Jiang, Zhuang Wang, Ruibin Tu, Yang Wang, Zhenhai Xu
College of Electronic Science, National University of Defense Technology,
Changsha, Hunan Province, People's Republic of China
zibo_travel@163.com

Abstract—**High speed targets (e.g., aircraft, satellite) imaging is crucial for air traffic safety and space surveillance. Based on the target motion model, the characteristics of the multi-component linear frequency modulation (LFM) signal caused by the high speed motion are analyzed in detail. Furthermore, a novel method based on the chirp Fourier transform and Shannon minimum entropy principle for high speed targets Inverse Synthetic Aperture Radar (ISAR) imaging is proposed. Firstly, according to the velocity scope, the chirp rate interval is established. Secondly, the corresponding phase term is constructed to compensate the quadratic phase term caused by the high speed motion. After the range compression, the range profile with minimum entropy is regarded as the optimal compensated profile, and finally the required ISAR image is formed by the cross-range compression. The simulation experiments demonstrate that the proposed method can obtain better ISAR images than the classic range doppler algorithm and fractional Fourier transform algorithm.**

Keywords-high speed targets; Inverse Synthetic Aperture Radar (ISAR); chirp-Fourier transform; minimum entropy.

I. INTRODUCTION

Radar can actively transmit electromagnetic waves, and then extract the target information from the received echoes. In this sense, radar can explore targets in any time and under any circumstance. Due to the limitation of resolution, the targets observed by the traditional radars are generally considered as point targets with position and motion parameters. With the development of modern wideband radar, the capability of radar has been expanded from target detection, location, and tracking to target imaging, which greatly improves the ability of radar targets recognition. Therefore, radar imaging has become a research frontier in the field of radar signal processing. Inverse Synthetic Aperture Radar (ISAR), as a representative application in the radar imaging domain, has the ability of acquiring target image with electromagnetic information. In detail, based on the scattering point model, ISAR obtains high range resolution by transmitting wideband signal, and derives high cross-range resolution from the Doppler effect produced by relative rotation between radar and target [1].

As a classical imaging method in the domain of ISAR imaging, the Range-Doppler (RD) algorithm forms a two-dimensional high resolution ISAR image by using a two-dimensional Fourier transform along the range and the cross-range directions respectively [2][3]. However, the RD algorithm is only valid for the low speed moving targets and is not suitable for the high speed targets. The reason lies in the fact that, within a pulse duration time, the moving distance of a high speed target with approximately a few kilometers per second (e.g., satellite, space station) will exceed one range cell, which is in contradiction with the "stop and go" preconditions required by the RD algorithm and may cause the problem of range profile distortion [4][5][6].

Many methods have been proposed to solve the problem of range profile distortion of the high speed targets. Zhang et at. [6] proposed a velocity compensation method, where Wigner Distribution and Radon transform were utilized to estimate the velocity of high speed targets in advance. But the cross terms generated by Wigner Distribution made the velocity difficult to estimate. Fractional Fourier transform (FRFT) and Shannon minimum entropy principle were combined for velocity estimation in [7]. However, the multiple scattering points model has a great impact on the peak search in FRFT, and may lead to pseudo-peak location. A novel high speed motion compensation method based on Keystone transform and FRFT was proposed by Li et al. [8] in 2017. It should be noted that the numerous approximations in the method may lead to a series of biases in the results. In conclusion, most of the existing ISAR imaging methods follow the strategy of 'velocity estimation, velocity compensation, range compression and cross-range compression', which complicates the imaging process and magnifies the error propagation of the velocity estimation.

Since the velocity estimation is only an intermediate step of ISAR imaging, this paper proposes a method to accomplish velocity estimation and range compression simultaneously by using chirp Fourier transform and Shannon minimum entropy principle. After that, the Fourier transform along cross-range direction is implemented to obtain the ISAR image. This method can avoid the peak search biases in FRFT and reduce the complexity of the imaging algorithm, while maintaining the quality of ISAR imaging results.

The rest of this paper is organized as follows: Section II deals with the high speed target echo model and the origin of range distortion. Section III is devoted to the definition of chirp Fourier transform, the concrete process of velocity compensation, and the range compression based on chirp Fourier transform. The simulation results are demonstrated and discussed in Section IV. Section V draws conclusion on the proposed imaging method.

II. High Speed Targets Echo Model and Range Distortion

The geometry configuration of a monostatic two-dimension ISAR imaging system is shown in Fig. 1. According to the electromagnetic scattering theory, when radar works in the high frequency domain, the total echo received from the target can be modeled as the sum of echoes from different isolate scattering points within the target.

Denoting that the radar transmits LFM signal with the carrier frequency f_c, bandwidth B, pulse duration time T_p, pulse interval T_r, and intensity σ_i for the ith scattering point, then the mth echo received from the target can be modeled as follows:

$$s_r(\hat{t},t_m)=\sum_i \sigma_i rect\left(\frac{\hat{t}-\tau_i}{T_p}\right)\exp\left[-j2\pi\left(f_c(\hat{t}-\tau_i)+\frac{1}{2}\gamma(\hat{t}-\tau_i)^2\right)\right] \quad (1)$$

Where $t_m=mT_r$ is the slow-time, $\hat{t}=t-mT_r$ is the fast-time, $\gamma=B/T_p$ is the chirp rate, $\tau_i=\frac{2R_{im}}{c}=\frac{2(R_{im0}+v_m\hat{t})}{c}$ is the time delay, R_{im0} is the original distance between the radar and the ith scattering point at mth pulse, v_m is the velocity of the target component on the radar-target direction at the mth pulse.

Denoting the reference distance of mth pulse as R_{ref}, then the reference time delay is $\tau_{ref}=\frac{2R_{ref}}{c}$. With the same carrier frequency f_c and chirp rate γ as the transmitted signal, the reference signal can be denoted as:

$$s_{ref}(\hat{t},t_m)=\sum_i rect\left(\frac{\hat{t}-\tau_{ref}}{T_{ref}}\right)\exp\left[-j2\pi\left(f_c(\hat{t}-\tau_{ref})+\frac{1}{2}\gamma(\hat{t}-\tau_{ref})^2\right)\right] \quad (2)$$

The result of the dechirp process, i.e., multiplying the conjugate of (2) with (1), can be written as:

$$s_{if}(\hat{t},t_m)=s_r(\hat{t},t_m)\times s_{ref}^*(\hat{t},t_m) \quad (3)$$

Then the precise echo model after the dechirp process can be modeled as:

$$s_{if}(\hat{t},t_m)=\sum_i \sigma_i rect\left(\frac{\hat{t}-\tau}{T_p}\right)\exp\left[-j2\pi\left(\varphi_i+f_i\hat{t}+\frac{1}{2}K\hat{t}^2\right)\right] \quad (4)$$

$$\varphi_i=f_c\frac{2(R_{im0}-R_{refm})}{c}-\gamma\frac{2(R_{im0}^2-R_{refm}^2)}{c^2} \quad (5)$$

$$f_i=\frac{2v_m}{c}f_c+\gamma\frac{2(R_{im0}-R_{ref})}{c}-\frac{4\gamma R_{im0}v_m}{c^2} \quad (6)$$

$$K=\gamma\frac{4v_m}{c}\left(1-\frac{v_m}{c}\right) \quad (7)$$

As for the low speed targets like airplanes, the moving distance along range direction within the pulse duration time does not exceed one range cell ($v_mT_p<<\frac{c}{2B}$). Hence, the velocity item v_m/c can be neglected. Consequently, (4) is simplified to single-frequency signal, which means that implementing Fourier transform along range direction can achieve the high range resolution. Nonetheless, as for the high speed targets like satellites, their velocities no longer meet the above condition, sometimes even $v_mT_p>>\frac{c}{2B}$ will occur. In such cases, the velocity term v_m/c cannot be ignored anymore.

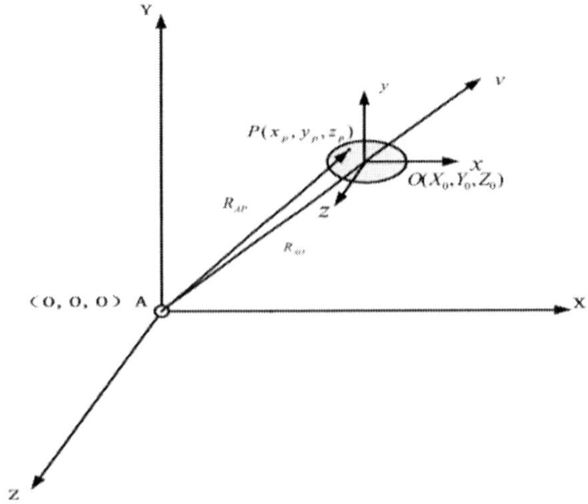

Figure 1. Geometry of imaging system

According to (4) - (7), due to the velocity v_m, the echo of the high speed target after dechirp process is a multi-component LFM signal. However, since R_{im0} changes with different scattering point, the carrier f_i of multi-component LFM signal also varies consequently. Furthermore, since the pulse duration time is very short (a fraction of a millisecond), v_m can be regarded as invariant within the pulse duration time. Therefore, the chirp rate K in (4) and (7) can also be considered constant. In view of the wide bandwidth of the LFM signal, the direct Fourier transform makes the spectrums of multiple LFM signals overlap, which is so-called range distortion. Consequently, the range resolution will be degraded and the ISAR image will be defocused. For high resolution range profile, multi-component LFM signals should be changed to multiple single-frequency signals in advance. After that, the Fourier transform along cross-range can be taken to form the desired high resolution ISAR image.

III. Velocity Compensation Based on Chirp Fourier Transform

Chirp Fourier transform is an effective method to eliminate the quadratic phase term caused by the high speed motion. This section will introduce the definition of chirp Fourier transform and the velocity compensation method based on it.

A. Chirp Fourier transform

Chirp Fourier transform is a kind of parameter estimation method in signal processing field. Chirp Fourier transform of signal $s(t)$ is as follows:

$$F(f,\gamma)=\int s(t)\exp\left[j2\pi\left(ft+\frac{1}{2}\gamma t^2\right)\right]dt \quad (8)$$

Denote $s(t)$ as binomial signal:

$$s(t)=\exp\left[-j2\pi\left(f_1 t+\frac{1}{2}\gamma_1 t^2\right)\right] \quad (9)$$

Where f_1, γ_1 are the carrier and chirp rate of signal $s(t)$ respectively. Plugging (9) into (7), the result of chirp Fourier transform of $s(t)$ is:

$$F(f,\gamma)=\int \exp\left\{j2\pi\left[(f-f_1)t+\frac{1}{2}(\gamma-\gamma_1)t^2\right]\right\}dt \quad (10)$$

When $f_1=f$, $\gamma_1=\gamma$, the integration result of the signal $s(t)$ can accumulate coherently to a peak at (f_1,γ_1) . If not, the integrated signal will be cancelled out, and the amplitude after accumulation will be much lower. Therefore, after chirp Fourier transform, a peak in the amplitude map will be formed at (f_1,γ_1) , which are the parameters to be estimated.

B. Velocity compensation based on chirp Fourier transform

As discussed in (4), the received echo from the high speed target is a multi-component binomial signal. The spectrum will be shifted as an entirety, although the carrier frequency f_i varies within the slow-time domain. Range alignment and phase correction can eliminate the effect. It is known that the primary reason for range distortion is the quadratic phase term of the echo. As a result, compensation for the quadratic phase term can avoid range distortion effectively. The quadratic phase term for velocity compensation is constructed as follows:

$$S_{comp}=\exp\left[j2\pi\left(\frac{1}{2}K_1\hat{t}^2\right)\right] \qquad \hat{t}\in\left(-\frac{T_p}{2},\frac{T_p}{2}\right) \quad (11)$$

After multiplying (11) with (4) and taking Fourier transform within the fast-time domain, the range profile is:

$$\begin{aligned} S_r(f,t_m)&=\int\sum_i\sigma_i \,\mathrm{rect}\left(\frac{\hat{t}-\tau}{T_p}\right)\exp\left\{-j2\pi\left[\varphi_i+f_i\hat{t}+f\hat{t}+\frac{1}{2}(K-K_1)\hat{t}^2\right]\right\}d\hat{t} \\ &=\sum_i\sigma_i\exp(-j2\pi\varphi_i)\int \mathrm{rect}\left(\frac{\hat{t}-\tau}{T_p}\right)\exp\left\{-j2\pi\left[f_i\hat{t}+f\hat{t}+\frac{1}{2}(K-K_1)\hat{t}^2\right]\right\}d\hat{t} \end{aligned} \quad (12)$$

From (12), when $K_1=K=\frac{4v_m}{c}\gamma$, the quadratic phase term will be eliminated efficiently, and LFM signal will be converted to single-frequency signal, which means that the range distortion is avoided.

After chirp Fourier transform, the range profile will focus well. Additionally, for the sake of simplicity, the real chirp rate is changed to the form of digital chirp rate $k=K/f_s^2$. Constructing the compensation phase as follows:

$$S_{comp}=\exp\left[j2\pi\left(\frac{1}{2}kn^2\right)\right] \qquad n\in\left[-\frac{N}{2},\cdots\cdots,\frac{N}{2}-1\right] \quad (13)$$

According to the velocity scope, the digital chirp rate $k=\frac{4\gamma v}{cf_s^2}$ interval is determined by:

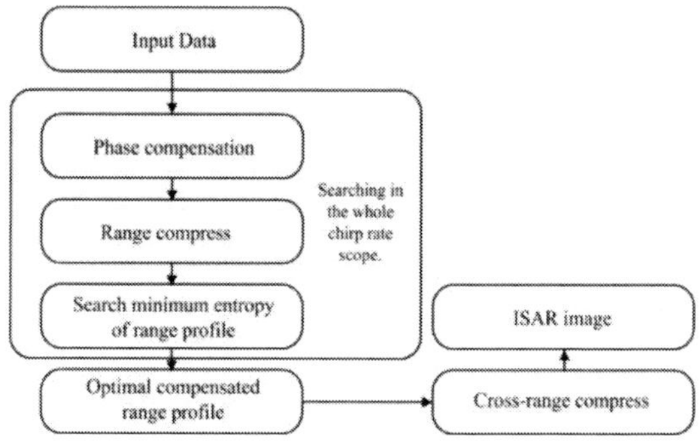

Figure 2. Concrete flowchart of the proposed method

$$k\in\left[\frac{4\gamma v_{min}}{cf_s^2},\frac{4\gamma v_{max}}{cf_s^2}\right] \quad (14)$$

As the quadratic phase term is compensated by chirp Fourier transform over the entire range of the digital chirp rate k, many range profiles are obtained. The entropy of each range profile is then calculated, and the specified range profile with the smallest entropy is considered as the optimal one. The exact definition of entropy can be written as (15). Through the above process, the high resolution range profile with the optimal velocity compensation is obtained. The concrete flowchart of the proposed method is shown in Fig. 2.

After chirp Fourier transform, the cross-range Fourier transform and the Keystone transform are combined to form the ISAR image of the target. The image entropy and the image contrast are introduced to evaluate the quality of the ISAR image. Larger contrast and smaller entropy indicate that an ISAR image has better quality. Denoting ISAR image as $I(m,n)$, the definition of ISAR image entropy and contrast can be written as [9]:

$$\begin{aligned} H&=-\sum_{m=1}^{M}\sum_{n=1}^{N}P(m,n)\ln P(m,n) \\ P(m,n)&=\frac{|I(m,n)|}{\sum_{m=1}^{M}\sum_{n=1}^{N}|I(m,n)|} \end{aligned} \quad (15)$$

$$C=\frac{\sqrt{E\left\{\left[I(m,n)-E(I(m,n))\right]^2\right\}}}{E\left[I(m,n)\right]} \quad (16)$$

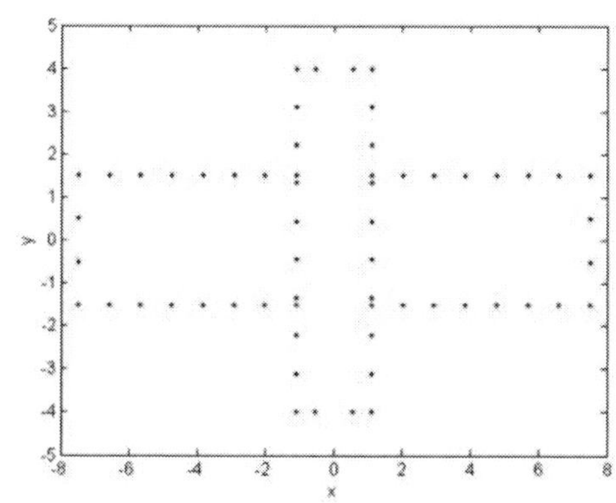

Figure 3. Scattering point model

TABLE I. RADAR AND TARGET PARAMETER CONFIGURATION

Target parameter	**Real size**		**Flying height**	**Velocity scope**	**Ideal scattering point number**
	15m X 8m		*100Km*	*(6100-6450) Km/s*	*64*
Radar parameter	f_c	B	T_p	PRF	f_s
	16GHz	*1GHz*	*0.1ms*	*256Hz*	*5.12MHz*

TABLE II. ISAR IMAGE QUALITY

Image quality/ algorithm	**RD algorithm**	**FRFT algorithm**	**The proposed method**
Entropy	*9.7180*	*9.5759*	*9.0735*
Contrast	*5.4974*	*6.9348*	*7.7437*

IV. EXPERIMENT RESULT

To demonstrate the compensation performance of the quadratic phase term with chirp Fourier transform, a simple satellite scattering model with 64 scattering points is established, as is shown in Fig. 3. Simulation experiments are taken under Signal Noise Ratio (SNR) of 5dB, and the parameter configurations for the radar and the target are shown in Table I.

The concrete target scattering point model is presented in Fig. 3. Fig. 4 illustrates the range profiles of the 50th pulse obtained by the proposed method and Fast Fourier transform (FFT), wherein the result of FFT is shown in red dotted line, and the result of the proposed method is shown in the blue full line. Owing to the wide bandwidth of LFM signal, direct Fourier transform without velocity compensation will lead to the spectrum overlap between multi-component LFM signals. As a result, the range profile distortion will occur, as shown

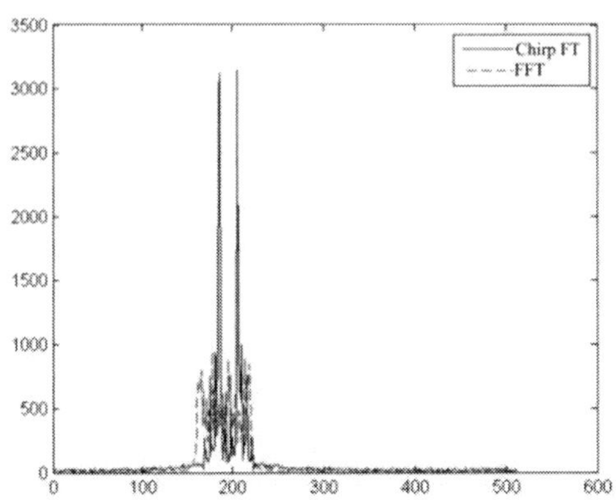

Figure 4. Range profile of 50th echo

in red dotted line in Fig. 4. Since chirp Fourier transform can convert LFM signal to single-frequency signal, the range distortion can be avoided efficiently, as is shown in blue full line in Fig. 4. In conclusion, the range profile of the proposed method focuses better than that of FFT.

Fig. 5, Fig. 6 and Fig. 7 are the ISAR imaging results obtained by RD, FRFT and the proposed algorithm respectively. In addition, the image entropy and image contrast of these three methods are shown in Table II. The image entropy and image contrast of Fig. 5, Fig. 6 and Fig. 7 are (9.7180,5.4974), (9.5759,6.9348), and (9.0735,7.7437) respectively.

Furthermore, as is shown in Fig. 5, the imaging result obtained by the RD algorithm is severely defocused and the scattering points cannot be resolved from each other. Although the ISAR image of the FRFT algorithm shown in Fig. 6 is better focused than that of the RD algorithm, there are still many scattering points difficult to resolve in the target model. Comparing to the above methods, the imaging result obtained by the proposed method is better focused, as is shown in Fig. 7. According to the energy convergence level, the image resolution of the proposed method is higher than that of the RD and FRFT algorithms. Therefore, through qualitative analysis, the ISAR image obtained by the proposed method is much clearer than that of the RD and FRFT algorithms. It can also be noticed that the entropy of the ISAR image obtained by the proposed method is smaller than that of the other two methods, while its contrast is greater than the other two methods. The quantitative comparison on the image entropy and the image contrast demonstrates that the image quality of the proposed method is better than that of RD and FRFT algorithms. In summary, the ISAR image of the proposed method has a higher level of energy convergence.

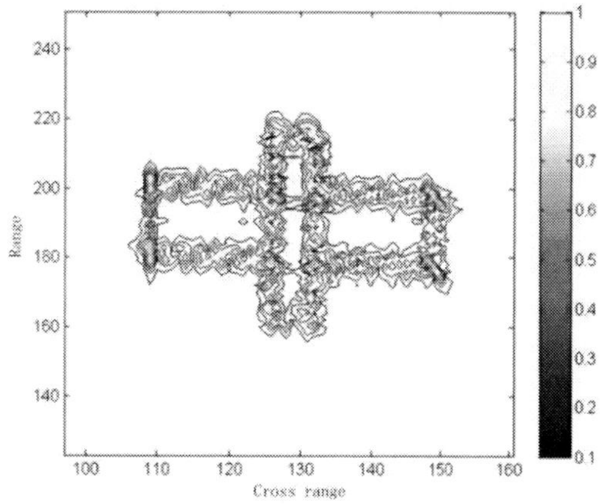

Figure 5. Image of RD algorithm

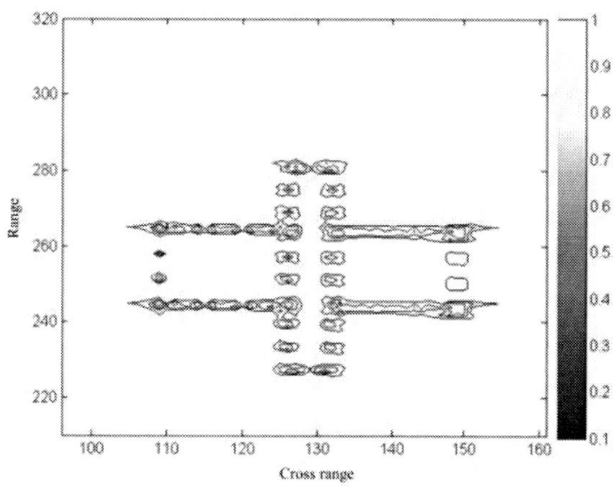

Figure 6. Image of FRFT algorithm

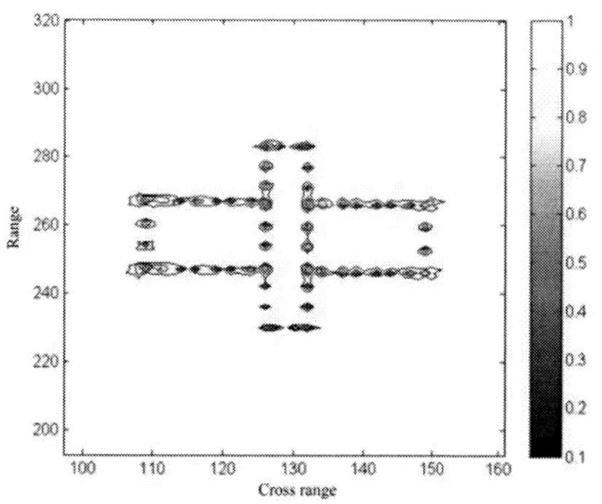

Figure 7. Image of the proposed method

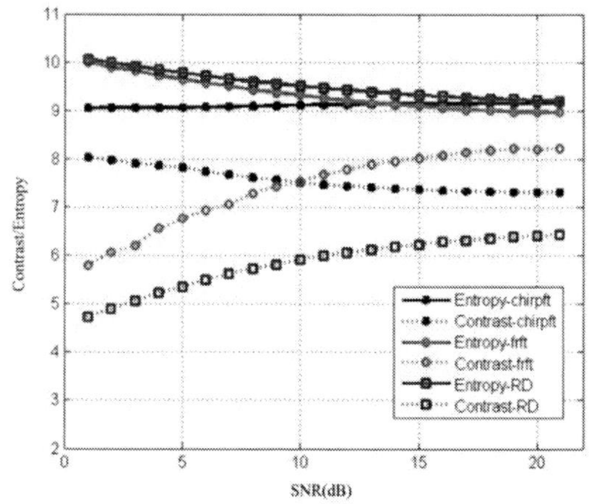

Figure 8. Image quality for different SNR

In conclusion, the simulation experiment results demonstrate that the proposed method can compensate the quadratic phase terms better than the RD algorithm and the FRFT algorithm. Consequently, the proposed method can obtain better ISAR imaging results for the high speed targets

Fig. 8 shows the imaging results of the three methods under different SNR levels (0~20dB). According to the curves in Fig. 8, the image entropy and the image contrast of the proposed method are much smoother than that of the RD algorithm and the FRFT algorithm, which means that the proposed method is more robust to the SNR level. Especially compared with RD and FRFT algorithms, the ISAR image obtained by the proposed method has less entropy and greater contrast at low SNR level, as is shown in Fig. 8. Thus, the proposed method is more suitable to low SNR level situation.

In conclusion, the imaging results presented in this paper are superior to the classic RD and FRFT algorithms. Meanwhile, the proposed algorithm is more robust to the SNR level.

V. CONCLUSION

The echo of the high speed target is a multi-component LFM signal, therefore, the direct Fourier transform will bring about range distortion, which leads to a blurred ISAR image. This paper proposes a novel imaging method based on chirp Fourier transform and Shannon minimum entropy principle, which can eliminate quadratic phase term caused by high speed motion and achieve range compression simultaneously. The proposed method can simplify the complexity of the algorithm, while maintain the quality of the ISAR imaging result. Additionally, the proposed method is more robust to the SNR level. The simulation experiments show that the imaging results obtained by the proposed method are better than that of RD and FRFT algorithms.

REFERENCES

[1] C.C. Chen, and H.C. Andrews. "Target-motion-induced Radar Imaging," IEEE Trans. AES., vol.AES-16, pp. 2-14, 1980.

[2] J Li, R.B. Wu, and V.C. Chen. "Robust Autofocus Algorithm for ISAR Imaging of Moving Targets," IEEE Trans. AES., vol.AES-37, pp.1056-1068, 2001.

[3] J. Yu, J. S. Yang, Motion compensation of ISAR imaging for high-speed moving target, IEEE Int. Symp. KAM, (2008) 124-127.

[4] J. Yu and J. Yang. Motion compensation of ISAR imaging for high speed moving target. IEEE International Symposium on Knowledge Acquisition & Modeling Workshop, 2009:124-127.D.

[5] X. Rao, H.H. Tao, J. Xie, J. Su, and W.P. Li. Long-time coherent integration detection of weak maneuvering target via integration algorithm, improved axis rotation discrete chirp-Fourier transform. IET Radar, Sonar & Navigation, Vol.9, Issue:7, 8 2015: 917-926.

[6] D.C. Zhang, Y Zhang, W.D. Chen, and D.J. Wang; Three dimensional ISAR Imaging of High Speed Space Target. 9th International Conference on Signal Processing (ICSP'08), Beijing, China, 2008, P2485-2488.J. Clerk Maxwell, A Treatise on Electricity and Magnetism, 3rd ed., vol. 2. Oxford: Clarendon, 1892, pp.68–73.

[7] A.F. Liu, X.H. Zhu, and L. Jin. Application of the fractional Fourier transform to ISAR range profile compensation of fast-moving target. Statistical Signal Processing, Bordeaux, France, 2005, P950-955.K. Elissa, "Title of paper if known," unpublished.

[8] D. Li, M.Y. Zhan, H.Q. Liu, Y. Liao, and G.S. Liao. A Robust Translational Motion Compensation Method for ISAR Imaging Based on Keystone Transform and Fractional Fourier Transform Under Low SNR Environment. IEEE transactions on aerospace and electronic systems. Vol. 53, No.5.2017, P2140-2156.Y.

[9] W.Z. Wu, P.J. Hu, S.Yu Xu, Z.P Chen, and J. Chen. Image registration for InISAR based on joint translation motion compensation. IET Radar, Sonar & Navigation. Vol.11, Issue:10, 2017. P1597-1603.

Automatic Traffic Light Recognition for Mobile Robot Applications

Chi-Hsun Chiang
Department of Engineering Science
National Cheng Kung University
Tainan, Taiwan 70101
Email: a0921986456@gmail.com

Cheng-Kang Wen
Department of Information Management
Tainan University of Technology
Tainan, Taiwan 71002
Email: ckwenisme@gmail.com

Chun Mu Wu
Department of Mechanical and Automation Engineering
Kao Yuan University
Kaohsiung, Taiwan 82151
Email: wtm@cc.kyu.edu.tw

Jung-Hua Chou*
Department of Engineering Science
National Cheng Kung University
Tainan, Taiwan 70101
*Corresponding author, email: jungchou@mail.ncku.edu.tw

Abstract—**In this study, we present a method to enhance the quality of traffic light images captured by a webcam using hardware filters for mobile robot applications. The images are processed through pre-processing, detection, and recognition steps to recognize the status of traffic lights. The results show that the status of traffic lights is recognized successfully; the overall recognition rate is about 99% while the recognition time is about 41ms to 76ms per frame. By using the method of support vector machine (SVM), the recognition rate is higher with the cost of a larger processing time.**

Keywords-traffic light; image processing; HOG; SVM; filters.

I. INTRODUCTION

With the growing concern about the traffic accidents around the world yearly, the big auto industry set the goal of achieving automatic driving by the year of 2025. However, with the progress being made, now the target time is moved forward to the year around 2020 or 2021. The ambition is admirable and the challenge is by no means simple. Researches on Advanced Driver Assistance System (ADAS) are becoming deeper and more extensive in recent years. A tremendous amount of efforts have been put into developing related techniques. Among them, real time recognition of traffic lights in the street is of a necessity. Automatic traffic light recognition plays an important role in traffic safety and traffic flow smoothness. However, traffic lights are hard to detect just by image processing in urban driving conditions due to the complex backgrounds and different illuminations. A worse situation is that some objects may even have visual features similar to traffic lights. Therefore, it is difficult to develop a universal real-time and robust traffic light recognition system for different environments, illuminations, and weather conditions.

Because of its importance, various traffic light recognition algorithms based on image processing have been proposed in the literature [1]-[6], even with machine learning [7] via Adaboost algorithm [8]. In general, researchers are usually divided into traffic light detection and traffic light recognition for the whole recognition algorithm of traffic lights. This is because traffic lights are very small as compared to other objects in the road environment, which may have street lights of similar geometric shapes. Thus, it is necessary to detect the region of interest for traffic lights first to exclude unnecessary background objects to verify the status of traffic lights more easily.

Since the goal of this study is traffic light recognition for mobile robot applications, all of the information has to be processed by the on-board computing facility without relying on external extensive computing powers. That is, an on-board notebook computer was used for all of the image processing task. The images were captured by a webcam (Logitech C525).

Following this Introduction section, Section II describes the methodology, Section III presents the results and discussion, and Section IV draws the conclusions. Details are as follows.

II. METHODOLOGY

As mentioned above, Logitech Webcam C525 was used to capture the traffic light images for the present application. Its resolution is 1280 by 720 pixels with a frame rate of 30 frames per second. In capturing the images, two types of filters were applied. One is a Circular Polarizer (CPL) filter and the other is a Neutral Density (ND) filter. The CPL filter was used to enhance the color contrast and to reduce light reflection to improve the image quality. The ND filter [9] was used to avoid image over exposure and to remove the halo around the traffic lights due to improper background lighting conditions, especially in the evening situations.

The effects of CPL and ND filtering can be clearly observed from the photos shown in Figures 1-4. The former two for CPL filtering; whereas the latter two for ND filtering. By comparing the original and the corresponding filtered photos, it is clear that the CPL filter enhances the color contrast to make the objects in the photos more distinguishable. For the ND filter, both light effect and halo around the traffic light are removed; 'the traffic light shows its complete round shape. Thus, by these two filters, the image quality captured by the webcam is improved greatly to ease and facilitate subsequent image processing.

Figure 1. Original photo without CPL filtering.

Figure 2. CPL filtered photo of Figure 1.

Figure 3. Original traffic light photo.

Figure 4. ND filtered photo of Fig. 3.

After the image was filtered and captured by the webcam, it is processed to determine whether it is a traffic light. If it is a traffic light, its status is further determined. All of this processing was performed by using Visual Studio C++ and OpenCV function libraries, executed by the notebook computer on the mobile robot designed for validating the recognition methods.

As shown in Figure 5, the traffic light recognition from the images captured by the webcam consists of mainly three steps in sequence: One is the pre-processing, the second is the detection of the traffic light, and the third is the recognition of the status of the traffic light. For the first step of image pre-processing, the red, green, and blue components (referred to as RGB colors hereafter) of the color image captured by the webcam is converted into H (hue), S (saturation), and V (value) color space as the latter is less sensitive to the environmental lighting conditions. Then, the region of interest, which contains the traffic light, is selected to increase the speed of processing.

For the second step of traffic light detection, typical image operations were conducted, including erosion/dilation, open/close operations to remove the noises embedded in the image. Thus, connected regions of interest can be deduced. Then, morphological operations taking care of the geometry, size, and aspect ratio of the traffic light were performed to segment out the traffic light for its status recognition.

In the last step of the recognition, the method of histogram of gradients (HOG) [10][11] is used to extract the features of the traffic light. A database of red, green, yellow, and non-traffic light was also established using the HOG descriptors. This database is constructed mainly for the recognition of using the approach of support vector machine (SVM) [12], which is also trained by the information in the database. That is, recognition is divided into two parts: one for daytime and the other for nighttime. For daytime traffic lights, HOG is combined with SVM for the recognition. For nighttime traffic lights, only features in the color space are used to recognition. If we detect zero or more than one candidate region, the loop will break back to the beginning of the input images for restarting. The image processing algorithm is verified by experiments using a mobile robot

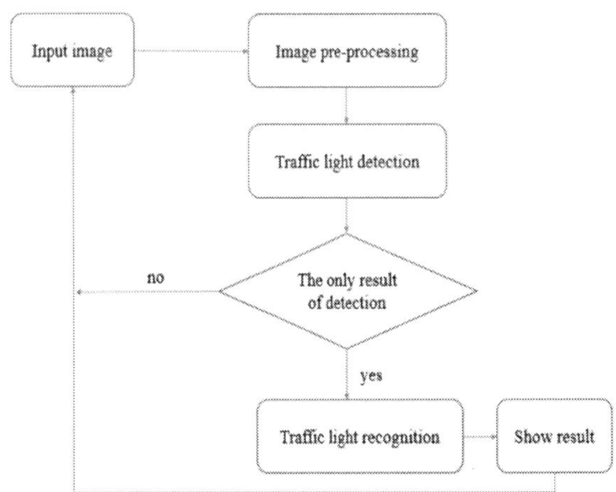

Figure 5. Flow of the traffic light algorithm.

In this study, SVM was selected for enhancing image recognition with HOG. The reasons for this choice are two. One is that the environment around the traffic light is fairly complex, especially at night when lighting sources around the street become the noise of traffic lights. The other is that SVM guarantees a convex space for classification, which can effectively avoid the trapping of the recognition algorithm to local maximum as compared to other classifiers.

III. RESULTS AND DISCUSSION

The experimental environments with traffic light images are shown in Figure 6 and Figure 7 for the red lights at daytime and nighttime, respectively. It is evident that in the daytime, surrounding objects are all captured in the image; whereas, at the nighttime, the lights have halos around them. The recognition process and result are shown in Figure 8, taking the green light recognition as a typical example. The result shows that even under a fairly complex background and illumination of the traffic light, the detection and recognition are successfully achieved.

In order to understand the details of the recognition results, we record every experimental result in different environments and the computation time from traffic light recognition. The results indicate that for the sunny daytime, the recognition rate is about 99.7%, for cloudy day about 99.8%, and 99.1% for nighttime. For the process time, it takes 76ms/frame and 41ms/frame for the daytime and nighttime, respectively. Most of the time is spent in the process of detecting the traffic light while recognition by using SVM also consumes about the same amount of time as the detection process. That is, it takes less time for the method through color recognition, but the correct rate is also slightly lower due to difficulties in distinguish the red from yellow lights.

Figure 6. Daytime traffic light captured and recognized.

Figure 7. Nighttime traffic captured and recognized.

IV. CONCLUSIONS

A notebook computer based algorithm for real-time robust traffic light recognition using images captured from a webcam is developed. The goal is to design a traffic light recognition system which can conquer influences from complex backgrounds and different illuminations for mobile robot applications. Thus, mobile robots can recognize traffic light signals automatically and work in an appropriate way. This algorithm adopts filters to enhance the captured images for detecting traffic lights.

Overall results show that the developed method performs well for image detection in a general environment. The SVM method combines with HOG feature extraction not only can reach real time but also has high accuracy for recognition. Although the recognition method with color feature takes less time than that of the SVM method, it is not efficient to recognize the difference between red and yellow lights. The experimental results show that our algorithm can detect and recognize circular lights in different environment robustly and in real-time with recognition rate around 99%. Further studies are being conducted to improve this recognition rate.

REFERENCES

[1] C. Yu, C. Huang and Y. Lang, "Traffic light detection during day and night conditions by a camera," IEEE 10th International Conference on Signal Processing Proceedings, pp. 821-824, 24-28 Oct., 2010.

[2] H. Moizumi, Y. Sugaya, M. Omachi, S. Omachi, "Traffic light detection considering color saturation using in-vehicle stereo camera," Journal of Information Processing, vol. 24, no. 2, pp. 349-357, 2016.

[3] O. Masako and O. Shinichiro, "Traffic light detection with color and edge information," 2009 2nd IEEE International Conference on Computer Science and Information Technology, pp. 284-287, 8-11 Aug., 2009.

[4] M. Diaz-Cabrera, P. Cerri, P. Medici, "Robust real-time traffic light detection and distance estimation using a single camera," Expert Systems with Applications, vol. 42, no. 8, pp. 3911-3923, 2015.

[5] S. Sooksatra and T. Kondo, "Red traffic light detection using fast radial symmetry transform," International Conference on Electrical Engineering/Electronics, Computer, Telecommunications and Information Technology (ECTI-CON), pp. 1-6, 2014.

[6] Y. Jie, C. Xiaomin, G. Pengfei, X. Zhonglong, "A new traffic light detection and recognition algorithm for electronic travel aid," 2013 Fourth International Conference on Intelligent Control and Information Processing (ICICIP), pp. 644-648, 9-11 June 2013.

[7] J. Gong, Y. Jiang, G. Xiong, C. Guan, G. Tao, H. Chen, "The recognition and tracking of traffic lights based on color segmentation and CAMSHIFT for intelligent vehicles," 2010 IEEE Intelligent Vehicles Symposium, pp. 431-435, 21-24 June, 2010.

[8] J. Zhu, H. Zou, S. Rosset, T. Hastie, "Multi-class adaboost," Statistics and its Interface, vol. 2, no. 3, pp. 349-360, 2009.

[9] R. Robilotto and Q. Zaidi, "Perceived transparency of neutral density filters across dissimilar backgrounds," Journal of Vision, vol. 4, no. 3, pp. 5-5, 2004.

[10] K. v. d. Sande, T. Gevers, C. Snoek, "Evaluating color descriptors for object and scene recognition, " IEEE Transactions on Pattern Analysis and Machine Intelligence, vol. 32, no. 9, pp. 1582-1596, 2010.

[11] T. Barbu, "Pedestrian detection and tracking using temporal differencing and HOG features," Computers and Electrical Engineering, vol. 40, no. 4, pp. 1072-1079, 2014.

[12] C.-C. Chang and C.-J. Lin, "LIBSVM: a library for support vector machines," ACM Transactions on Intelligent Systems and Technology (TIST), vol. 2, no. 3, pp. 27, 2011.

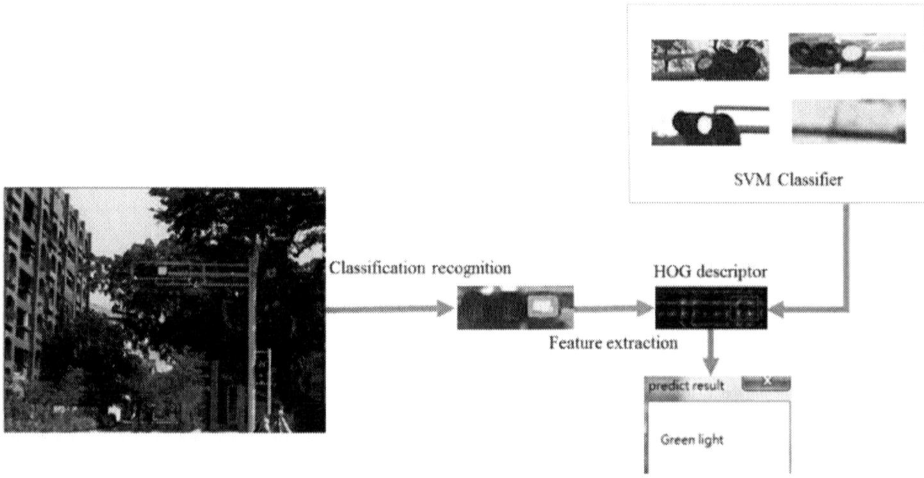

Figure 8. Overall recognition process and result.

Real Time Hyperspectral Imaging using High Frame Rate Video Camera and GPGPU Processing

Enagnon Aguénounon, Manon Schmidt, Foudil Dadouche, Wilfried Uhring, Sylvain Gioux
ICube, UMR 7357, Université de Strasbourg and CNRS, 300 bd Sébastien Brant - CS 10413 - F-67412 Illkirch Cedex, France
Email: wilfried.uhring@unistra.fr

Abstract—**This paper presents a new method to get real time hyperspectral images using time modulation of light and demodulation by means of General-Purpose computing on Graphics Processing Units (GPGPU). Three different Compute Unified Device Architecture (CUDA) implementations of real time hyperspectral images demodulation are presented. These methods are compared using a numerical simulation. The results show an execution time as low as 18 µs per wavelength and per frame for the Custom-made proposed implementation for a 512x512 pixels frame.**

Keywords-hyperspectral imaging; GPGPU; C CUDA; real time, FFT.

I. Introduction

The purpose of hyperspectral imaging is to obtain more information on the scene (objects, samples) by adding a spectral dimension. This additional information may be useful in many applications ranging from microscopy [1] to astronomy. Among these applications we can quote geosciences [2][3], medical applications [1][4], food quality and safety [5], art work [6] and many others. To address the specific constraints of those applications, from the infinitely small to the infinitely large, several methods have been developed over time. In terms of instrumentation, these methods are commonly classified in 3 main categories [7]: (1) methods based on the dispersive elements (grating, prism, grism) which deviates the light differently according to the wavelength, (2) the methods based on filter elements that allow to get one wavelength or a spectral band at a time makes use of a filter wheels or tunable filters to get all spectral information and (3) interferometer systems based methods. Alternatively, it is possible to classify the methods in 3 other categories depending of the field of view: whiskbroom, pushbroom and framing [7]. The whiskbroom category refers to a point system using one of the aforementioned instrumentation methods and that requires to scan the entire scene to get the hyperspectral data. The pushbroom category is usually composed of several whiskbrooms that each acquires a line by scanning the scene in the opposite direction. Finally, the framing category, built around a whiskbroom or a pushbroom, is able to scan an entire scene at a time. It may use filters to acquire spectral information over time or be designed by stacked detectors, sensitive to different incident radiation spectrum. Most of these techniques are nowadays integrated into systems and many manufacturers offer both sensors technology and hyperspectral cameras.

In this article, we propose a new method to get real time hyperspectral images using time modulation of light and GPGPU processing. The proposed method allows using a classic monochrome camera to acquire several wavelengths simultaneously. It is robust to noise, does not require a complex optical or mechanical system and offers at the same time a very high spectral and spatial resolution.

The details of this method are described in the following sections. First, the operating principle of the hyperspectral method is introduced in Section II. Section III presents the Graphics Processing Units (GPU) implementation of the wavelengths extraction algorithm. The testing methods are reported in Section IV and the obtained results are presented in Section V where the advantages and current limitations of the proposed method are also discussed. Section VI provides some final observations, as well as future work required to improve reliability, robustness, efficiency and practicality of this hyperspectral imaging method.

II. Proposed Method

A. *Principle*

The principle of the method is inspired from amplitude modulation and demodulation used in telecommunication [8]. As shown in the block diagram "Figure 1", the typical system is composed of a camera, several modulated laser sources, a projection system, a high speed acquisition frame grabber and a GPU.

The approach is composed of two consecutive steps. The first one consists of time modulation of k laser sources with different wavelengths λ_k in a sinusoidal manner at different frequencies F_k. The chosen frequencies are exact frequencies in the discrete Fourier domain given by the formula (1): they depend on the camera framerate (fps), the number of images (N), which will be used later for the demodulation and the spectrum position (k) in Fourier domain. In a case where a modulation frequency does not match an exact discrete Fourier frequency, it will spread its energy on the two adjacent modulation frequencies, leading to possible crosstalk, as illustrated in "Figure 2".

$$F_k = \frac{k \times fps}{N} \qquad (1)$$

In the second step, the spectral contribution of each wavelength can be isolated by using discrete Fourier transform during a demodulation process on a computer. In order, to keep a high framerate at the end of the process the temporal demodulation is performed by using a GPU processing.

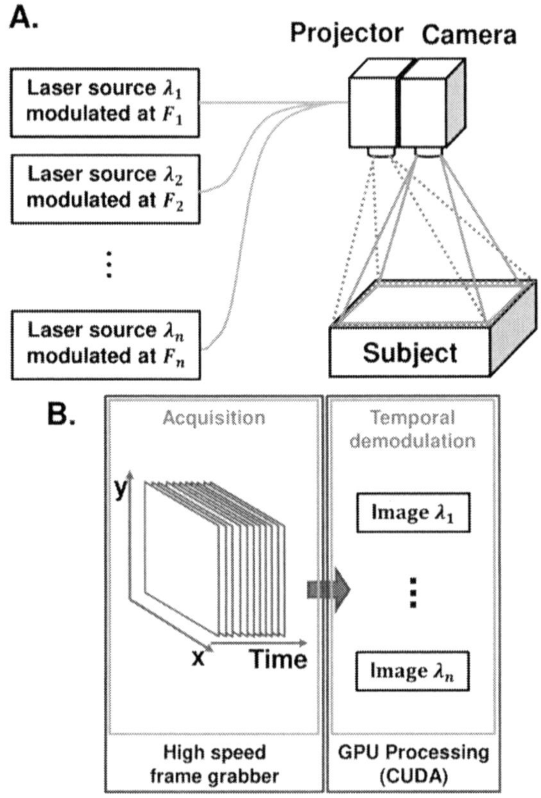

Figure 1. Real time hyperspectral acquisition and processing setup (A: Projection system and camera, B: Acquisition and processing system).

B. Spectral information extraction

In order to get the spectral contributions of each wavelength, a discrete Fourier transform is used from the N acquired images referred in (1).

The discrete Fourier transform of one pixel in time is given by:

$$X_k = \sum_{n=0}^{N-1} x_n * e^{-i2\pi\frac{nk}{N}} \tag{2}$$

With

$$e^{-i2\pi\frac{nk}{N}} = \cos\left(-2\pi\frac{nk}{N}\right) + i\sin\left(-2\pi\frac{nk}{N}\right) \tag{3}$$

Thus:

$$X_k = \sum_{n=0}^{N-1} x_n \cos\left(-2\pi\frac{nk}{N}\right) + i\sum_{n=0}^{N-1} x_n \sin\left(-2\pi\frac{nk}{N}\right) \tag{4}$$

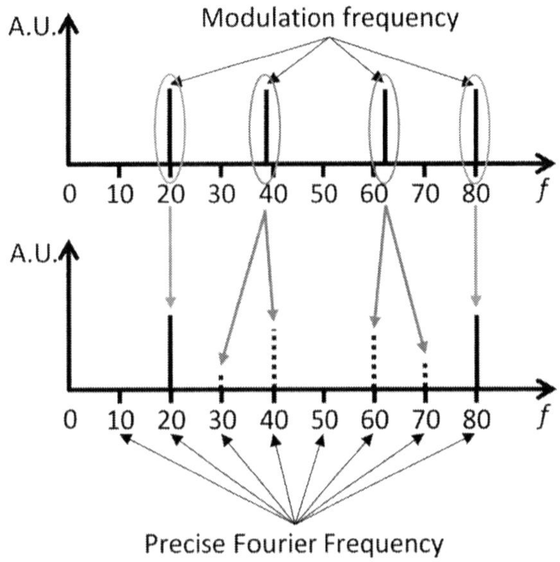

Figure 2. Sample of good/bad Frequency positioning in Fourier domain - arbitrary unit (A.U.).

And the amplitude value of (4) is the spectral contributions of the wavelength modulated at a given frequency.

$$\|X_k\| = \sqrt{\left(\sum_{n=0}^{N-1} x_n \cos\left(-2\pi\frac{nk}{N}\right)\right)^2 + \left(\sum_{n=0}^{N-1} x_n \sin\left(-2\pi\frac{nk}{N}\right)\right)^2} \tag{5}$$

Depending on the application, a windowed step or rolling window is used. According to our experience, the best way to extract a hypercube data is to use the rolling window method. Indeed, the next pixel in time is given by (6) and can be rewritten with (7) and (8):

$$X_k = \sum_{n=1}^{N-1+1} x_n \cos\left(-2\pi\frac{(n \bmod N)k}{N}\right) + i\sum_{n=1}^{N-1+1} x_n \sin\left(-2\pi\frac{(n \bmod N)k}{N}\right) \tag{6}$$

$$\begin{aligned}\sum_{n=1}^{N-1+1} x_n \cos\left(-2\pi\frac{(n \bmod N)k}{N}\right) &= \sum_{n=0}^{N-1} x_n \cos\left(-2\pi\frac{(n \bmod N)k}{N}\right) \\ &-x_0 \cos\left(-2\pi\frac{(0 \bmod N)k}{N}\right) + x_N \cos\left(-2\pi\frac{(N \bmod N)k}{N}\right)\end{aligned} \tag{7}$$

$$\begin{aligned}\sum_{n=1}^{N-1+1} x_n \sin\left(-2\pi\frac{(n \bmod N)k}{N}\right) &= \sum_{n=0}^{N-1} x_n \sin\left(-2\pi\frac{(n \bmod N)k}{N}\right) \\ &-x_0 \sin\left(-2\pi\frac{(0 \bmod N)k}{N}\right) + x_N \sin\left(-2\pi\frac{(N \bmod N)k}{N}\right)\end{aligned} \tag{8}$$

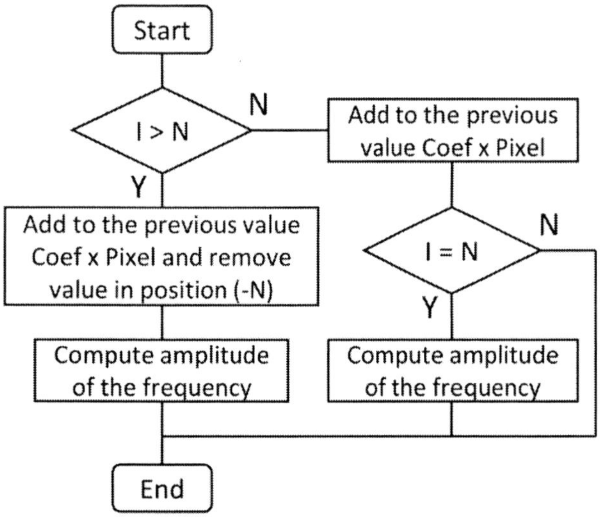

Figure 3. Demodulation algorithm applied to all the pixels of the images from the high-speed camera.

This technique, depicted in the "Figure 3", where I is the number of acquired frames, replaces N multiplications with the subtraction of the contribution of the first sample of the rolling windows and the addition of the new sample contribution, resulting in a significant gain of resources since processors use more resources for multiplication than for addition or subtraction.

III. GPU PROCESSING

Each pixel being totally independent in time from its neighbors, the method is perfectly adapted for General Purpose GPU computing, because GPU is particularly useful for operations on arrays thanks of its massive parallel architecture.

In this section, we present three different ways to implement the temporal demodulation on the GPU and their important operations are illustrated by CUDA code snippets. Two of them consist of using CUDA Fast Fourier Transform (FFT) library of NVIDIA based on one dimension cudaFFT real to complex (R2C) function. The third one consists of a custom-made implementation inspired by the equations shown previously.

A. *Implementation using cuFFT 1D*

The first implementation starts with the initialization where the GPU resources are allocated for the N images of the FFT.

A ring buffer, having a dimension N corresponding to the number of images, is used for this purpose. It also requires resources for the output images of the function "cudaFFT 1D R2C" and for the amplitudes of the images, which represent the spectral contribution of each wavelength. Once the allocations have been made, it is necessary to configure the execution plan of the "cudaFFT 1D R2C" function. The role of this operation is to provide information on how the data will be read and stored and how many FFTs shall run. In our case, the function must find pixels in time in a cube of N images before executing the FFT and then reform the images. The loop processing follows the initialization. In the loop, once the buffer is full and for each new image, the function "cudaFFT 1D R2C" executes the temporal FFT. The call of the "cudaFFT 1D R2C" function is followed each time by the function that calculates the amplitudes. These amplitudes must be calculated using custom functions, because the "cudaFFT 1D R2C" function only returns complex values. "Figure 4" summarizes these different steps, starting from the creation of the plan, the transfer of the image to the GPU, the execution of the function cudaFFT and the calculation of the amplitudes by our custom function.

```
cufftHandle plan;
cufftPlanMany(&plan, 1, N, 0, (Size_X * Size_Y), 1, 0, (Size_X *
Size_Y), 1, CUFFT_R2C, (Size_X * Size_Y));
cudaMemcpy((d_image + (Size_X * Size_Y * position)), h_datain,
Size_X * Size_Y * sizeof(cufftReal), cudaMemcpyHostToDevice);
cufftExecR2C(plan, d_image, d_outdata);
amplitude_function << < grid, block >> > (d_outdata, d_ amplitude);
cudaDeviceSynchronize();
```

Figure 4. A part of cuFFT 1D (Direct) C CUDA code.

B. *Improved implementation using cuFFT 1D*

The idea behind the second implementation with the "cudaFFT 1D R2C" function is to reduce the time taken to perform pixel search and alignment by directly controlling it with a custom GPU function. The function created has the role of temporally aligning the pixels by respecting the ring buffer setup. This implementation requires a modification of the code for the function that calculates the amplitudes allowing the reconstitution of the images after FFT execution. The resources needed for this operation are allocated as before and the execution plan of the function "cudaFFT 1D R2C" is configured. In loop processing, as soon as an image arrives, the pixels are aligned in the buffer. As described in "Figure 3", when the system has received at least the N number of images needed by the FFT, the "cudaFFT 1D R2C" function executes. The amplitudes are then calculated and the images reformed. "Figure 5" is given below to summarize this improved implementation.

```
cufftHandle plan;
cufftPlanMany(&plan, 1, N, 0, 1, N, 0, 1, (N / 2 + 1), CUFFT_R2C,
(Size_X * Size_Y));
cudaMemcpy(d_image, h_datain, Size_X * Size_Y * sizeof(uint16),
cudaMemcpyHostToDevice);
alignment_function << < grid, block >> > (d_image, d_image_
aligned);
cufftExecR2C(plan, d_image_ aligned, d_outdata);
reformation_and_amplitude_function << < grid, block >> >
(d_outdata, d_ amplitude);
cudaDeviceSynchronize();
```

Figure 5. A part of cuFFT 1D (Improved) C CUDA code.

C. *Custom-made DFT 1D Implementation*

This last implementation is inspired from the equations shown in the previous Section. As usual it needs to reserve the GPU memory spaces necessary for processing: (1) a memory space is reserved for the sin () and cos ()

coefficients needed for the calculation of the Discrete Fourier Transform (DFT), (2) a ring buffer with a dimension of N+1 is setup for the camera output images, (3) a memory space is reserved for the images after treatment, and finally (4) another memory space is allocated to store intermediate results of real and imaginary parts. After accomplishing memory allocation, the coefficients for the DFT are then calculated on the CPU and they are transferred to the GPU.

Once the initialization is finished, the processing loop can begin "Figure 6". In this step, each time an image arrives it is stored in the ring buffer of size N+1. The function of the "Figure 7" is then called to compute the DFT as explained above. This function directly returns an image for each demodulated wavelength.

```
cudaMemcpy((d_image + (Size_X * Size_Y * position)), h_datain,
Size_X * Size_Y * sizeof(uint16), cudaMemcpyHostToDevice);
DFTcomputationGPU << < grid, block >> > (d_image, d_amplitude,
Reel, Imag, Cos_coef, Sin_coef);
cudaDeviceSynchronize();
```

Figure 6. A part of DFT 1D custom implementation C CUDA code.

```
__global__ void DFTcomputationGPU(uint16 *d_image, float
*d_amplitude, ...) {
unsigned int id = (threadIdx.y + (blockIdx.y * blockDim.y)) *
Size_X[0] + (threadIdx.x + (blockIdx.x * blockDim.x));
...
for (int i = 0; i < N_lambda[0]; i++) {
...
if (Num_image[0] < N[0]) {
Reel[idx] = Reel[idx] + (d_image (id + Present_idx[0]) *
Cos_coef[ind]);
Imag[idx] = Imag[idx] + (d_image (id + Present_idx[0]) *
Sin_coef[ind]);
if (Num_image[0] == (N[0] - 1)) {
d_amplitude[idx] = (sqrtf((Reel[idx]^2) + (Imag[idx]^2)));
}}
if (Num_image[0] >= N[0]) {
Reel[idx] = Reel[idx] - (d_image (id + Past_idx[0]) * Cos_coef[ind])
+ (d_image (id + Present_idx[0]) * Cos_coef[ind]);
Imag[idx] = Imag[idx] - (d_image (id + Past_idx[0]) * Sin_coef[ind])
+ (d_image (id + Present_idx[0]) * Sin_coef[ind]);
d_amplitude[idx] = (sqrtf((Reel[idx]^2 ) + (Imag[idx]^2)));
}}}
```

Figure 7. Custom-made DFT 1D computation function.

IV. NUMERICAL SIMULATION

A. Measurement simulation

In order to evaluate the performance of these three CUDA codes, we measured the execution time considering a one dimension DFT on stack of 8, 16, 32, 64, 128 and 256 images of size 512 x 512 pixels. These images allow extracting respectively 5, 9, 17, 33, 65 and 129 wavelengths by demodulation. The numbers of images have been chosen so that functions based on the cudaFFT library produce optimal performance [12]. The images used in this experience are created using Matlab (MathWorks) calculation tools by addition of multiple sinus signal for one pixel and then simply duplicating M times to obtain the desired image size.

B. GPU configuration

In GPGPU computing, the processing time depends strongly on the configuration. For our implementation, the major configuration we chose is related to the number of threads and their organization for the execution of the written functions. In our study, since we have been working on 512 x 512 pixel size images, and the pixels are independent in time, we chose to create one thread for each pixel, which implies 512 x 512 = 262144 threads that we broke down into 4096 blocks of 64 threads.

V. RESULTS AND DISCUSSION

The measurements of the different implementations depending of the number of images used for demodulation were performed. These measurements were performed with two configurations; one with the GPU Quadro K2200 which has 640 CUDA cores and another with the Geforce GTX 1080 Ti with 3584 CUDA cores. The obtained results are shown in "Figure 8" and "Figure 9". As we can see, the implementation "Custom DFT 1D algorithm" is the fastest in execution time followed by the two implementations "cuFFT 1D (improved)" and "cuFFT 1D (direct)". The relatively long execution time of the two last implementations (compared to the Custom implementation) is explained by the many matrix transpositions they performed. Indeed, the performance of matrix transpositions is strongly limited by the bandwidth and the memory accesses [9]. For the fastest implementation, the Quadro K2200 took 11400 µs for the demodulation of 129 wavelengths, corresponding to 88 µs per wavelength, and the Geforce GTX 1080 Ti took 2250 µs for the same number of frames, or 18 µs per wavelength.

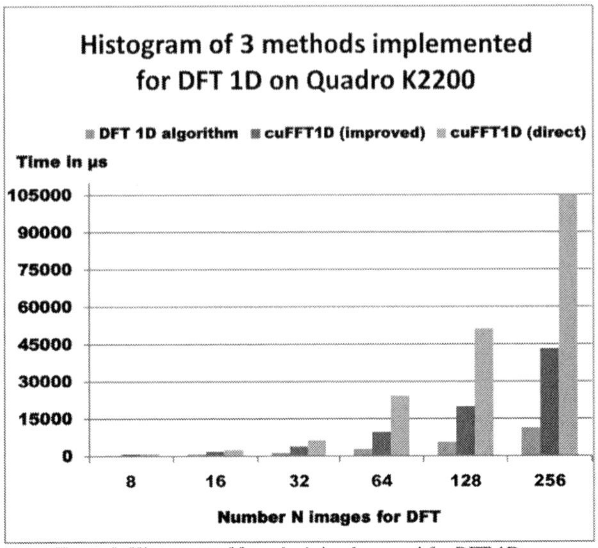

Figure 8. Histogram of 3 methods implemented for DFT 1D on Quadro K2200.

The first conclusion drawn from these results is that the execution time is inversely related with the number of

CUDA cores: here multiplying the number of CUDA cores by 5 results in dividing the execution time by 5. This leads to suppose that we can still reduce the execution time and therefore increase the acquisition frame rate with additional GPU cores. Another important point is that the custom-made implementation has the particularity to allow the user to just compute the chosen modulation frequency.

Nevertheless, this method also has some limitations. A first limitation is the constant delay due to the first number of images needed to execute the first demodulation. Depending on the application, such a delay may be or not a drawback. This delay also implies no motion of the sample during the acquisition, or at least motion that is much slower that the time needed to acquire N frames. A way to mitigate this issue consists of reducing the number of wavelengths wanted by taking fewer frames for the FFT. A second limitation is the number of wavelengths that can be acquired, a direct consequence of the dynamic range of the camera. Indeed, the bit depth of a camera is generally 8, 10, 12 or 16 bits. Consequently, the higher the number of modulated wavelengths, the more the dynamic will be subdivided. And with low modulation amplitude the demodulated image quality will decrease due to a low signal to noise ratio. One solution to circumvent this limitation would be to use one or more camera with tunable or wheel band filter at the cost of a more complex and expensive system.

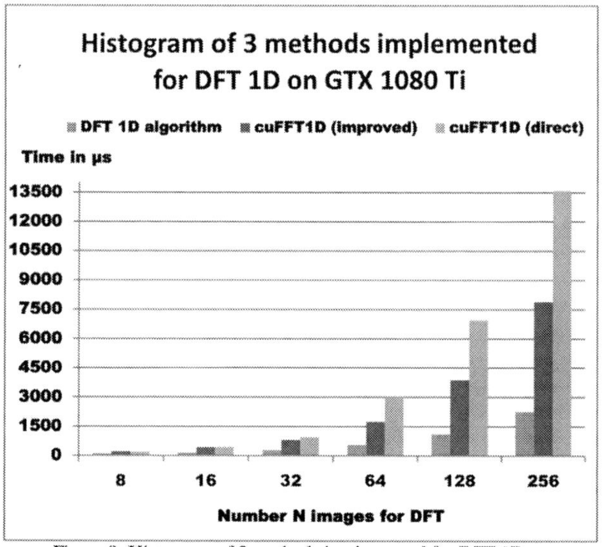

Figure 9. Histogram of 3 methods implemented for DFT 1D on GTX 1080 Ti.

VI. CONCLUSION

A new method to acquire hyperspectral images was presented by combining temporal modulation of light and temporal demodulation using GPGPU processing. Three CUDA codes allowing to get spectral information are presented and are compared. With a simulation test we demonstrate that it is possible to reach very high acquisition frame rate by calculating the DFT with accumulation and subtraction at the arrival of each image. We also discussed about hardware system limitations essentially due to the cameras dynamics. As a future work, it will be interesting to study with a real system the effect of increasing the number of wavelengths on the quality of demodulated images.

ACKNOWLEDGMENT

Funding for this research was provided by European Research Council (ERC) under the European Union's Horizon 2020 research and innovation program under grant agreement No 715737 (QuantSURG), France Life Imaging, University of Strasbourg IdEx, and ICube Laboratory.

REFERENCES

[1] L. Gao and R. T. Smith, "Optical hyperspectral imaging in microscopy and spectroscopy – a review of data acquisition", J Biophotonics, vol. 8(6), June 2015, pp. 441-456, doi:10.1002/jbio.201400051.

[2] T. Adão et al, "Hyperspectral Imaging: A Review on UAV-Based Sensors, Data Processing and Applications for Agriculture and Forestry", Remote Sensing, vol. 9(11), Oct. 2017, pp. 1-30, doi:10.3390/rs9111110.

[3] L. Rousset-Rouviere et al, "SYSIPHE system: a state of the art airborne hyperspectral imaging system. Initial results from the first airborne campaign", Proc. SPIE, vol. 9249, Oct. 2014, doi:10.1117/12.2066643.

[4] G. Lu and B. Fei, "Medical hyperspectral imaging: a review", J Biomed Opt, vol. 19(1), Jan. 2014, pp. 1-23, doi:10.1117/1.JBO.19.1.010901.

[5] Y. Liu, H. Pu, D.-W. Sun, "Hyperspectral imaging technique for evaluating food quality and safety during various processes: A review of recent applications", Trends in Food Science & Technology, vol. 69, part A, Nov. 2017, pp. 25-35, doi.org/10.1016/j.tifs.2017.08.013.

[6] A. Polak et al, "Hyperspectral imaging combined with data classification techniques as an aid for artwork authentication", Journal of Cultural Heritage, vol. 26, July-August 2017, pp. 1-11, doi.org/10.1016/j.culher.2017.01.013.

[7] R. G. Sellar and G. D. Boreman, "Classification of imaging spectrometers for remote sensing applications", Optical Engineering, vol. 44(1), Jan. 2005, pp. 1-3, doi:10.1117/1.1813441.

[8] A. B. Carlson and P. B. Crilly, Communication Systems: An introduction to signals and noise in electrical communication, McGraw-Hill Education, 2009.

[9] J. Cheng, M. Grossman, T. McKercher, Professional CUDA C Programming, John Wiley & Sons, 2014.

[10] J. Sanders and E. Kandrot, CUDA by Example: An introduction to general-purpose GPU programming, Addison-Wesley Professional, 2010.

[11] Nvidia, docs.nvidia.com, "CUDA C Programming Guide", [Online] Available from: http://docs.nvidia.com/cuda/pdf/CUDA_C_Programming_Guide.pdf, [retrieved: March, 2018].

[12] Nvidia, docs.nvidia.com, "CUFFT Library", [Online] Available from: http://docs.nvidia.com/cuda/pdf/CUFFT_Library.pdf, [retrieved: March, 2018].

Detecting UAVs Using Acoustic Camera

Jurica Ivošević, Tomislav Radišić, Mario Muštra
Faculty of Transport and Traffic Sciences
University of Zagreb
HR-10000 Zagreb, Croatia
Email: jivosevic@fpz.hr, tradisic@fpz.hr, mmustra@fpz.hr

Ivan Bublić, Ivan Tudor, Darije Varžić
Testing Laboratory
The Institute for Advancement of Safety
HR-31000 Osijek, Croatia
Email: ivan.bublic@zus.hr, ivan.tudor@zus.hr, darije.varzic@zus.hr

Abstract— **Over the past decade, a huge increase in production and operation of Unmanned Aerial Vehicles (UAVs) has been present on a global scale. To maintain the required level of safety and to accommodate the expanding traffic, the governments worldwide have implemented regulations to operations of UAVs. Nonetheless, in recent years there have been numerous safety and security incidents with UAVs, which prompted an increase in research of surveillance and interdiction methods tailored for UAVs. Detection of UAVs using acoustic camera, which is the primary topic of this paper, is possible due to UAV's propeller noise which is predominant noise source, at least in multicopter UAVs. We performed a detectability test of a commonly used custom made UAV type – multirotor with 6 motors. We concluded that small multirotor UAVs can be detected with acoustic camera, a human interpreter is necessary for detection due to the background noise, maximum detection range can be greater than with visual detection, and UAV detectability depends on UAV noise spectrum, its ratio to background noise, the dynamic range of acoustic camera, and its frequency resolution.**

Keywords-UAV; acoustic camera; surveillance; detection.

I. Introduction

Over the past decade, a huge increase in production and operation of UAVs has been present on a global scale. According to Federal Aviation Administration (FAA) Aerospace Forecast for fiscal years 2017-2037, there are currently over 1.1 million registered UAVs in the United States (US). By the year 2021, in the US alone, the number of registered UAVs is expected to reach 6 million units. Of these, three quarters will be hobbyist UAVs and model aircraft in the 0.25 kg – 25 kg category [1].

To maintain the required level of safety and to accommodate the expanding traffic, the governments worldwide have implemented regulations to operations of UAVs. In 2012, US government regulated operation of UAVs by publishing *Public Law 112-95 - FAA Modernization and Reform Act of 2012* [2]. Operation of UAVs in Europe has been regulated by the act of European Comission in 2008 with *Regulation (EC) No 216/2008* for UAVs heavier than 150 kilograms, and with national regulations for UAVs lighter than 150 kg [3]. In 2017, however, a new regulation was proposed with the purpose of regulating all categories of UAVs in European Union (EU) and it is expected to be adopted during the 2018 [4].

Notwithstanding the attempts at regulating the UAV operations, the increase in number of operations alone has increased the probability of incidents. In [5], UAV sighting reports published by FAA dating from December 17, 2013 to September 12, 2015 were analyzed. FAA reports were organized in two categories: *Sightings*, which included incidents where a pilot or an air traffic controller spotted an UAV flying within or near the flight paths of manned aircraft though not posing an immediate threat or collision, and *Close Encounters*, where a manned aircraft came close enough to an UAV that it met the FAA's definition of a "near mid-air collision" or close enough that there was a possible danger [5]. They have analyzed 921 incident reports and deduced that 35.5 % of recorded incidents were *Close Encounters* and that over 90 % of all incidents occurred above allowed maximum altitude [5].

For safety and security reasons, it is necessary to develop methods for detection and monitoring of UAV operations in predetermined areas. Conventional methods of UAV detection are using radars, visual detection, and thermal or acoustic sensors. Radar detection of UAVs based on differentiating Doppler signatures of various UAVs was successfully performed and described in [6] and [7]. However, there are obvious difficulties in using this method in urban areas. Visual detection method by analyzing images from cameras with image processing algorithms was proven somewhat successful, with shortcomings typical of visual identification systems, namely false positives in case of other flying objects (e.g., birds) [8].

Another method of UAV detection is thermal imaging, which can be used for ground-based detection or for airborne collision avoidance during night-time operations. To prove that UAV detection using thermal imaging can be used as a viable detection system, thermal images obtained via *FLIR Lepton* micro thermal camera mounted on a Raspberry Pi processing unit were analyzed [9]. UAVs used for testing were *DJI Phantom 4*, *Parrot AR.drone 2*, and one custom made hexacopter.

Beside conventional methods of detection, possibility of detecting UAVs controlled via wireless devices (such as *Parrot AR Drone*) was successfully tested [10]. Authors have successfully detected and gained control of targeted drone as third party users. One shortcoming of this detection method is requirement for a wireless receiver installed on UAV.

Detection using acoustic sensors relies on sound emission of different units. Authors in [11] state that UAV detection with acoustic array, unlike radar detection and visual detection methods, does not depend on the size of observed object for detection, but rather on the sound of the engine. For their method, however, a requirement is a comprehensive database of UAV sounds.

Detection of UAVs using acoustic camera, which is the primary topic of this paper, is possible due to their propeller noise, the predominant noise source, at least in multicopter UAVs. Propeller noise is composed of tonal and broadband components. Tonal component contains basic frequency and harmonics. The basic frequency f_1 or Blade Pass Frequency (BPF) is the product of propeller rotation speed and number of propeller blades [12]:

$$BPF = N_R\, N_B\, 60^{-1}, \quad (1)$$

where is:
BPF - basic frequency of tonal propeller component,
N_R - propeller rotation speed (rotations per minute),
N_B - number of propeller blades.

Besides the base frequency harmonic components also appear [12]:

$$f_N = f_1\, N, \quad (2)$$

where is:
f_N - frequency of the n-th harmonic,
f_1 - basic tonal frequency,
N - number of particular harmonic.

Besides propeller noise, UAV's noise consists of airframe and structure borne noise. Airframe noise is the result of air flow (wind around airframe). It is of the broadband flow mixing type, except where a resonant cavity is formed. Its main characteristic is a great dependence on UAV's speed. In multirotors, this type of noise is quite low. Structure borne noise results from airframe vibrations. Various vibration modes excite structural modes. Acoustic space again has its acoustic modes that are excited by structural modes. This noise is quite complex and in UAV operations it does not have a great importance.

The primary scope of this paper is detection possibility of UAVs using acoustic camera. In Section 2 of the paper, we describe the methods and apparatus used for the test. In Section 3, we show and interpret results of the test, and in the Section 4, we draw conclusions and suggest ideas for the future work.

II. Method and Apparatus

A. *Test track*

In order to test the ability of acoustic camera to detect small airborne UAV, we flew custom built UAV over a 170 m long test track (Figure 1). The goal was to determine at what distance the UAV could be detected without trying to identify it. UAV was flown at the approximately 15 m – 45 m above ground level and at a steady velocity of around 2 m/s. The test was performed on a relatively cold winter day (4 °C) with little to no wind. The terrain of the polygon was grassy, without significant noise sources and without any sound sources with predominant tonal components. The test was performed in the early afternoon. Equivalent A-weighted residual (background) noise was 42.5 dB with 41.3 dB exceeded for 99 % of the measured time.

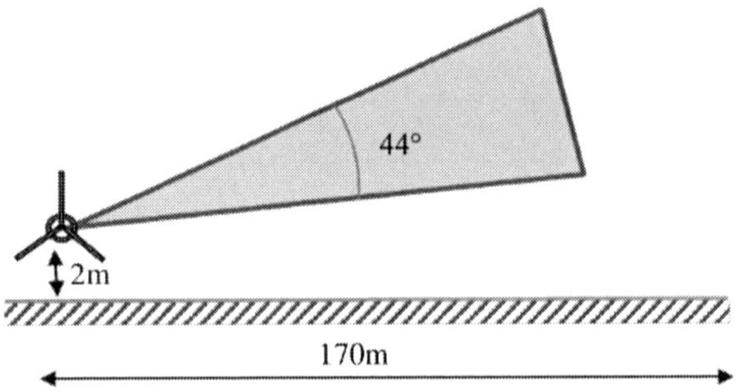

Figure 1. Test track

B. *Acoustic sensor*

For this test, the acoustic camera produced by The Faculty of Mechanical Engineering from Ljubljana, called SoundEye, has been used. SoundEye consists of a microphone array and an optical camera in the center. It can work in two different configurations, basic (Figure 2, left), with 30 microphones equally distributed on the circular disc carrier, and extended, with 54 microphones – 3 flat extensions with 8 microphones each attached to the basic circular carrier at the angle of 120° to each other (Figure 2, right). The camera has fixed Field-of-View (FOV) angles, horizontal FOV of 58° and vertical FOV of 44° (these are angles at which the scene is covered by both optical and acoustic camera). Detailed camera specifications can be found in Table 1.

The working principle of an acoustic camera is based on the microphone array's properties to form a highly directional beam. The signals from the microphones are acquired simultaneously or with known relative time delays to be able to use the phase difference between the signals. As the sound propagates in the air at a finite known speed, a sound source is perceived by the microphones at different time instants and at different sound intensities that depend on both the sound source location and the microphone location.

TABLE I. SOUNDEYE ACOUSTIC CAMERA SPECIFICATIONS

Specification	Description
Function	Imaging device used to locate and characterize sound sources
Producer	Faculty of mechanical engineering, Ljubljana, Slovenia
Configuration	Basic and extended
Number of microphones	30 (basic), 54 (extended)
Microphone frequency range	20 Hz – 20 kHz
Mapping frequency range	800 Hz – 12.5 kHz (basic), 100 Hz – 12.5 kHz (extended)
Sampling frequency of AD converter	48 kHz
Sampling resolution	16 bit/sample
Algorithm	Cross Spectral Matrix Beamforming
Analysing spectrum	1/1 octave, 1/3 octave, FFT
Optical/acoustic covering angle	± 58° horizontal, ± 44° vertical
Optical camera frame rate	30 fps
Operating distance	>5 m
Mains supply	USB
Disc diameter	0.4 m
Extension length	1 m
Weight	10 kg

One of the methods to obtain an acoustic image from the measurement of the microphone array is to use beamforming. By delaying each microphone signal relatively to each other and adding them together, the signals coming from a specific direction are amplified while signals coming from other directions are canceled. The power of this resulting signal is then calculated and reported on a power map at a pixel corresponding to the specific direction. The process is iterated for each direction where the power needs to be computed. The algorithm to obtain acoustic picture used by SoundEye acoustic camera is Cross Spectral Matrix Beamforming. The working principle is presented graphically in Figure 3.

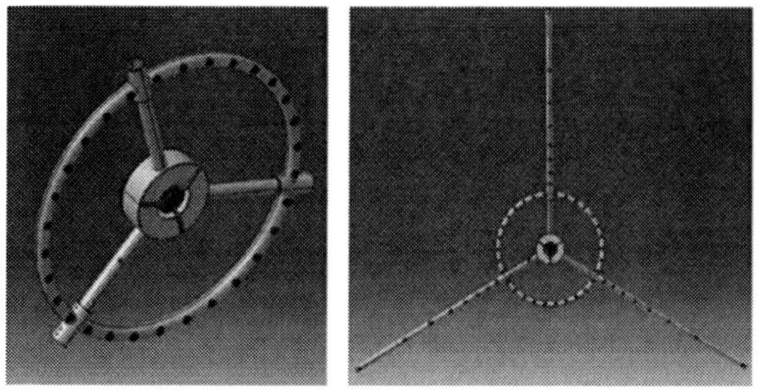

Figure 3. Two configurations of acoustic camera

The dynamic range of acoustic image (the ratio of the largest to the smallest intensity of sound that can be presented, measured in decibels) depends on the frequency of the sound source. For the frequencies above the 1000 Hz, dynamic range is 24 dB, while for the lowest frequencies is smaller – at the frequency of 100 Hz it is about 2 dB. This understanding is crucial for interpretation of acoustic images.

Figure 4 - Figure 6 present examples to better understand the interpretation of acoustic images. Directivity function of acoustic camera for a certain angle depending on the frequency is presented in Figure 4. For this theoretical example extended configuration of camera was used and the source that emits white noise (random signal having equal intensity at different frequencies, giving it a constant power

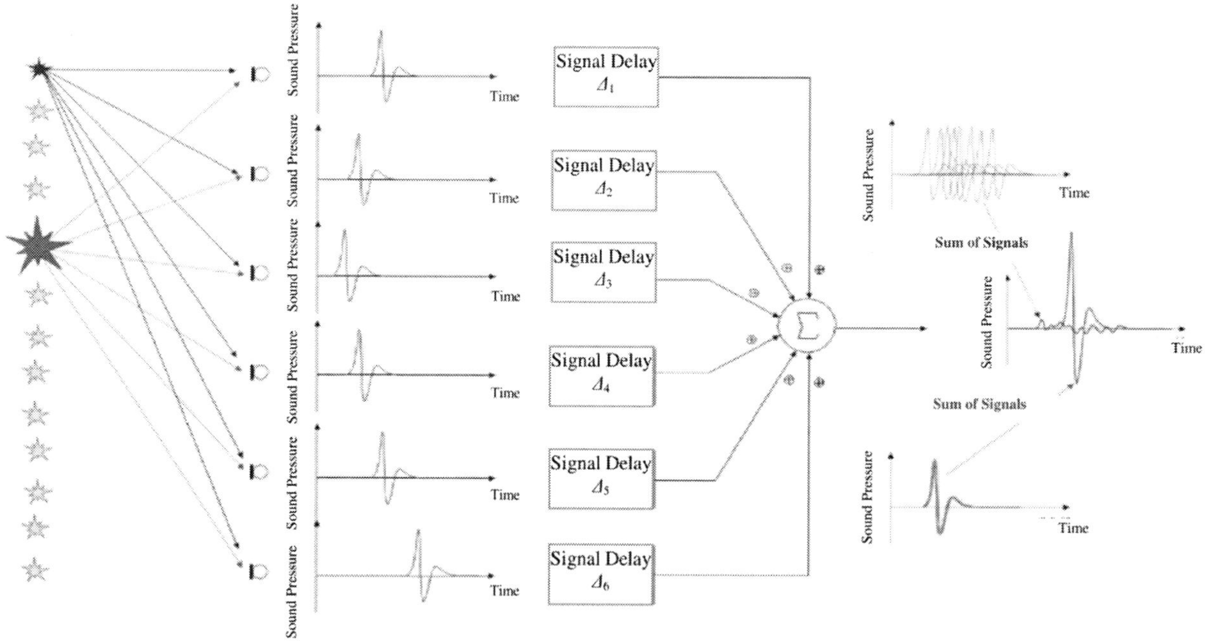

Figure 2. Working principle of the acoustic camera

spectral density) is situated right in the middle of the camera's FOV at the distance of 100 m (far field). Figure 4 shows the ability to distinguish the emitted sound levels of a single source at a selected frequency. The range of angles on the vertical axis is chosen to correspond to the horizontal FOV of acoustic camera and is equal to 58°. The angle of 90° is situated at the middle of the axis. Based on the calculation, the camera would show the acoustic image of the same size at a given frequency as presented in Figure 4. For example, at the frequency of 1000 Hz the red area (highest level) will be slightly larger than the red area at a frequency of 10000 Hz, although the noise emission at both frequencies is the same. The ratio between dark red and dark blue color is 24 dB. At the frequency range between 1000 Hz and 12500 Hz, the dynamic range of the acoustic image is 24 dB. This does not apply to a frequency range below 1000 Hz.

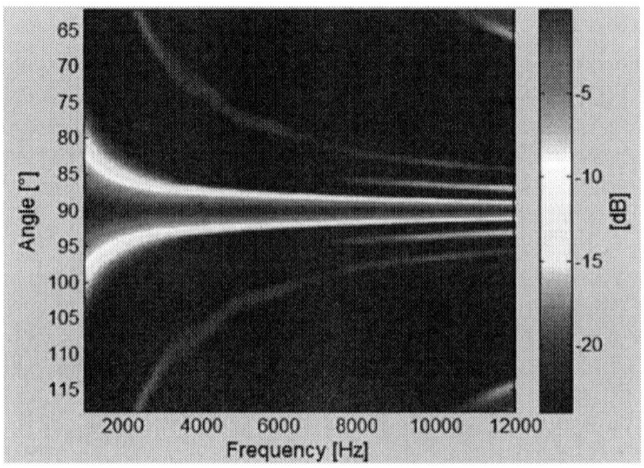

Figure 4. Directivity function of acoustic camera in the frequency range 1000 Hz - 12000 Hz with acoustic image dynamic range of 24 dB

Figure 5 shows directivity function of acoustic camera in the frequency range 100 Hz - 1000 Hz with acoustic image dynamic range of 5 dB.

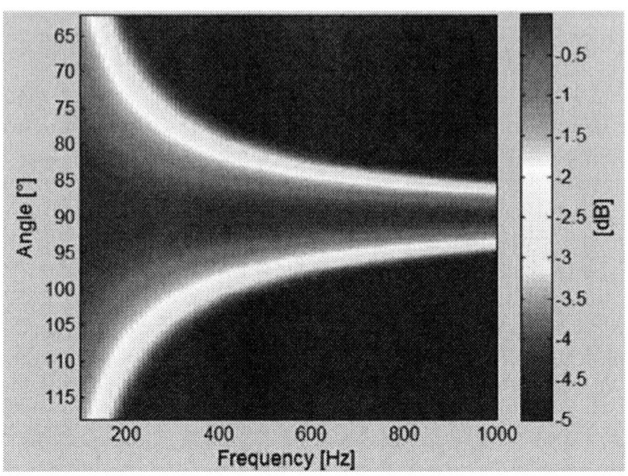

Figure 5. Directivity function of acoustic camera in the frequency range 100 Hz - 1000 Hz with acoustic image dynamic range of 5 dB

As can be seen, dynamic range is much narrower than that in Figure 4, especially at frequencies lower than 200 Hz (for the same sound emission at all frequencies). If the source would emit a sound at 100 Hz (source location right in the middle of the camera's FOV and at the distance of 100 m) and if the camera would have image dynamics (scale on the right side of the characteristics) 5 dB, the algorithm would calculate the acoustic image, which would be shown in red over the entire picture.

If the dynamic range would be reduced to 0.5 dB, the algorithm would calculate the acoustic image with characteristics as shown in Figure 6. A large red circle would be displayed in more than half of the image.

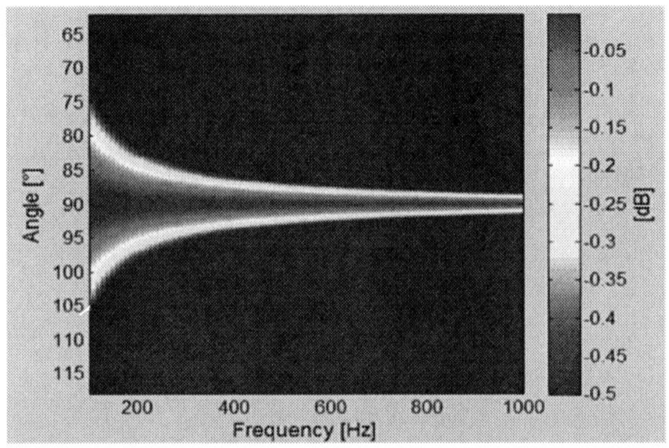

Figure 6. Directivity function of acoustic camera in the frequency range 100 Hz - 1000 Hz with acoustic image dynamic range of 0.5 dB

The results of the calculation of the acoustic image by an acoustic camera algorithm at frequencies lower than 1000 Hz and especially lower than 500 Hz should be considered only conditionally, both in terms of the range of noise level and in terms of the exact position of the noise source. At these frequencies, the dynamic range of acoustic images, some of which are presented in the results at the next paragraph, is set to lower values - from 0.1 dB to 2 dB.

C. *UAV*

A custom built hexacopter was used in this test. The specifications are available in Table 2.

TABLE II. SPECIFICATIONS OF THE HEXACOPTER USED IN TESTING

Parameter	Description
Size (w/o propellers)	75 × 75 × 37 cm
Weight	4420 g
Number of motors	6
Motor power	480 W
Motor type	Outrunner
Battery	LiPo, 6S, 5000 mAh
Propeller type	2-blade
Propeller size	12"

The most important parameter which determines UAVs acoustic footprint is propeller rotation speed. This UAV has 6 motors and their rotation speed varies within certain limits to achieve a satisfactory control and stability of the UAV. This rotation speed range is unknown so we did 1/3 octave band premeasurements of its noise to define a frequency band where basic frequency of tonal propeller component and its harmonics are situated.

III. Results and Discussion

First, we did 1/3 octave band measurements of UAV's noise to define a predominant frequency bands. The noise was measured by means of Nor140 Sound Analyzer with an extensive set of functions available in its expanded version. UAV's noise was recorded in time period of 5 s at the distance of 20 m at stabilized UAV flight mode. The noise levels were calculated and the characteristics are presented in Figure 7.

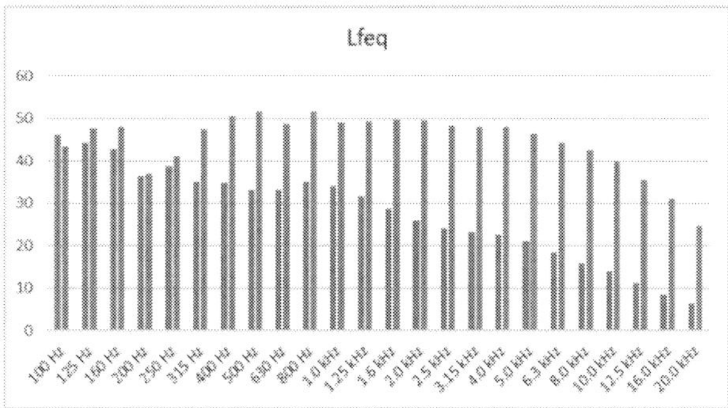

Figure 7. One-third octave band measurement results of UAVs noise

Residual noise is presented in blue color and the UAV's noise in green color. It is obvious that the UAV has broadband noise with basic frequency of tonal propeller component in 1/3 octave bands of central frequency of 125 Hz or 160 Hz. The difference of UAVs noise and background noise is at least 20 dB for the frequency range 100 Hz – 20 kHz.

Next four figures present the most interesting results of UAV visibility measurements using acoustic camera. All figures consist of four parts. At the top left side is situated a black and white photograph with the indicated position of the UAV. At the top right side is the overall spectrogram with the indicated part of the spectrogram (frequency components which originate from the UAV) used for calculation of specific acoustic image.

At the bottom left side is the acoustic image calculated from overall spectrogram and at the bottom right side is the acoustic image calculated from indicated part of the spectrogram. Measurement results at the distance of the 20 m are presented in Figure 8.

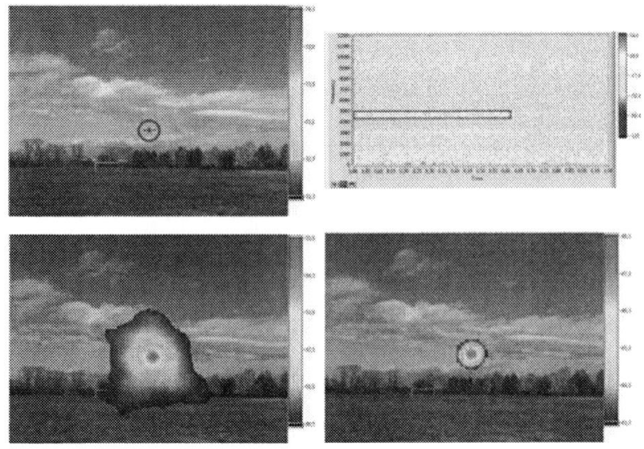

Figure 8. Measurement results at the distance of 20 m

UAV is visually clearly visible. It stands out as the dominant noise source within the overall sound image. The overall spectrogram highly expresses frequency components that come from the UAV. By using the selected part of the spectrogram, after signal processing, it is possible to determine the location of the UAV very well.

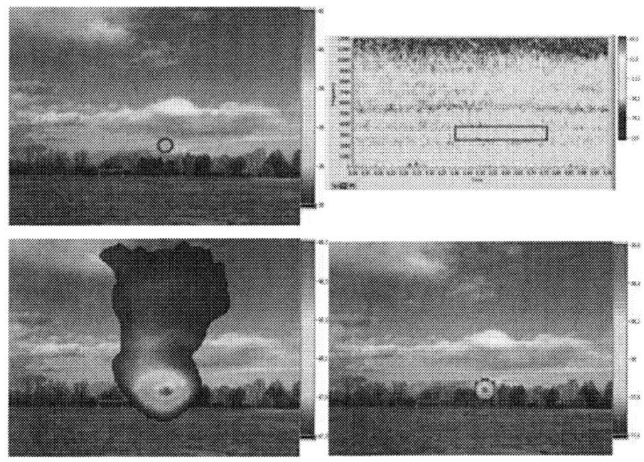

Figure 9. Measurement results at the distance of 60 m

Results of the measurements at the distance of 60 m are presented in Figure 9. UAV is discernible visually. It stands out as the dominant noise source within the overall sound image. The spectrogram shows frequency components that come from the UAV. By using the selected part of the spectrogram, after signal processing, it is possible to determine the location of the UAV.

Measurement results at the distance of the 100 m are presented in Figure 10. The UAV is visually noticeable. Within the overall sound image it does not stands out. In the spectrogram, the frequency components that come from the UAV are poorly visualized. By using the selected part of the spectrogram, after signal processing, it is possible to determine the location of the UAV.

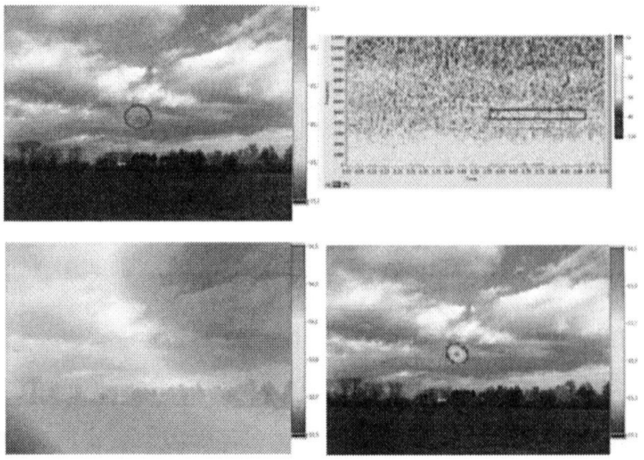

Figure 10. Measurement results at the distance of 100 m

Measurement results at the distance of the 170 m are presented at Figure 11.

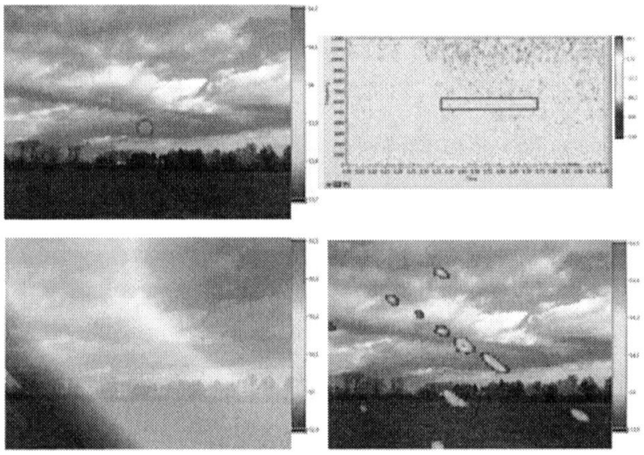

Figure 11. Measurement results at the distance of 170 m

The UAV is visually hardly noticeable. Within the overall acoustic image, it does not stand out. In the spectrogram, the frequency components that originate from the UAV are poorly visualized. By using the selected part of the spectrogram, after signal processing, it is possible to determine the location of the UAV with uncertainty. This is the detection limit based on the existing background noise.

IV. CONCLUSIONS

We have performed a detectability test of commonly used custom-made type UAVs. Our goal was to determine whether an acoustic sensor could be used to detect multirotor UAVs for the purpose of air traffic surveillance or collision avoidance. To achieve this, we have flown a custom-built UAV over a test track and recorded its movement with the SoundEye acoustic camera.

We concluded that:

- Small multirotor UAVs can be detected with acoustic camera in some conditions;
- Basic four parameters on which detectability depends on are: UAV noise spectrum, its ratio to background noise, the dynamic range of acoustic camera, and its frequency resolution;
- Due to background noise, human interpreter is necessary in the detection process;
- Maximum range of detection can be greater than visual detection;
- Due to necessity of human interpreter and time for processing, it is questionable whether the acoustic camera can be used for air traffic surveillance purposes.

In the future work, we will test detectability of UAVs against noisier background conditions. A more rigorous test of detectability will be performed with UAVs appearing from unknown directions. Finally, we will test methods for reducing the noise signature of an UAV.

REFERENCES

[1] Federal Aviation Administration, "FAA Aerospace Forecast - Fiscal Years 2017-2037", United States Department of Transportation, Washington, 2017.

[2] United States, "Public Law 112 - 95 - FAA Modernization and Reform Act of 2012", U.S. Goverment Publishing Office, Washington, 2012.

[3] European Comission, "Regulation (EC) No 216/2008", Official Journal of the European Union, Brussels, 2008.

[4] European Aviation Safety Agency, "Notice of Proposed Amendment 2017-05 (A), Introduction of a regulatory framework for the operation of drones, Unmanned aircraft system operations in the open and specific category", EASA, 2017.

[5] D. Gettinger and M.A. Holland, "Drone Sightings and Close Encounters: An Analysis", Center for the Study of the Drone at Bard College, New York, 2015.

[6] F. Hoffmann, M. Ritchie, F. Fioranelli, A. Charlish, and H. Griffiths, "Micro-Doppler Based Detection and Tracking of UAVs with Multistatic Radar", in IEEE Radar Conference, Philadelphia, 2016, pp. 1-6

[7] A. Moses, M. J. Rutherford, and K. P. Valvanis, "Radar-Based Detection and Identification for Miniature Air Vehicles", in 2011 IEEE Multi-Conference on Systems and Control, Denver, 2011, pp. 933-940

[8] T. Zsedrovits et al., "Collision avoidance for UAV using visual detection", in 2011 IEEE International Symposium of Circuits and Systems, Rio de Janeiro, 2011, pp. 2173-2176

[9] P. Andraši, T. Radišić, M. Muštra, and J. Ivošević, "Night-time Detection of UAVs using Thermal Infrared Camera", InAIR Conference 2017, Prague, 2017, pp. 183-190

[10] M. Peacock and M. N. Johnstone, "Towards detection and control of civilian unmanned aerial vehicles", in 14th Australian Information Warfare Conference, Perth, 2013, pp. 9-15

[11] E. E. Case, A. M. Zelnio, and B.D. Rigling, "Low-Cost Acoustic Array for Small UAV Detection and Tracking", in Aerospace and Electronics Conference, Dayton, 2008, pp. 110-113

[12] D. Miljković, J. Ivošević, and T. Bucak, "Two vs. three blade propeller - cockpit noise comparison", International Congress Alps Adria Acoustics Association 2012 Proceedings, Zadar, Croatia, 2012, pp. 1-5

Shaping Electromagnetic Emissions of Event-Driven Circuits Thanks to Genetic Algorithms

Sophie Germain[1,2], Sylvain Engels[1,2], Laurent Fesquet[1]

[1]Univ. Grenoble Alpes, CNRS, Grenoble INP*/ TIMA
F38000 Grenoble, France
e-mail: {*First name*}.{*Last name*}@univ-grenoble-alpes.fr

[2]STMicroelectronics
F38920 Crolles, France
e-mail: {*First name*}.{*Last name*}@st.com

***Abstract*—This paper presents a method to shape by design the electromagnetic spectrum of any event-driven circuits. Contrarily to synchronous circuits, which are driven by a clock, event-driven or asynchronous circuits can be tuned to adjust their computation instants by setting appropriated delays in their local synchronization mechanisms. Thanks to this prominent feature, shaping their electromagnetic spectrum is feasible. For that purpose, a mask in the frequency domain is defined to constrain their electromagnetic spectrum. Thanks to a genetic algorithm, well-suited delays are computed to be compliant with the mask. This approach has been evaluated on an event-driven micropipeline circuit. We observe that the resulting spectrum fits within the mask and does not present harmonics as its synchronous counterparts. Moreover, the highest peak of the event-driven circuit is 3.2 times smaller than the highest peak in the spectrum of the synchronous design.**

Keywords-Event-Driven Circuit; Micropipeline; Electromagnetic Spectrum.

I. Introduction

Electromagnetic compatibility (EMC) specifications are established in order to ensure the correct operation of different equipment in a common electromagnetic environment. Indeed, the unwanted generation, propagation and reception of electromagnetic energy in integrated circuits may cause unwanted effects, such as electromagnetic interference (EMI) or, even worst, physical damage. A device that emits, whether deliberate or unwanted, electronic emissions in its environment is referred to the aggressor. On the contrary, the circuit that is made malfunctioning or destroyed by the emission is referred to the victim. These kinds of issues are well-known by the circuit designers when they implement on the same die a RF transceiver and a baseband digital controller [1]. Indeed, the digital baseband controller tends to generate huge electromagnetic emissions disturbing the operations of the analog RF part of the circuit [2]. The clock signal of the digital circuit especially generates strong periodic current pulses on the power supply, producing a wide spectrum able to make inoperative a sensitive analog block [3].

Techniques for shielding the sensitive parts of electronic circuits are developed, for a long time, by designers in order to develop immunity against electromagnetic aggressions [4]. Techniques for hardening the circuitry have also been developed in order to make the circuit more robust [5][6]. Several techniques exist for synchronous designs to reduce their electromagnetic emissions [7][8]. Nevertheless, the clocked activity still produces periodic current pulses that pollute the electromagnetic spectrum. Contrarily, the asynchronous designs, also known as clockless circuits, show a spread electromagnetic spectrum. Philips Research and Philips Semiconductors developed an asynchronous version of the 80C51 microcontroller for a contactless smartcard application [9]. In comparison with the 80C51 synchronous version, the asynchronous one consumes about four times less energy and its spectrum does not have clock harmonics [10]. In this example, the advantage of asynchronous design for EMC has been presented but no strategy has been developed to control the electromagnetic spectrum by design.

The first attempt to control the electromagnetic emissions by design is made in [11] using asynchronous circuit and the Force Directed Scheduling (FDS). Their method has been applied to a finite impulsion response filter. This study shows a 9dB reduction of the highest peak component of the electromagnetic spectrum.

Nevertheless, to the best of our knowledge, there does not exist efficient strategy for shaping and controlling the electromagnetic spectrum by design.

In this paper, we present a genetic algorithm approach, for asynchronous circuits, not only to minimize the electromagnetic spectrum peaks but also the way to respect a spectral mask, like for example the Federal Communications Commission (FCC) spectral mask.

Section II of this paper describes the micropipeline event-driven circuitry used to apply the method. The current modelling is introduced in Section III. Section IV describes the genetic algorithm for shaping and controlling the electromagnetic spectrum. The simulation results are presented in Section V and a conclusion is given in Section VI.

* UGA Institute of Engineering

II. MICROPIPELINE

In order to shape the electromagnetic emission, using event-driven circuits is required. In our method, the Micropipeline class [12] is used, but other classes, such as Quasi-Delay Insensitive, Speed-Independent or Burst-mode circuits [13] for instance could be easily used.

Sutherland introduces first the Micropipeline in 1989 [12]. In the micropipeline architecture, the data path is kept from synchronous circuits and the global clock signal is removed. The synchronization between the registers, in the control path, is made by local controllers using a handshake protocol [12]. The controller sends a request signal when valid data are at the inputs of its registers and an acknowledgement signal to notify to the previous stage that its registers are ready to receive new data. To be valid, data have to be captured after their processing by the combinational logic. In order to ensure that the timing assumption, given in (1), the request signal has to be delayed of a value at least equal to the critical path of the corresponding combinational logic (see Figure 1).

$$D_{Capture} > D_{Launch} \quad (1)$$

Our method keeps the architecture of the micropipeline circuit and uses the set of delays to shape and control the emitted electromagnetic spectrum. This approach can be considered as a generic method.

III. CURRENT MODELLING

As far field EM measurements are targeted in this study, the EM spectrum directly depends on the circuit current consumption [1].

In synchronous CMOS circuits, the modelling of the current consumption is based on the following considerations:

- Gate switching produces the current consumption.
- The clock tree and the clock switching activity of the flip-flops produce an important part of the current consumption.
- Most of the gate switching activity is localized in time just after the clock edges.

Figure 2 shows a CMOS circuit current consumption with peaks on the clock edges. Therefore, current pulses may simply model the consumption of a digital CMOS circuit.

In synchronous circuits, because of the clock signal, all the registers capture data at the same time producing a uniform distribution in time of the current peaks and strongly impacting the electromagnetic spectrum by generating

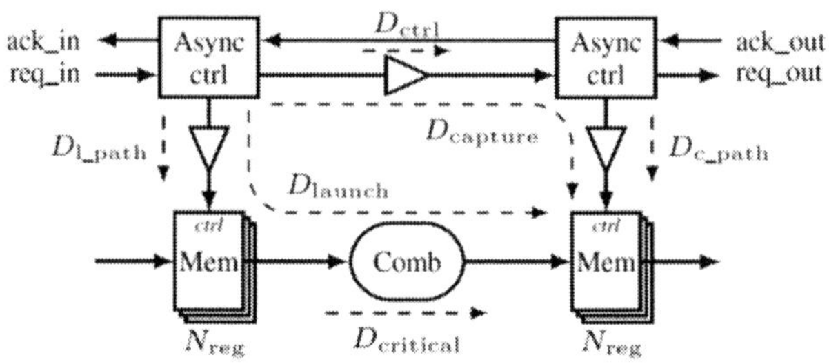

Figure 1. Architecture of a micropipeline circuit.

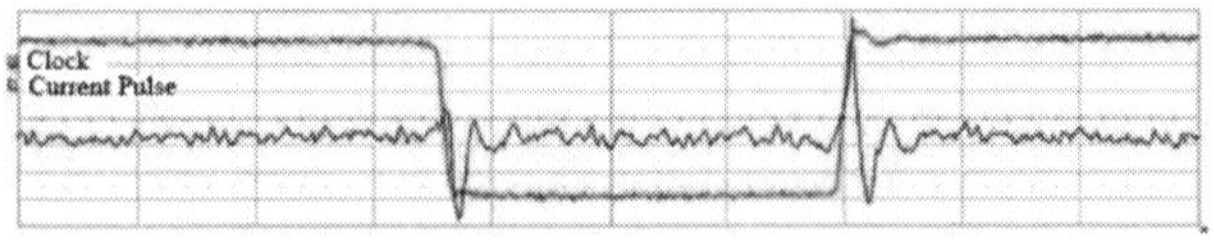

Figure 2. CMOS current consumption with peaks on the clock edges.

harmonics. In asynchronous designs, as the global clock is removed, the peaks distribution is no more uniform. This helps to reduce the harmonics. Therefore, the memorization instant of the registers can be seen as an event that introduces a peak in the current signal. These events could be distributed in time in order to shape the electromagnetic spectrum. To simply evaluate the current consumption a current pulse is placed on the current waveform when registers capture data.

Figure 3 illustrates the architecture on an n-stage linear micropipeline. The request signal of each stage n of the micropipeline is delayed of d_n. The total current consumption of this design is modeled as in Figure 4. The current consumption is seen as a sum of current peaks, which are distributed in time in function of the circuit delays.

Once the current curve is obtained, a Fast Fourier Transform (FFT) is performed in order to evaluate the electromagnetic spectrum.

IV. GENETIC ALGORITHM

A mask in the frequency domain is used to specify the targeted electromagnetic spectrum and to evaluate the circuit spectrum. A genetic algorithm (GA) is used to find the delays of micropipeline circuits to fit within the spectral mask.

The GA is a technique dedicated to optimization problems. Introduced by Professor Holland from the University of Michigan [14], this algorithm is inspired from the biology and natural phenomenon as the reproduction and the mutation. GA manipulates populations of individuals where, originally in biology, individuals are considered as chromosomes that evolve and mutate. This evolution can be interpreted as solutions to an optimization problem. Each chromosome is composed of genes that are the binary encoding of the parameters. The algorithm process (see Figure 5) begins with an initial population composed of N chromosomes that are candidate solutions to the problem. For each given chromosome x, a cost is evaluated with a fitness function $f(x)$. Then, they are classified from the stronger to the weaker, so that the rank increases from the best to the worst chromosome. Afterwards the parents of the next generation are selected among the current population. To select the parents, a line is created where each chromosome is a section of the line. The algorithm moves along that line in steps of equal size and allocates parents. The first parent is selected with a random number smaller than the step value. This method is called a stochastic uniform selection. During the selection, a chromosome can be selected more than once as a parent. In this case, its genes will contribute for more than one child. In the selection

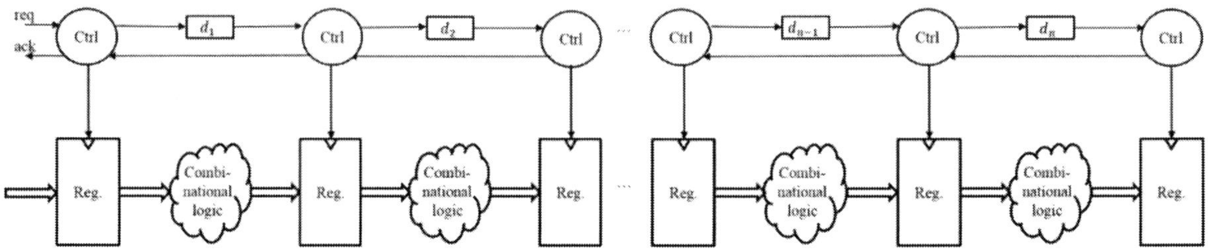

Figure 3. Architecture of an n-stage micropipeline

process, the chromosomes that have a better cost function are privileged. Then, the next generation is created in three steps.

Firstly, the elite children, the individuals with the best fitness value, in the current generation, are automatically selected. A proportion of the population has to be kept because there is no guarantee that the children will be better than the parents.

Secondly, the crossover children are created by the combination of two parents, this is similar to the reproduction in biology. A random binary vector is created and when its value is 1 the gene is selected from the first parent otherwise it is picked up from the second parent.

Finally, mutation children are created by applying random changes in a single individual. The mutation adds a random number chosen from a Gaussian distribution to each entry of the parent vector. The amount of mutation, which is proportional to the deviation of the distribution, decreases at each generation. This mutation step allows to explore different solutions and avoid to be locked.

To finish, the new generation is evaluated with the fitness function and the process of the algorithm is repeated. All the generations must have the same size to avoid the death of the population. The GA allows to find solutions for an optimization problem but not necessarily to find the best one (if it exists!).

In our case, we used the GA to find the delays that distribute the events in time in order to shape the electromagnetic spectrum. Therefore, the delays of the micropipeline are the genes of the individuals. The number of stages in the micropipeline defined the number of genes for the individuals. In our case, each gene has a minimal value corresponding to the critical path of the combinational logic associated to the stage. A maximal value is also determined by the designer in order to hold the expected speed performances of the circuit. The initial population is randomly chosen.

For each individual, we are able to determine the shape of the current when data are processed by the micropipeline circuit. Then, we apply a Fast Fourier Transform to have the frequency spectrum corresponding to this individual. The matching difference between this spectrum and the frequency mask is evaluated by the fitness function. When this difference is positive, the value is added to the chromosome cost. The algorithm is stopped when the best chromosome has a cost of zero. This last solution is chosen for setting the delays in the micropipeline circuit.

V. SIMULATION RESULTS

The simulations have been performed using the Matlab genetic algorithm function with the matching difference between the spectrum and the frequency mask as a fitness function.

We applied our method to an asynchronous circuit and then compared its electromagnetic spectrum to the spectrum of its synchronous counterparts. Both of them have one hundred stages. For the test case, the synchronous design has a clock period of 10 ns. The asynchronous version is designed in micropipeline [12]. We constrained the GA with delays covering a range between 5 ns to 10 ns with a resolution step of 0.1 ns. The upper bound, for the delays,

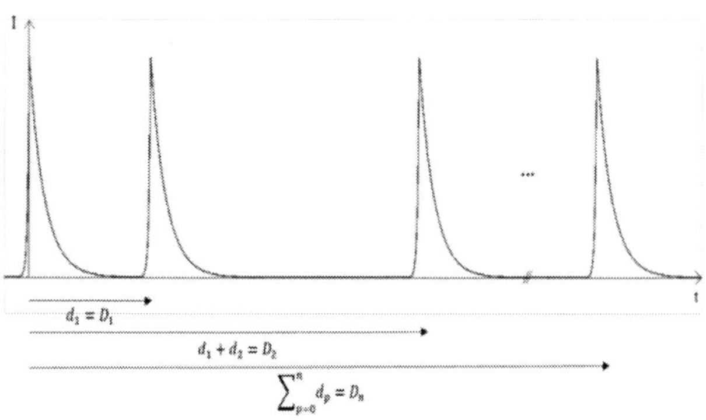

Figure 4. Shape of the total current consumption in time.

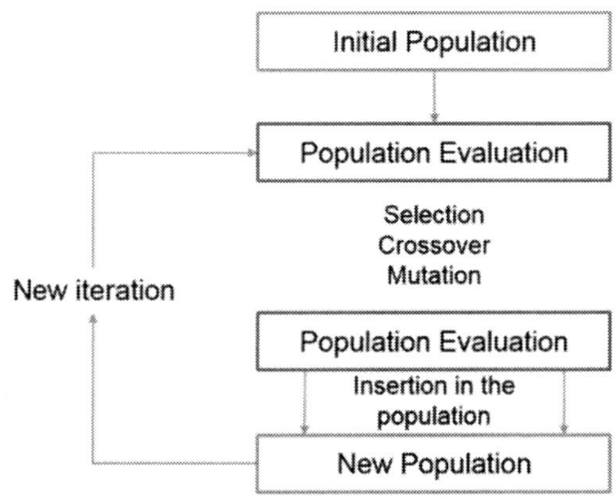

Figure 5. Genetic Algorithm Process.In our case the initial population is randomly chosen.

ensures that the total latency of the pipeline is maintained during optimization. The lower bound is the length of the critical path.

Figure 6 represents the architecture of a micropipeline stage where d_{min} is equal to the delay of the critical path in order to ensure the capture of valid data. Then, d_{GA} is the delay found by the genetic algorithm in order to fit the spectrum of the circuit within the spectral mask.

A mask is chosen as an electromagnetic spectral template in order to control the magnitude of the emissions in the frequency domain. The blue curve in Figure 7 is an example of spectral mask. In our example, we want to reduce the amplitude of some low frequencies. As already mentioned, the genes are delays selected in the range of 5 to 10 ns by step of 0.1 ns. The result of the simulations is showed in Figure 7. The green curve represents the electromagnetic spectrum of the synchronous design with a period of 10 ns. As expected, the spectrum presents harmonics every 100 MHz. The blue curve represents the spectral mask used in the fitness function to evaluate the individuals. The red curve is the resulting spectrum obtained by applying our method on the micropipeline design. Its magnitude now matches the spectral mask as expected. Moreover, the spectrum of the asynchronous design does not show harmonics anymore and its highest peak is 3.2 times smaller than the highest peak in the spectrum of the synchronous design.

To enhance the spectrum quality and ease the result convergence, the architecture of the design can be modified to add delays [15]. Indeed, increasing the number of stages in the design facilitates the search of delay solutions. The range and the step of the delays are also two important parameters that can be tuned to more easily fit the spectral mask [15].

VI. CONCLUSION

This paper presents a design method for shaping the emitted electromagnetic spectrum by an integrated circuit. With such a strategy, fitting within a spectral mask should become a specific step in the integrated circuit design flow. In order to apply this approach, event-driven asynchronous circuits have to be targeted. We chose for this purpose micropipeline circuits because they offer an event-driven behavior and an easy implementation for most of the circuit

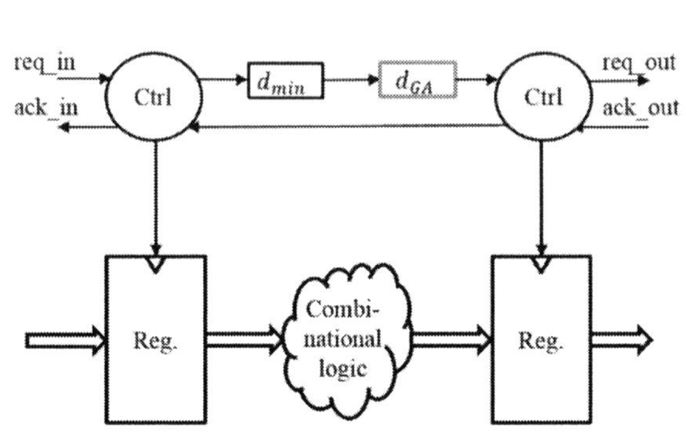

Figure 6. Micropipeline stage with the minimal delay that cover the critical path and the delay added to control the spectrum.

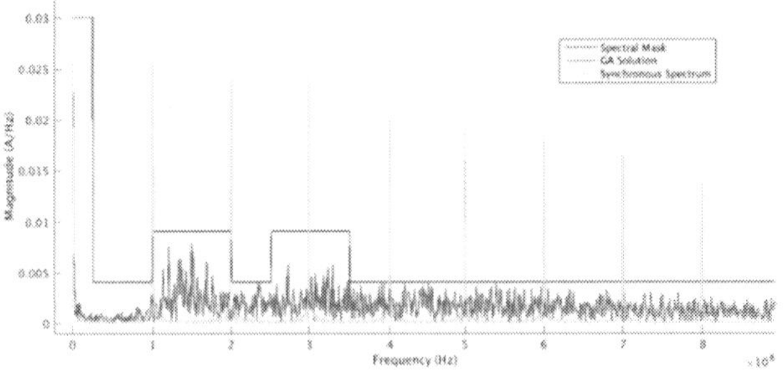

Figure 7. Simulation results, where the blue curve is the spectral mask and the red curve is the resulting spectrum of our method. The green curve is the spectrum of the synchronous version.

designers. We can notice that this design strategy can be applied to any kind of asynchronous designs.

Once the event-driven circuit is designed, the designer has to determine the minimal and the maximal values for each delay and the spectral mask. Then, the genetic algorithm is performed. The GA determines the value of the delays so that the electromagnetic spectrum of the circuit fits within the spectral mask.

Finally, we are able to obtain with event-driven circuits an electromagnetic spectrum fitting within a spectral mask and without harmonics in comparison to the spectrum emitted by their synchronous counterparts. Moreover, we obtain a significant reduction of the electromagnetic spectral peaks with this strategy.

A test chip has been designed and fabricated. The latter is under validation with real EM measurements. Moreover, we emphasize that our EM shaping technique can be fully automated and a specific design tool should be implemented.

ACKNOWLEDGMENT

This work has been partially supported by the Labex PERSYVAL-lab (ANR-11-LABX-0025-01) and the ANRT (Convention Cifre N° 2016/0718).

REFERENCES

[1] M. Ramdani et al., "The Electromagnetic Compatibility of Integrated Circuits—Past, Present, and Future," IEEE Trans. Electromagn. Compat., vol. 51, no. 1, pp. 78–100, 2009.

[2] C. M. Hung and K. Muhammad, "RF/Analog and Digital Faceoff-Friends or Enemies in an RF SoC," VLSI Technology Systems and Applications (VLSI-TSA), 2010 International Symposium on, pp. 19–20, 2010.

[3] M. Cazzaniga et al., "Evaluating the impact of substrate noise on conducted EMI in automotive microcontrollers," Electromagnetic Compatibility of Integrated Circuits (EMC Compo), 2013 9th Intl Workshop on, pp. 129–133, 2013.

[4] R. Rossi, G. Torelli, and V. Liberali, "Model and verification of triple-well shielding on substrate noise in mixed-signal CMOS ICs," ESSCIRC 2004 - 29th European Solid-State Circuits Conference (IEEE Cat. No.03EX705), pp. 643–646, 2003.

[5] M. J. Schneider, "Design Considerations to Reduce Conducted and Radiated EMI," Electrical and Computer Engineering Technology, 2009.

[6] M. Mardiguian, Controlling Radiated Emissions by Design, 3rd ed. Norwell, Massachusetts: Kluwer Academic Publishers, 2014.

[7] K. B. Hardin, J. T. Fessler, and D. R. Bush, "Spread spectrum clock generation for the reduction of radiated emissions," 1994, pp. 227–231.

[8] T. Steinecke, "Design-in for EMC on CMOS large-scale integrated circuits," 2001, vol. 2, pp. 910–915.

[9] G. Stegmann et al, "An asynchronous low-power 80C51 microcontroller," Advanced Research in Asynchronous Circuits and Systems, 1998. Proceedings. 1998 Fourth International Symposium on, pp. 96–107, 1998.

[10] K. V. Berkel, M. B Josephs, and S. M. Nowick, "Scanning the technology: applications of asynchronous circuits," Proc IEEE, pp. 223–233, 1999.

[11] D. Panyasak, G. Sicard, and M. Renaudin, "A current shaping methodology for lowering EM disturbances in asynchronous circuits," Microelectron. J., vol. 35, no. 6, pp. 531–540, 2004.

[12] I. E. Sutherland, "Micropipelines," Commun. ACM, vol. 32, no. 6, pp. 720–738, 1989.

[13] J. Sparsø and S. Furber, Principles of asynchronous circuit design: a systems perspective. Boston: Kluwer, 2010.

[14] J. H. Holland, Adaptation in natural and artificial systems: an introductory analysis with applications to biology, control, and artificial intelligence. Ann Arbor: University of Michigan Press, 1975.

[15] S. Germain, S. Engels, and L. Fesquet, "Event-based design strategy for circuit electromagnetic compatibility," presented at the 3rd International Conference on Event-Based Control, Communication and Signal Processing (EBCCSP), 2017, pp. 1–7.

Infinite Impulse Response Filters for Nonuniform Data

Brigitte Bidegaray-Fesquet* and Laurent Fesquet†
*Univ. Grenoble Alpes, CNRS, Grenoble INP, LJK, 38000 Grenoble, France
Email: Brigitte.Bidegaray@univ-grenoble-alpes.fr
†Univ. Grenoble Alpes, CNRS, Grenoble INP, TIMA, 38000 Grenoble, France
Email: Laurent.Fesquet@univ-grenoble-alpes.fr

***Abstract*—Capturing and storing samples only when needed is a way to ensure a drastic reduction of the data to be processed, which is a crucial issue in many applications, such as autonomous and communicating smart devices (Internet of Things). This leads to nonuniform data for which specific processing chains have to be designed. In this paper, we discuss the issues to be address to generalize Infinite Impulse Response filters to the nonuniform case. We illustrate the performance of the constructed filters on an electrocardiogram signal, for two ways to obtain the nonuniform samples, and select linear decimation and the bilinear scheme as a good combination for this application.**

Keywords–Nonuniform sampling; Infinite Impulse Response Filters; Asynchronous and Event-Driven Systems; Electrocardiogramm.

I. Introduction

For many applications, a way to drastically reduce the number of data in order to make their processing tractable with light platforms such as autonomous and communicating smart devices (often named Internet of Things) is to only capture and store samples when needed. For instance, analog-to-digital converters capture samples only when events occur or signals vary significantly. This induces data that are sampled irregularly in time, also called nonuniform data. The subject on how to sample the right data for a target application is out of the scope of this paper, but is an active research subject [1] [2].

Usual signal processing chains strongly rely on the fact that samples are taken regularly in time, or are the output of decimated regular data. When addressing genuine nonuniform data, we need to rethink the whole processing chain, in particular filtering devices.

Two main directions have been explored for constructing nonuniform filters: 1. the use of existing filters, originally designed for uniform signal and adapted to nonuniform signal [3]–[7]; 2. the design of specific filters [8]. Here we explore the first direction, and more specifically Infinite Impulse Response (IIR) filters. The case of finite impulse filters is somewhat simpler since the coefficients of the filter in the time domain can be directly used and there is only the need to interpolate correctly both the signal and the filter [3]. As will be shown in this paper, IIR filtering has to stem from a continuous representation of the filters in the Laplace domain, then in the time domain, eventually discretized at the sampling times. Other approaches in processing nonuniform sampled signals may also be found, e.g., in [9] or [10].

The design flow presented here has already been studied in [11] and its performances illustrated on a toy signal, namely a superposition of two sine signals. In particular, stability proofs can be found there. In this paper, we are more precise on the strategies to implement IIR filters on nonuniform data and give a more realistic numerical illustration.

The outline is as follows. In Section II, we describe the filter and the signal representation, and define most of the useful notations for the sequel. We particularly justify the choice of the state equation representation. In Section III, we show various ways to discretize the state equation and recall existing results on stability issues. In Section IV, we explore the filtering of an electrocardiogram (ECG) signal, using two types of sampling, level-crossing and linear decimation.

II. Signal and Filter Representations

In the usual uniform world, an IIR filter is often represented thanks to a difference equation that links the new output sample to previous samples of both the input and output signals. The coefficients in this difference equation are the feedforward and feedback filter coefficients. This representation of the filter strongly relies on the fact that samples are uniformly spaced. Another representation directly stems from the difference equation using the Z-transform. Both these representations are not possible to extend to a nonuniform context. A third possible representation is the state representation, which makes use of the representation of the filter in the Laplace domain. In this representation the output signal Y is simply the product of the filter transfer function H and the input signal I: $Y(s) = H(s)I(s)$. The filter transfer function can be written as a rational function of the Laplace variable s:

$$H(s) = \frac{\sum_{j=0}^{N} \alpha_j s^j}{\sum_{j=0}^{N} \beta_j s^j},$$

where N is the filter order.

Coming back to the time domain, this is classically cast as a system of ordinary differential equations

$$\frac{dx(t)}{dt} = Ax(t) + Bi(t), \quad (1)$$
$$y(t) = Cx(t) + Di(t), \quad (2)$$

where the state matrix A, the command vector B, the observation vector C, and the direct link coefficient D are expressed in terms of the α_j and β_j, $j = 0, \dots, N$. The advantage of this formulation is that it addresses *a priori* a continuous time, and can be considered at equally spaced time instants, in the case of classical uniform signal, or at irregularly spaced time instants in the nonuniform case, which we consider in this paper.

A uniform signal is described by a series of amplitudes, and the time delay between two samples is implicit, or even more usually renormalized to 1. In the case of nonuniform samples, time cannot clearly remain implicit and the samples consist of amplitude–delay couples (a_n, dt_n), where the delay dt_n is the time elapsed since the previous sample was taken (see Figure 1). This choice, compared to the choice of amplitude–time couples has two reasons. First, it has been applied to systems in which the samples are captured on the fly thanks to an asynchronous technology where no global clock synchronizes the whole system but where the synchronization is implemented with local handshakes [12]. Second, as we will see, the stability of the scheme depends on the values of the delays and not the time instants themselves.

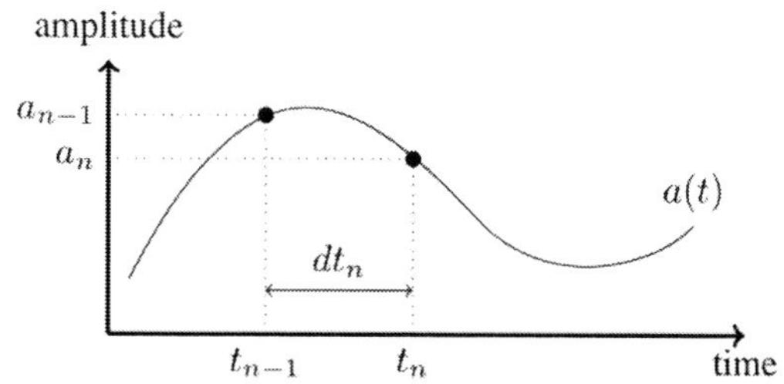

Figure 1. Non-uniform data.

In [11], the samples were collected using a level crossing algorithm. This gives extra information on the signal, but this is not an important feature for the application of a filtering scheme. In the world of nonuniform signals, we have to assume at some point that the right samples have been taken for the targeted application. In view of (2), it seems natural to define and compute the state signal $x(t)$ and the output signal $y(t)$ at the same time instants as the input signal. Another choice could be made, but this would necessitate the interpolation of signals and introduce interpolation errors. Hence, to an input signal (x_n, dt_n) will naturally correspond an output signal (y_n, dt_n) with the same time delays.

III. Discretization of the State Equation and Stability Issues

Once the filter is chosen and written in the state representation, there are various ways to discretize the system. Stability is the main issue to address, as well as the ability to implement efficiently the algorithm in an autonomous device.

A. Principle

The stability of the IIR filter depends on two choices: the choice of the filter and the choice of the scheme to discretize it. The impact of the choice of the filter is already present in the continuous time domain. The criterion is the following: the eigenvalues of the state matrix A should have a negative real value. These eigenvalues are solution to the characteristic polynomial of A which only depends on the feedback filter coefficients:

$$\det(\lambda \mathrm{Id} - A) = \lambda^N + \beta_{N-1}\lambda^{N-1} + \cdots + \beta_1\lambda + \beta_0,$$

where Id is the $N \times N$ identity matrix.

In the time discretization of the state equation (1), the N eigenvalues λ are transformed in the complex plane into a set of N other eigenvalues $\mu_n = \mathcal{T}_n(\lambda)$. For a constant time delay, the new eigenvalues are the same for the whole filtering process. In the nonuniform case, the set of eigenvalues varies through time, since it depends on dt_n. Therefore, we have to find a scheme which is uniformly stable for a range of time delays.

For the discretized scheme, the condition is that the eigenvalues lie in the unit circle of the complex plane. This can be easily understood from the integral representation of the solution to (1), namely

$$x(t) = e^{At}x(0) + \int_0^t e^{A(t-\tau)}Bi(\tau)d\tau. \tag{3}$$

Indeed, the eigenvalues of A lie in the left half plane, if and only if the eigenvalues of e^{At} lie in the unit circle.

B. A simple example: the Euler scheme

The simplest example to illustrate this principle is the Euler scheme, although it will not prove to be a "good" scheme. The Euler scheme reads

$$\frac{x_n - x_{n-1}}{dt_n} = Ax_{n-1} + Bi_{n-1}, \tag{4}$$

or equivalently

$$x_n = (\mathrm{Id} + dt_nA)x_{n-1} + Bdt_ni_{n-1}.$$

If we compare to the integral form, we see that e^{Adt_n} is simply approximated by $(\mathrm{Id} + dt_nA)$, and even by Id in the integral which is calculated with a left rectangle method. Here, $\mathcal{T}_n(\lambda) = 1 + dt_n\lambda$.

We have two ways to discuss this. If we want to address with this scheme all possible IIR filtering methods, with all possible eigenvalues in the left half-plane. Then, we can only say that $\mathcal{T}_n$ maps the left half-plane in an other half-plane (see Figure 2) and certainly the Euler scheme will not lead to a stable digital filter.

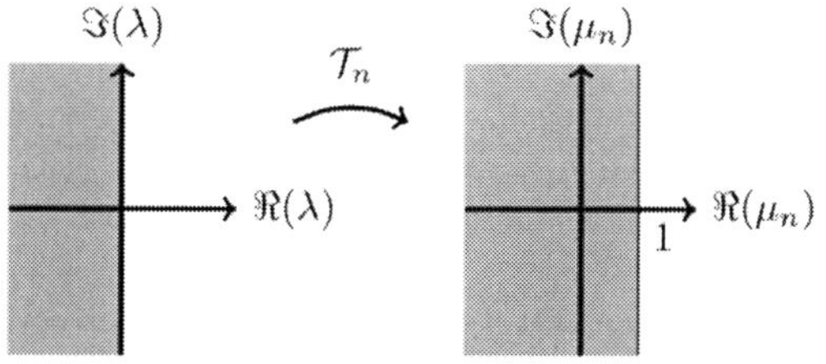

Figure 2. Action of the $\mathcal{T}_n$ transform for the Euler scheme. Eigenvalues λ (left) and eigenvalues μ_n (right).

An other point of view is to compute the inverse transform of the unit circle, which is also a circle for the Euler scheme, as shown on Figure 3. If it contains all the eigenvalues λ of the original filter, the discrete filter will be stable. This has to be valid for all the values of dt_n, i.e., for the maximum value of dt_n which yields the smallest inverse image of the unit circle. This leads to give a maximal bound for the time delay, that is to integrate these issues in the sampling procedure in a global signal processing chain.

C. Review of other schemes

The discretization of the state equation is either made on its integral form (3) or on the differential equation (1).

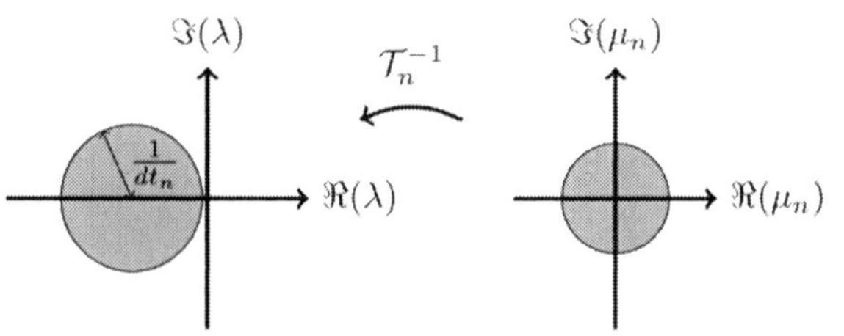

Figure 3. Backward action of the $\mathcal{T}_n$ transform for the Euler scheme. Eigenvalues λ (left) and eigenvalues μ_n (right).

1) Discretization of the integral form: Some of schemes are directly based on the integral formulation of the solutions. This is the case in [5], where the only approximation consists in replacing the continuous signal $i(t)$ by a sample-hold or piecewise linear interpolation on the time interval $[t_{n-1}, t_n]$, and compute exactly the integral. For example, for sample-hold interpolation

$$x_n = e^{Adt_n} x_{n-1} - A^{-1}(\mathrm{Id} - e^{Adt_n}) B i_{n-1}. \quad (5)$$

Since e^{Adt_n} is not approximated, this leads by construction to stable schemes. Another feature in this reference is the use of cascading filters, splitting the original filter into second- (or first-) order filters. This leads to a simpler calculation of $\exp(Adt_n)$ and make possible the implementation on asynchronous architectures [3] [13].

2) Discretization of the differential equation: The first example of this approach can be found in [6] [7] where they use the bilinear method to approximate the time derivative in (1):

$$\frac{x_n - x_{n-1}}{dt_n} = A\frac{x_n + x_{n-1}}{2} + B\frac{i_n + i_{n-1}}{2}. \quad (6)$$

For this scheme, the eigenvalue transform is the homographic function

$$\mathcal{T}_n(\lambda) = \frac{1 + dt_n\lambda/2}{1 - dt_n\lambda/2},$$

which is well known to map the left half-plane in the unit circle.

Other schemes have been reviewed in [11], backward Euler, various Runge-Kutta schemes. The results are well-known results when using difference methods to discretize ordinary differential systems of equations. In particular it is possible to construct unconditionaly stable implicit or semi-implicit schemes, i.e., schemes that are stable whatever the value of dt_n. This is the case of the backward Euler and bilinear methods. Explicit schemes, such as Runge-Kutta methods, can be easier to implement but they will always have a stability condition, and as for the Euler scheme an upper bound has to be set on the intersample time. This has to be integrated in the processing chain or, if no control on the input data is possible, extra data has to be interpolated in very quiescent parts of the signal. Practical implementations have shown that the bound on dt_n is not a crucial point and is not also a practical technical issue for the asynchronous systems [14]. In [11], the complexities of the various schemes are also compared. This proves not to be a crucial point either, if the filters are decomposed in one- or two- order filters, to avoid the computation of matrix exponentials.

TABLE I. COMPRESSION OF THE ECG SIGNAL VIA LEVEL-CROSSING.

number of levels	4	8	16
number of samples	584	1377	2414
compression	2%	4.8%	8.5%

IV. FILTERING AN ECG SIGNAL

To study the stability performances of the IIR filters in [11] sine signals were chosen. These signals are always active and no gain in the number of samples can be hoped since even with a non-uniform sampling the Nyquist rate should be ensured at last in average [15] [16]. If the signal frequency-range is constant over the signal duration, no reduction of the number of samples can be obtained, and since the processing of the samples could be more complex when nonuniform, the overall performances would be lower than with classical uniform sampling and classical filtering techniques. Notice that this point is not obvious and the processing is not always more costly such as in [17].

Here we consider an ECG signal. Such a signal is interesting to address with nonuniform sampling, since it has quiescent parts and for applications, such as pacemakers or disease diagnosis, we very often want to isolate specific patterns in the signal and not process the signal as a whole. The signal shown in the next experiments has a 14.27 s duration which corresponds to about 22 cardiac cycles. The initial signal, sampled at 2000 Hz, has 28548 samples.

All the computations have been performed using the SPASS Matlab toolbox [18].

A. Nonuniform sampling of the input signal

Two types of nonuniform sampling are explored, a level-crossing sampling scheme and linear decimation, which can be more or less assimilated to a slope crossing scheme.

1) Level-crossing: A simple and widely used way of nonuniformly sampling signals is level-crossing sampling [19] [20] [10]. It consists in defining levels within the range of the input signal. These levels can be either equally spaced, for simplicity or implementations reasons [3], or on the contrary very carefully chosen in order to capture the important features of the signal for a specific application [21].

Figure 4 displays the samples obtained of our ECG sample. Here 8 equally-spaced levels have been chosen, which leads to 1377 samples, and hence 4.8% of the initial samples. To have an idea of the compression obtained with this technique, we give in Table I the number of samples and compression for 4, 8 and 16 levels.

2) Linear decimation: We propose here another way to decimate the initial samples, which can be performed on the fly, which is of practical interest for hardware implementations. The principle of this decimation is shown in Figure 5.

It consists in defining a tolerance on the surface of the polygon between the curve with all the initial samples and the kept samples. Let us suppose that we begin with sample S_1. If the surface of the triangle $S_1S_2S_3$ is above threshold, then we keep S_2 and explore the next samples taking S_2 as new initial sample. If this surface is below threshold, then we consider the surface of the polygon $S_1S_2S_3S_4$, if it is above threshold,

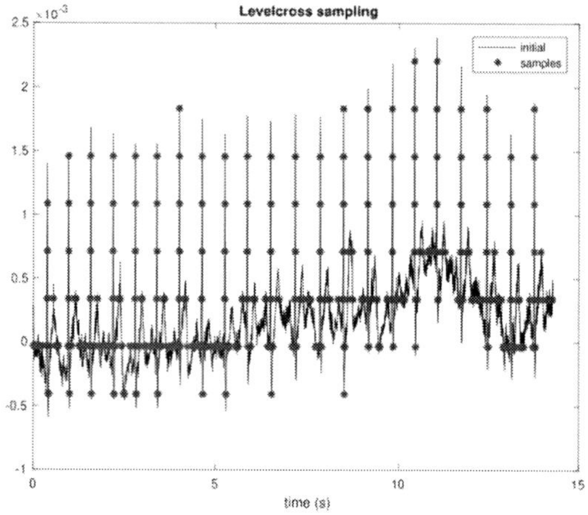

Figure 4. 8-level-crossing sampling of an ECG signal.

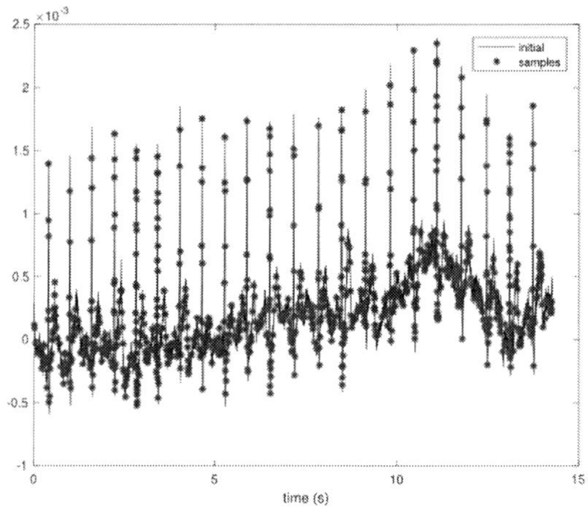

Figure 6. Linear decimation sampling of a ECG signal. range criterion, 916 vs. 284548 samples.

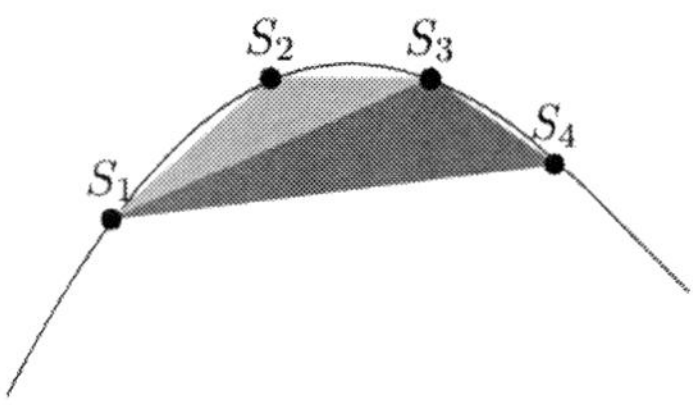

Figure 5. Principle of linear decimation.

we keep S_3 and take it a new initial sample, otherwise we go on exploring S_5, etc.

Figure 6 displays the samples obtained for our ECG signal. Here we chose a tolerance equal to twice the width of the range of the signal, which leads to 916 samples, and hence 3.2% of the initial samples. Again, a few other choices for the tolerance and the associated compression are given in Table II.

With less samples than with 8-level-crossing the description of the signal seems better. This will be confirmed by the filtering results. Of course there is a drawback, although possible, the hardware implementation of this type of sampling is much harder.

B. Filtering results

We use an order-10 Butterworth filter with a cut-off frequency at 200 Hz. We have tested the various methods described in [11] but only plot results for the backward Euler scheme

$$\frac{x_n - x_{n-1}}{dt_n} = Ax_n + Bi_n, \quad (7)$$

TABLE II. COMPRESSION OF THE ECG SIGNAL VIA LINEAR DECIMATION.

tolerance	2*range	range	range/2
number of samples	916	1548	2341
compression	3.2%	5.4%	8.2%

and the bilinear scheme (6). For this test case, both the Euler scheme (4) and the Runge-Kutta 4 scheme are unstable and do not yield any result. Other Runge-Kutta schemes, such as RK23, are not unstable but give very distorted results.

Figure 7 displays the filtering of the ECG signal after level-crossing sampling with the backward Euler discretization of the state equation (7). For the sake of clarity, we have windowed the plot to see a small sequence of the signal.

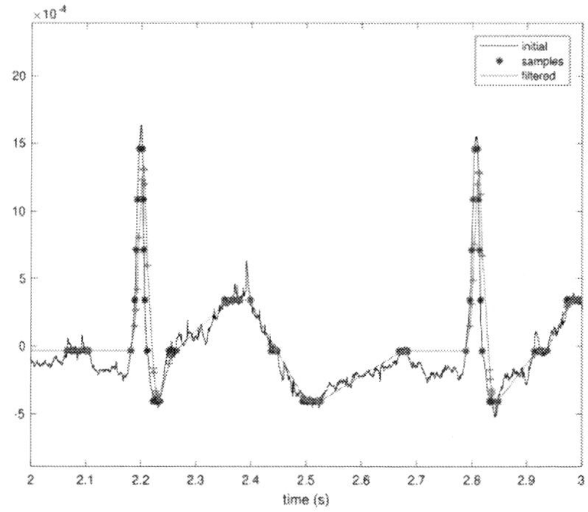

Figure 7. Backward Euler Butterworth filtering of ECG signal after level-crossing sampling.

We can notice two unwanted features: first, the filtered signal keeps the memory of the sampling levels; second, the P pattern is not captured. Indeed, physicians who read ECGs want to spot specific patterns in the ECG signal to diagnose diseases. These patterns are designated by the letters PQRST, see Figure 8. The reason why P has not been captured is not due to filtering but to sampling since no point has been set in this part of the signal. This can typically be corrected by a cleverer choice of the levels.

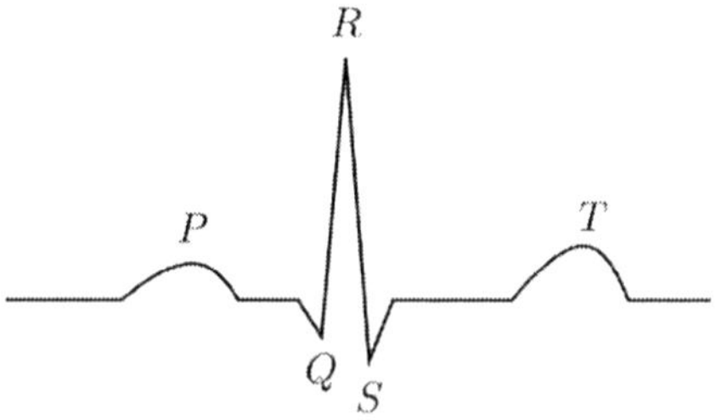

Figure 8. Patterns in a normal heart sinus rhythm.

Figure 9 displays the filtering of the ECG signal after the same level-crossing sampling but with the bilinear discretization. The previous bad features are always there because they were mainly due to sampling. They are present for all the (stable) schemes, the worst one from this point of view being the integral form (5). This is not due to the integral form itself which is exact, but to the sample-hold interpolation. You have to use piecewise linear or nearest neighbor interpolation for this application.

The bilinear discretization does nonetheless a little better than the backward Euler scheme. Indeed, the amplitude of the R pattern is much better captured.

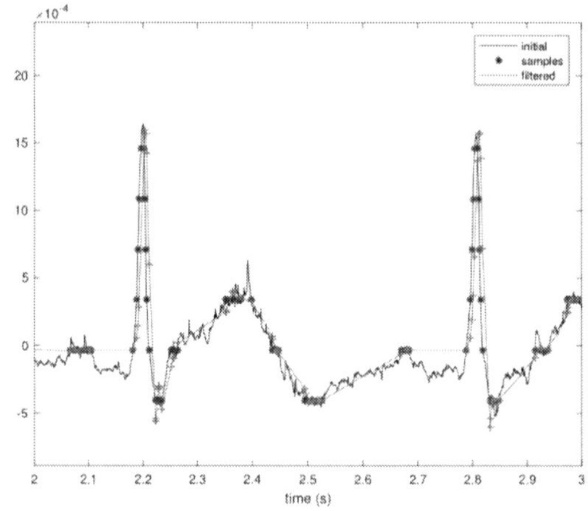

Figure 9. Bilinear Butterworth filtering of ECG signal after level-crossing sampling.

Now, we explore the simulations performed with a linear decimated sampled signal. Figures 10 and 11 yield the results for the backward Euler and bilinear discretizations of the Butterworth filter. The unwanted features of the level-crossing sampling are of course not present and the filtered result much resembles the theoretical pattern of Figure 8. The bilinear scheme is once more better than the backward Euler scheme, since it captures better the amplitude and times of the points of interest.

V. Conclusion and Future Work

We have discussed various issues which are important when having to generalize IIR filters to the nonuniform case:

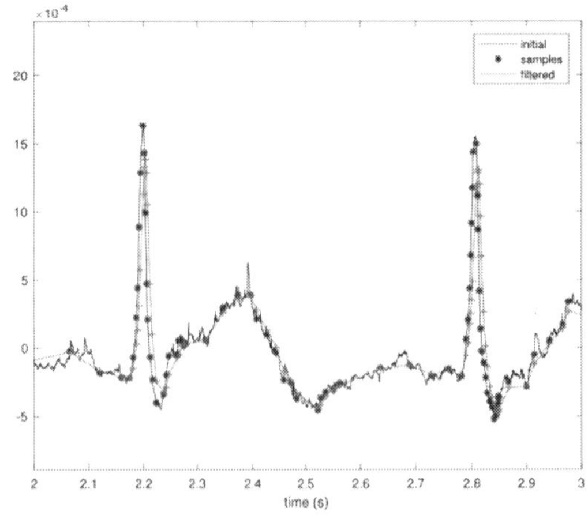

Figure 10. Backward Euler Butterworth filtering of ECG signal after linear decimation sampling.

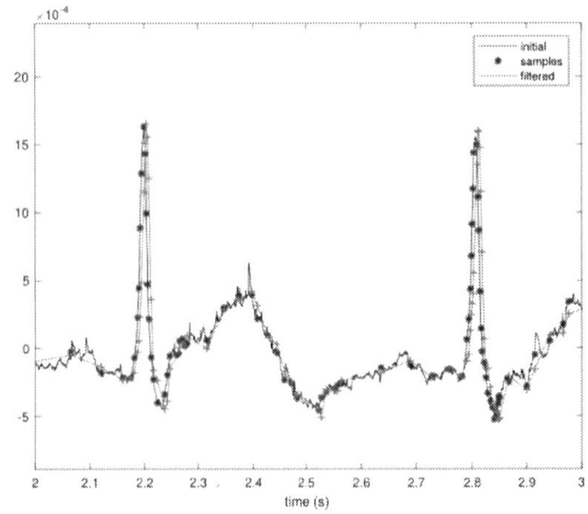

Figure 11. Bilinear Butterworth filtering of ECG signal after linear decimation sampling.

which representation of such filters is the more adapted to this generalization?

We illustrate the performance of the constructed filters on an electrocardiogram signal, for two ways to obtain the nonuniform samples. We select linear decimation and the bilinear scheme as a good combination for this application. This discretization of the equation gives stable and accurate results. We have seen on an ECG example that if the choice of the discrete filtering method is important, the way the nonuniform samples have been chosen is also a very crucial issue. The method, we call linear decimation, seems to be adapted to the ECG case, but there is clearly a lot of work to be done in this direction to reduce more drastically the number of samples and therefore the computational cost.

Acknowledgment

This work has been partially supported by the LabEx PERSYVAL-Lab (ANR-11-61 LABX-0025-01).

References

[1] F. Marvasti, Nonuniform Sampling. Theory and Practice, ser. Information Technology: Transmission, Processing and Storage. Kluwer Academic Publishers, 2001.

[2] B. Bidégaray-Fesquet and L. Fesquet, "Levels, peaks, slopes... which sampling for which purpose?" in 2nd International Conference on Event-Based Control, Communications, and Signal Processing (EBCCSP16). Krakow, Poland: IEEE, Jun. 2016, pp. 1–6.

[3] F. Aeschlimann, E. Allier, L. Fesquet, and M. Renaudin, "Asynchronous FIR filters: Towards a new digital processing chain," in 10th International Symposium on Asynchronous Circuits and Systems (Async'04). Hersonisos, Crete: IEEE, Apr. 2004, pp. 198–206.

[4] B. Bidégaray-Fesquet and L. Fesquet, "A fully non-uniform approach to FIR filtering," in 8th International Conference on Sampling Theory and Applications (SampTa'09), L. Fesquet and B. Torrésani, Eds., Marseille, France, May 2009, pp. 129:1–4.

[5] L. Fontaine and J. Ragot, "Filtrage de signaux à échantillonnage irrégulier [Filtering irregularly sampled signals]," Traitement du Signal, vol. 18, no. 2, 2001, pp. 89–101.

[6] D. Poulton and J. Oksman, "Digital filters for non uniformly sampled signals," in Nordic Signal Processing Symposium (NORSIG 2000), Vildmarkshotellet Kolmarden, Sweden, Jun. 2000, pp. 421–424.

[7] ——, "Filtrage des signaux à échantillonnage non uniforme [Filtering nonuniformly sampled signals]," Traitement du Signal, vol. 18, no. 2, 2001, pp. 81–88.

[8] B. Bidégaray-Fesquet and L. Fesquet, "Non-uniform filter interpolation in the frequency domain," Sampling Theory in Signal and Image Processing, vol. 10, no. 1–2, 2011, pp. 17–35.

[9] S. M. Qaisar, L. Fesquet, and M. Renaudin, "Adaptive rate sampling and filtering based on level crossing sampling," EURASIP Journal on Advances in Signal Processing, vol. 2009, no. Article ID 971656, 2009, p. 13 pages.

[10] C. Vezyrtzis and Y. Tsividis, "Processing of signals using level-crossing sampling," in IEEE International Symposium on Circuits and Systems, ISCAS 2009. Taipei, Taiwan: IEEE, May 2009, pp. 2293–2296.

[11] L. Fesquet and B. Bidégaray-Fesquet, "IIR digital filtering of non-uniformly sampled signals via state representation," Signal Processing, vol. 90, no. 10, Oct. 2010, pp. 2811–2821.

[12] J. Sparso and S. Furber, Eds., Principles of Asynchronous Circuit Design: A Systems Perspective. Springer, 2001.

[13] T. Beyrouthy and L. Fesquet, "An event-driven FIR filter: design and implementation," in 22nd IEEE International Symposium on Rapid System Prototyping (RSP 2011). Karlsruhe, Germany: IEEE, May 2011, pp. 59–65.

[14] E. Yahya, L. Fesquet, Y. Ismail, and M. Renaudin, "Statistical static timing analysis of conditional asynchronous circuits using model-based simulation," in 19th International Symposium on Asynchronous Circuits and Systems (ASYNC). IEEE, 2013, pp. 67–74.

[15] F. J. Beutler, "Sampling theorems and bases in a hilbert space," Information and Control, vol. 4, no. 2-3, 1961, pp. 97–117.

[16] ——, "Error-free recovery of signals from irregularly spaced samples," SIAM Review, vol. 8, no. 3, 1966, pp. 328–335.

[17] G. Roa, T. Le Pelleter, A. Bonvilain, A. Chagoya, and L. Fesquet, "Designing ultra-low power systems with non-uniform sampling and event-driven logic," in 27th Symposium on Integrated Circuits and Systems Design (SBCCI 2014). Aracaju, Sergipe, Brazil: IEEE, Sep. 2014, Article No. 5:1–6.

[18] B. Bidégaray-Fesquet and L. Fesquet, "SPASS 2.0: Signal Processing for ASynchronous Systems," Software, May 2010. [Online]. Available: https://ljk.imag.fr/membres/Brigitte.Bidegaray/SPASS/ [retrieved: April, 2018]

[19] N. Sayiner, H. V. Sorensen, and T. R. Viswanathan, "A level-crossing sampling scheme for A/D conversion," IEEE Transactions on Circuits and Systems II, vol. 43, no. 4, Apr. 1996, pp. 335–339.

[20] E. Allier, G. Sicard, L. Fesquet, and M. Renaudin, "A new class of asynchronous A/D converters based on time quantization," in 9th International Symposium on Asynchronous Circuits and Systems, Async'03. Vancouver, Canada: IEEE, May 2003, pp. 196–205.

[21] T. Le Pelleter, T. Beyrouthy, R. Rolland-Girod, A. Bonvilain, and L. Fesquet, "Non-uniform sampling pattern recognition based on atomic decomposition," in 10th International Conference on Sampling Theory and Applications (SampTA 2013), Bremen, Germany, Jul. 2013, pp. 236–239.

Analysis of Emotions from Body Postures Based on Digital Imaging

Bruno Barbosa, António J. R. Neves
DETI / IEETA
University of Aveiro
3810-193 Aveiro, Portugal
Email: {brunobarbosa, an}@ua.pt

Sandra C. Soares[1], Isabel D. Dimas[2]
[1]CINTESIS.UA, Departamento de Educação e Psicologia
[2]GOVCOPP/ESTGA
University of Aveiro
3810-193 Aveiro, Portugal
Email: {sandra.soares, idimas}@ua.pt

Abstract — **In this paper, we present a state of the art regarding computer vision systems for the detection and classification of human body postures. Although emotions conveyed by human body postures are an important means of socio-communicative functions in several contexts, a surprising lack of systems that enable the recognition and classification of postures for different emotional signatures, is acknowledged. The neglect of such systems is most likely due to the complexity of the emotions reflected in body postures, and to the wide range of variations in postures, particularly when assessing groups of individuals. Despite the existence of several sensors, allowing to obtain images of various types, from color images to thermal images, no one was yet used for this purpose. We propose the use of a recently developed algorithm, which has presented optimal results in several domains, to allow for the recognition of emotions from human body postures.**

Keywords - Pose Estimation; Digital Image; Emotions; Skeleton Detection.

I. INTRODUCTION

Emotions conveyed by facial expressions are powerful non-verbal cues for functional socio-emotional interactions. The study of body postures as another important non-verbal means to communicate emotions and behavioral intentions has been exponential in the past decade [1], particularly in the fields of cognitive, affective and social neuroscience [2][3]. Although these studies have been showing that emotion recognition performance depicted from body postures do not seem to differ from those of facial expressions, research work exploring the effectiveness of computer vision systems able to automatically detect and classify emotional categories and dimensions from human postures, are scant.

Herein, we present the state of the art regarding the development of computer vision systems for detection and classification of human body posture, including the type of existing sensors to obtain images that feed such systems and their operation, as well as human skeletal detection algorithms. We discuss the implications regarding the development of such systems for emotion detection from body posture in several contexts, in which emotions are relevant for socio-communicative purposes.

With the advancement in the study of emotions associated with body postures, it is necessary to investigate, technologically, how emotions can be extracted, non-invasively, from human postures. This is of high relevance to several areas of application, ranging from education, (e.g., posture of students in classrooms, denoting disinterest or excitement [4], to teamwork [5] and mental health contexts (e.g., postures associated with psychopathology, such as unipolar depression [6]).

Our proposal is that, by using digital cameras and algorithms that allow to extract human body postures, postures associated with different emotional dimensions should be mapped. We suggest the development of a system that allows the detection and classification of these postures, in groups of individuals, which are asked to freely interact in a dynamic. Hence, unlike the previous studies, participants will not be asked to perform specific postures that are expected to be associated with different socio-communicative patterns (e.g., expansive or constrictive) [7][8][9]. This raises the following questions: "How to use a PC and a camera to measure the body posture of the human body?" and "How to classify each posture as being associated with certain emotional dimensions and or categories?".

This article is organized as follows: Section 1 gives a brief introduction and presentation of problem, in Section 2 are presented the existing computer systems for the presented problem, Section 3 discusses the definition of digital image, presenting the various types of existing image sensors, Section 4 are addressed some of the existing posture detection algorithms and in section 5 a conclusion is made about everything that has been said previously.

II. EXISTING COMPUTATIONAL SYSTEMS FOR THE PRESENTED CONTEXT

Some work has been carried out in the development of systems for the detection and evaluation of the human body. However, no system was yet developed to allow the detection and classification to map emotions from body postures. This lack of systems' is due to the difficulty of classifying a posture. Moreover, in real life settings, the variations in postures are immense, making it difficult to infer emotions from dynamic interactions between individuals.

In [10], in a classroom context, the authors claim to provide important information to the teacher about their audience's attention. This study focused mainly on the capture of data through a camera system to detect movements, as well as the head and its orientation, thus obtaining the most significant patterns of behavior to infer this cognitive dimension (i.e., attention). However, the results failed to show a direct relationship between the movements of the students and their attention.

In [11], a system for the recognition of human actions based on posture primitives is described. This system, like [12], only focuses on perceiving/classifying if a person runs, walks, dance, etc. and not their emotions. In a learning phase, the representative parameters of posture are estimated through videos. After that, already in a classification phase, the method is used for both videos and static images. In this system, 3 disjoint problems are identified in the recognition of human action: detection of a person in the image, recognition of the posture expressed, and attribution of a category of action to its posture, the focus being the last 2 points. The results of this system are promising, resulting in a highly accurate recognition of actions, allowing us to conclude that the posture of human beings contains enough information about their activity. It is also mentioned that, the addition of other information besides posture, allows for a greater precision in the recognition of the activities.

In short, we were able to verify the existence of some systems for the recognition of posture with specific applications. However, no system is yet available to recognize and classify postures according to the emotions they are communicating.

III. Image Sensors

Typically, a digital image is represented by a rectangular matrix of scalar vectors, composed by a finite number of elements in each position and with a certain value. These elements are called pixels [13].

A pixel is the smallest unit of an image and has an intensity value and a location associated with it. Through the joining of many pixels and due to the filtering effect of the human eye, it is possible to create illusions, like gradients and shading.

Figure 1 shows an array of pixels relating to a digital image and Figure 2 represents the gradient of a Red, Green and Blue (RGB) image by merging pixels.

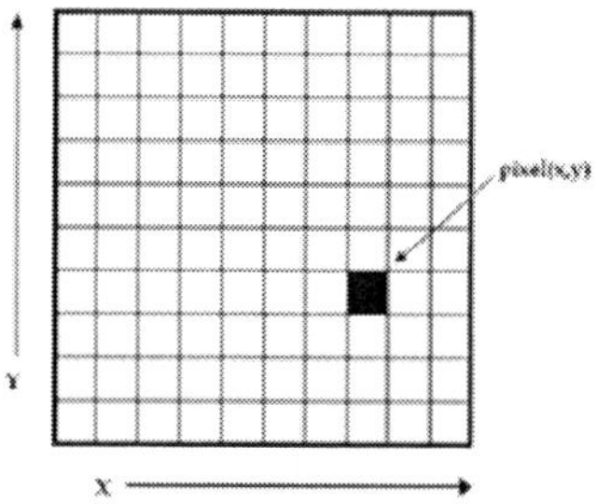

Figure 1. Representation of an array of pixels in an Image with Width X and Height Y [14].

The most common types of digital images are grayscale and RGB images. In grayscale images, the value associated with each pixel is black, white or a shade of gray, which can range, for 8 bits per pixel, from 0 to 255, where 0 is black and 255 is white. In color images, each pixel has associated with it a red, green and blue value, which combined in different amounts can generate any color. The values of red, green and blue also vary, for 8 bits per pixel, between 0 and 255, with 0 being the black color and 255 the maximum of the respective color. Figure 3 shows an intensity matrix of a grayscale image for a given area [16].

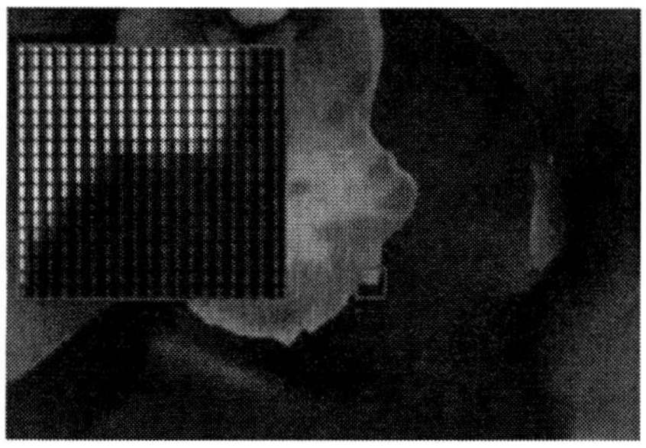
Figure 2. Gradient associated with a region of an RGB image [15].

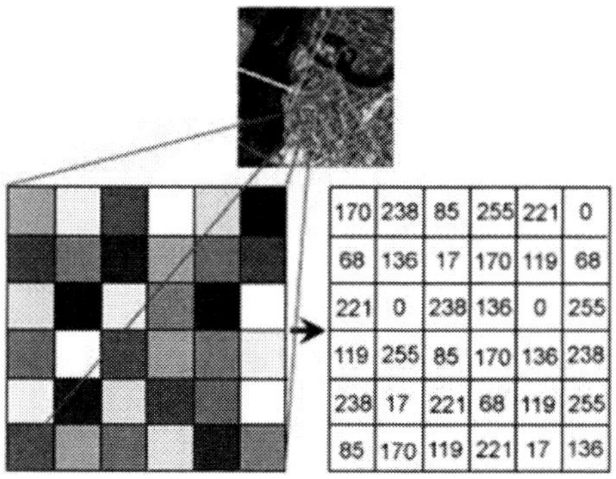

Figure 3. Matrix for certain area of a grayscale image [17].

The resolution of a digital image depends on the size of its array, that is, with increasing number of pixels, the resolution increases. However, the processing of this matrix becomes computationally slower.

There are several types of sensors able to obtain digital images. In the next subsections, some of these types of sensors will be discussed and their operation explained.

A. *Image Sensors in the Visible Spectrum*

For capturing digital images in the visible spectrum, mainly two types of sensors are used - the Charge-Coupled Device (CCD) and the Complementary Metal-Oxide-Semiconductor (CMOS) sensor.

Each of these sensors is composed by millions of photosensitive transducers whose function is to convert light energy into electric charge. They also have a photosensitive surface, which receives a charge of light to capture the image, so the larger the photosensitive surface, the better the image quality [18].

However, these sensors can only measure the energy of the radiation. To obtain color images, it is necessary to apply a filter that allows to target specific colors to their respective pixels. The most common filter is the Bayer filter. Figure 4 shows the operation of this type of filter.

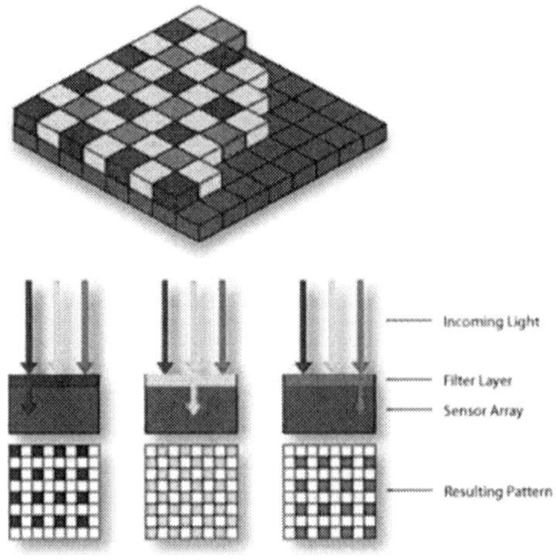

Figure 4. Application of a Bayer filter to obtain a color image [19].

The CCD sensor exists mainly in compact cameras, while the CMOS sensor is present from simple webcams and smartphone cameras to professional cameras.

Figure 5 shows an example of a CCD and CMOS sensor.

Figure 5. Example of CCD (left) and CMOS (right) sensor [20].

B. *Special Sensors*

In addition to the sensors mentioned earlier, there are also special sensors that allow to obtain other information besides the color image. These sensors are especially used for image processing in special cases, such as the measure of distances and temperatures.

In the next subsections, the modes of operation of these sensors will be explained.

1) *Thermal*

A thermal camera, unlike the cameras in the visible spectrum mentioned above, are composed of sensors capable of capturing radiation in the infrared spectrum, thus allowing the creation of an infrared image [21]. Normally, when displaying this type of images, a color table is applied so that it is possible to easily distinguish between hot and cold zones. Figure 6 shows a thermal image, obtained through a *Flir* [22] thermal camera, with the respective color table. Although this camera is commercial, it has a high cost due to its specific market and technology used in its manufacture.

Figure 6. Example of CCD (left) and CMOS (right) sensor [22] .

This type of sensor can be used even in low-light environments, as opposed to sensors, such as CCD and CMOS [21]. There are several areas where these apply. From security, where they can be used to detect intruders even in low light situations [23], to the industry, where they can be used to detect heating problems in machines, which are not detected by the human eye [21], passing through the detection of people through the temperature of the human body [24].

2) *Multi/Hyper Spectral*

The Multispectral and Hyperspectral sensors measure the energy in various bands of the electromagnetic spectrum. The spectral resolution is the main distinguishing factor between the images produced by these two types of sensors. The hyperspectral sensors contain a greater number of bands with narrow wavelengths, providing a continuous measurement in all the electromagnetic spectrum, whereas the multispectral sensors usually contain between 3 and 10 bands with wide wavelengths in each pixel of the image produced [25]. This way, the images captured by a hyperspectral sensor contain more data than the images captured by multispectral sensors. In a practical context, images produced by multispectral sensors can be used, for example, to map forest areas, while images produced by hyperspectral sensors can be used to map tree species within the same forest area [26].

Figure 7 shows the comparison between multispectral and hyperspectral images.

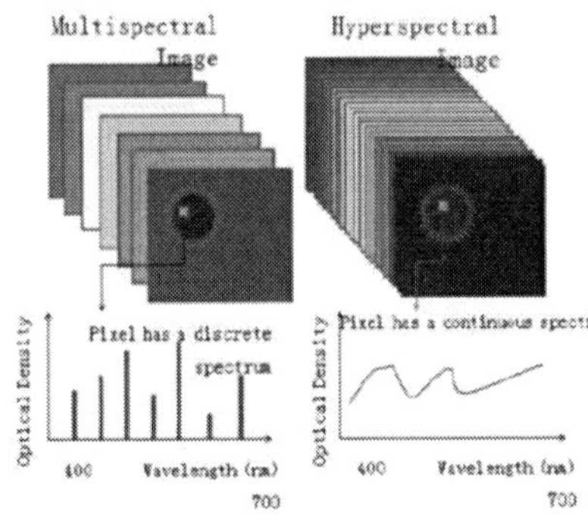

Figure 7. Comparison between a multispectral (left) and hyperspectral (right) image [27].

3) Distance

There are several types of distance image sensors. These types of sensors can obtain images where the closest and most distant objects are perceptible.

There are three major types of sensors, the sensors called Time Of Flight (TOF), Structured Light and Stereo. TOF sensors work on the principle of sending and receiving a signal by measuring the properties of the received signal. By determining the flight time and, consequently, through this time and the speed of the signal the distance to the object is obtained [28]. Structured Light sensors work by projecting a previously established pattern into scene, allowing the system, by capturing that same pattern, to calculate the depth of each pixel of the image received. This calculation is performed by deformation of each point of the pattern projected in combination with the original pattern [29]. Finally, the Stereo sensors allow to obtain distance image through two lenses, at a certain distance, so that the two captured images can be processed and compared, creating a 3D image [30].

IV. Algorithms for Posture Detection

There are many human posture detection algorithms, but few do it dynamically and in poorly controlled environments.

The main existing algorithms focus on the area of vision. This area has been increasingly explored as it allows everything to be done in a non-invasive way for the Human being. Thus, devices not directly in contact with it enable the ecological validity of the actions, hence increasing the accuracy and credibility of the algorithm. In this type of algorithm, the detection is done using external objects such as flags [9], or simply through the previous teaching of the system for the intended postures [8].

A posture emerges as well as the set of 2D or 3D locations of the joints, being possible, through these locations, to assess the position and displacement of all limbs. However, the problem that is common to these algorithms relates to critical body positions, such as lying, sitting, shrunken, sideways, etc. [8][31] and in situations that involving groups of people, where some parts of the body overlap [31]. In this type of positioning, the accuracy of these systems drops significantly.

All posture detection algorithms presented here are based on videos or a set of images collected from digital cameras. There are thus several types of cameras used with these algorithms. As described in the previous section, these cameras may differ in the type of image you can get. However, at present, the Kinect is the preferred device of most of these algorithms, since its own Software Development Kit (SDK) is one of the most used with respect to detection of the human skeleton. Kinect consists of an RGB camera, depth sensor, a three-axis accelerometer, a tilt motor and a microphone vector [32]. Thus, it is possible to obtain, with only one device, different types of images. Figure 8 shows the various components of a Kinect.

As mentioned previously, its software, Kinect Skeletal Tracking, is widely used in the detection of the human skeleton, which is carried out in three steps: In the first, an analysis, per pixel, is made to detect and classify body parts; In a second phase, a global centroid is found to define the joints of the body; finally, a mapping of the joints is done, so that they fit into a human skeleton, through data previously known about the human skeleton [34]. Figure 9 shows the steps explained above.

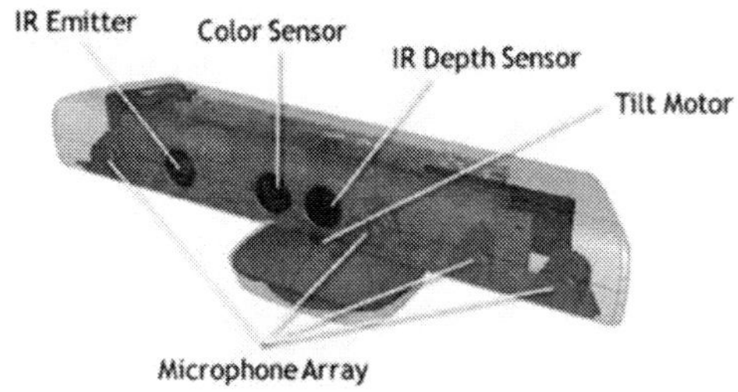

Figure 8. Hardware Configuration of a Kinect Device [33].

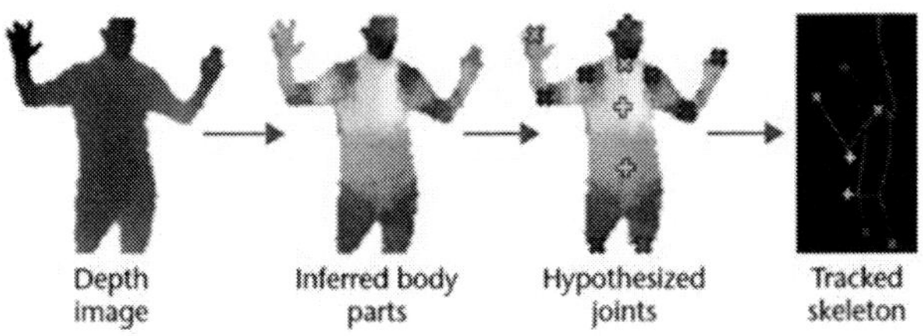

Figure 9. Detection steps of the Human Skeleton through the Kinect Skeletal Tracker Software [34].

In April 2017, the OpenPose library [35] was launched. Using only RGB images, this library can detect and extract 2D values from the main parts of the human body. In this library, it is possible to perform a detection of body, face and hands, in a total of 130 possible keypoints, 15 or 18 of them for body parts, 21 for each hand and 70 for the face.

For body detection, one of two data sets are used: Common Objects in Context (COCO) or MPII Human pose dataset, with people images, annotated with the human skeleton, still being used CMU Panoptic dataset during the development of the algorithm, since it contains about 65 sequences of approximately 5 hours and 30 minutes and 1.5 million 3D skeletons available. This detection is done through the approach described in [31], where a neural network is used to simultaneously predict confidence maps for body part detection (Figure 10b) and affinity fields for association of parts of the body (see Figure 10c), this process being done in several steps, so that this detection is credible.

Next, a set of two-part combinations is performed to associate the body parts, where a score is used to define which person belongs to the respective part and to make a correct connection of the parts in each person in the image/frame (Figure 10d). Through this approach, it is possible to detect several people in the image and define their posture. Finally, with a greedy inference algorithm, all parts are connected and the 2D points are defined for each of the joints (Figure 10e).

In [36][37], are presented approaches of detection multiple human skeletons in simple RGB images with efficient results, however fall short of [31].

Figure 10. Detection of the Human Skeleton through the OpenPose library [31].

V. Conclusion

In the presented state of the art, it is possible to recognize the lack of systems for the detection and classification of emotion systems from human body postures, as well as the difficulties associated to the already existing systems. However, there are many image sensor's alternatives, allowing to guide the system to several types of solutions, from skeleton detection based on distance image to the detection based on RGB image.

Finally, the Human Posture Detection algorithms research work [31] presents the algorithm with better results at all levels, which is possibly what will be used in the development of a system to allow the recognition of emotions from human body postures. This solution is not only optimal for its simplicity in terms of image, but also for its good results in detecting postures in groups of people. However, for this algorithm to work properly, it is necessary to have specific and expensive hardware, due to the parallel computing used and the GPU calculation performed.

References

[1] B. de Gelder, A. W. de Borst, and R. Watson, "The perception of emotion in body expressions," *Wiley Interdiscip. Rev. Cogn. Sci.*, vol. 6, no. 2, pp. 149–158, 2014.

[2] A. P. Atkinsonô, W. H. Dittrichô, A. J. Gemmell, and A. W. Young, "Emotion perception from dynamic and static body expressions in point-light and full-light displays," *Perception*, vol. 33, pp. 717–746, 2004.

[3] W. H. Dittrich, T. Troscianko, S. E. G. Lea, and D. Morgan, "Perception of Emotion from Dynamic Point-Light Displays Represented in Dance," *Perception*, vol. 25, no. 6, pp. 727–738, Jun. 1996.

[4] E. Babad, "Teaching and Nonverbal Behavior in the Classroom," in *International Handbook of Research on Teachers and Teaching*, Boston, MA: Springer US, 2009, pp. 817–827.

[5] H. A. Elfenbein, J. T. Polzer, and N. Ambady, "Team Emotion Recognition Accuracy and Team Performance," *Research on Emotion in Organizations*, vol. 3, pp. 87–119, 2007..

[6] F. Loi, J. G. Vaidya, and S. Paradiso, "Recognition of emotion from body language among patients with unipolar depression.," *Psychiatry Res.*, vol. 209, no. 1, pp. 40–9, Aug. 2013.

[7] T.-L. L. Le, M.-Q. Q. Nguyen, and T.-T.-M. T. M. Nguyen, "Human posture recognition using human skeleton provided by Kinect," *2013 Int. Conf. Comput. Manag. Telecommun.*, pp. 340–345, 2013.

[8] Z. Zhang, Y. Liu, A. Li, and M. Wang, "A Novel Method for User-Defined Human Posture Recognition Using Kinect," *Int. Congr. Image Signal Process.*, pp. 736–740, 2014.

[9] C. W. Chang, M. Da Nian, Y. F. Chen, C. H. Chi, and C. W. Tao, "Design of a Kinect Sensor Based Posture Recognition System," *2014 Tenth Int. Conf. Intell. Inf. Hiding Multimed. Signal Process.*, pp. 856–859, 2014.

[10] M. Raca and P. Dillenbourg, "Classroom Social Signal Analysis," *J. Learn. Anal.*, vol. 1, no. 3, pp. 176–178, 2014.

[11] C. Thurau and V. Hlavac, "Pose primitive based human action recognition in videos or still images," in *2008 IEEE Conference on Computer Vision and Pattern Recognition*, 2008, pp. 1–8.

[12] T. Zhao and R. Nevatia, "Tracking multiple humans in complex situations," *IEEE Trans. Pattern Anal. Mach. Intell.*, vol. 26, no. 9, pp. 1208–1221, Sep. 2004.

[13] R. Gonzalez and R. Woods, "Digital image processing and computer vision," *Comput. Vision, Graph. Image Process.*, vol. 49, no. 1, p. 122, Jan. 1990.

[14] M. Lyra, A. Ploussi, and A. Georgantzoglou, "MATLAB as a Tool in Nuclear Medicine Image Processing," *MATLAB - A Ubiquitous Tool Pract. Eng.*, no. October 2011, pp. 477–500, 2011.

[15] "Free How to Photoshop Tutorials, Videos & Lessons to learn Photoshop training | Photoshop Course." [Online]. Available: http://www.we-r-here.com/ps/tutorials/. [Retrived: Apr, 2018].

[16] G. Borenstein, *Making Things See: 3D Vision with Kinect, Processing, Arduino, and MakerBot*. 2012.

[17] "Naushadsblog." [Online]. Available: https://naushadsblog.wordpress.com/. [Retrived: Apr, 2018].

[18] N. Blanc, "CCD versus CMOS - has CCD imaging come to an end?," *Photogramm. Week 2001*, pp. 131–137, 2001.

[19] "Wikimedia Commons." [Online]. Available: https://commons.wikimedia.org/wiki/Main_Page. [Retrived: Apr, 2018].

[20] "Photography tips and tricks, Equipment, Photography News, Photography Books, Tutorial, and Lighting - OneSlidePhotography.com." [Online]. Available: http://oneslidephotography.com/. [Retrived: Apr, 2018].

[21] W. K. Wong, P. N. Tan, C. K. Loo, and W. S. Lim, "An effective surveillance system using thermal camera," *2009 Int. Conf. Signal Acquis. Process. ICSAP 2009*, pp. 13–17, 2009.

[22] "FLIR Systems | Thermal Imaging, Night Vision and Infrared Camera Systems." [Online]. Available: http://www.flir.eu/home/. [Retrived: Apr, 2018].

[23] T. Sosnowski, G. Bieszczad, and H. Madura, "Image Processing in Thermal Cameras," Springer, Cham, 2018, pp. 35–57.

[24] S. Hwang, J. Park, N. Kim, Y. Choi, and I. S. Kweon, "Multispectral pedestrian detection: Benchmark dataset and baseline," *Proc. IEEE Comput. Soc. Conf. Comput. Vis. Pattern Recognit.*, vol. 07–12–June, pp. 1037–1045, 2015.

[25] L.-J. Ferrato and K. W. Forsythe, "Comparing Hyperspectral and Multispectral Imagery for Land Classification of the

Lower Don River, Toronto," *J. Geogr. Geol.*, vol. 5, no. 1, pp. 92–107, 2013.

[26] "What is the difference between multispectral and hyperspectral imagery? - eXtension." [Online]. Available: http://articles.extension.org/pages/40073/what-is-the-difference-between-multispectral-and-hyperspectral-imagery. [Retrived: Apr, 2018].

[27] M. Aboras, H. Amasha, and I. Ibraheem, "Early detection of melanoma using multispectral imaging and artificial intelligence techniques Early detection of melanoma using multispectral imaging and artificial intelligence techniques," *Http://Www.Sciencepublishinggroup.Com*, vol. 3, no. November 2016, p. 29, 2015.

[28] S. B. Gokturk, H. Yalcin, and C. Bamji, "A time-of-flight depth sensor - System description, issues and solutions," *IEEE Comput. Soc. Conf. Comput. Vis. Pattern Recognit. Work.*, vol. 2004–Janua, no. January, 2004.

[29] P. Zanuttigh, C. D. Mutto, L. Minto, G. Marin, F. Dominio, and G. M. Cortelazzo, *Time-of-flight and structured light depth cameras: Technology and applications*. 2016.

[30] G. Calin and V. O. Roda, "Real-time disparity map extraction in a dual head stereo vision system," *Lat. Am. Appl. Res.*, vol. 37, no. 1, pp. 21–24, 2007.

[31] Z. Cao, T. Simon, S.-E. Wei, and Y. Sheikh, "Realtime Multi-person 2D Pose Estimation Using Part Affinity Fields," in *2017 IEEE Conference on Computer Vision and Pattern Recognition (CVPR)*, 2017, pp. 1302–1310.

[32] J. Han, L. Shao, D. Xu, and J. Shotton, "Enhanced Computer Vision With Microsoft Kinect Sensor: A Review," *IEEE Trans. Cybern.*, vol. 43, no. 5, pp. 1318–1334, Oct. 2013.

[33] "Kinect for Windows Sensor Components and Specifications." [Online]. Available: https://msdn.microsoft.com/en-us/library/jj131033.aspx. [Retrived: Apr, 2018].

[34] Z. Zhang, "Microsoft kinect sensor and its effect," *IEEE Multimed.*, vol. 19, no. 2, pp. 4–10, 2012.

[35] "OpenPose - Realtime Multiperson 2D Keypoint Detection from Video | Flintbox." [Online]. Available: https://cmu.flintbox.com/public/project/47343/. [Retrived: Apr, 2018].

[36] E. Insafutdinov, M. Andriluka, L. Pishchulin, S. Tang, E. Levinkov, B. Andres et al., "ArtTrack: Articulated Multi-person Tracking in the Wild," Dec. 2016.

[37] E. Insafutdinov, L. Pishchulin, B. Andres, M. Andriluka, and B. Schiele, "DeeperCut: A Deeper, Stronger, and Faster Multi-Person Pose Estimation Model," May 2016.

Human Body Posture Detection in Context: The Case of Teaching and Learning Environments

Rui Sacchetti, Tiago Teixeira,
Bruno Barbosa, António J. R. Neves
DETI / IEETA
University of Aveiro
3810-193 Aveiro, Portugal
Email: {ruisacchetti, tiagomaioteixeira, brunobarbosa, an}@ua.pt

Sandra C. Soares[1], Isabel D. Dimas[2]
[1]CINTESIS.UA, Departamento de Educação e Psicologia
[2]GOVCOPP/ESTGA
University of Aveiro
3810-193 Aveiro, Portugal
Email: {sandra.soares, idimas}@ua.pt

Abstract—**This paper describes an approach to detect and classify human posture in an individual context, more precisely in a classroom ambience. The posture can be divided into two main groups: "Confident/Not Confident", aiming for the teacher's posture evaluation, and "Interested/Not Interested", targeted for the students. We present some relevant concepts about these postures and how can they be effectively detected using the OpenPose library. The library returns the main key points of a human posture. Next, with TensorFlow, an open-source software library for machine learning, a deep learning algorithm has been developed and trained to classify a given posture. Lastly, the neural network is put to the test, classifying the human posture from a video input, labeling each frame. The experimental results presented in this paper confirm the effectiveness of the proposed approach.**

Keywords - Body language; Human Postures; Computer Vision; Digital Camera; Machine Learning.

I. INTRODUCTION

The advancement of computers and new technologies plays a key role in creating systems capable of better interacting with humans, which leads to an increasing number of systems that can analyze, classify and predict human behavior. Emotions are at the core of most of our overt behavior and plays a key role in socio-communicative interactions [1]. Facial expressions are exceptionally powerful nonverbal means to convey information about emotions [2] and have been the focus of an enormous amount of research for several decades.

More recently, studies have also been devoting a great deal of attention to human body postures, as they also express emotions, while adding important cues on behavioral intentions, which is critical for functional social interactions [3]. For instance, one may infer from Figure 1 that the person on the left seems to be more insecure/less confident than the person on the right.

Figure 1. Body language differences: insecure to the left and confident to the right [4].

The possibility to assess emotional and motivational dimensions in educational contexts, by means of machine learning techniques, was the main motivation of the current work. More specifically, within a classroom context, our goal was to test the feasibility of categorizing the speaker, either as confident or non-confident (see Figure 1), and the audience, with either interested or non-interested postures (as depicted in Figure 2). An effective two-way interaction between the audience and the speaker is deemed as crucial to engage the audience, which is why implementing non-invasive technological tools may provide meaningful improvements in educational settings.

Figure 2. Body language differences: Not Interested to the left and Interested to the right [5].

For the development of the proposed classifier, we used a state-of-the-art algorithm to calculate human postures: the OpenPose library [6][7]. Using a common RGB camera, it is possible to obtain the main key points of an individual on the scene. Then, after obtaining this information, we use a deep learning image classifier to train the neural network based on the TensorFlow library [8][9]. Later, we use the trained model to classify each frame of a given video, frame by frame, and label the posture of the individual. These procedures will be described in more detail in the next section. Finally, Section III presents the experimental results obtained, followed by a conclusion in Section IV.

II. PROPOSED APPROACH

This work was developed in well-defined gradual stages. In this section, we describe all the phases and technologies in detail. We begin with a brief description of the OpenPose library [6][7], how it was used to extract the key points, and the results obtained. Next, TensorFlow [8][9] machine learning library is described, as well as another library, Keras [10][11], which runs on top of TensorFlow and speeds up the development of deep learning models. Finally, we discuss how the generated models of deep learning were used to classify postures.

A. *OpenPose*

OpenPose is an open-source C++ library for detecting key points in human postures [6][7]. It was recently launched (2017) and, due to its potential, has been widely used for different purposes. In this work, in order to provide clear images about the human posture to the deep learning algorithm - that is, without noise or other elements that might compromise the efficiency of the algorithm - this library was used in order to obtain the best learning degree possible.

The library can detect 15 or 18 body key points, 21 key points per hand and 70 face key points. It can detect multiple individuals in one scene. However, with more than one person in the scene, the speed of detection is greatly reduced. It uses deep learning algorithms for better detection of the person's key points, using the Caffe framework [12].

It can be used with command-line demo, C ++ wrapper or C ++ API, and can receive as input images, videos, webcam images or IP cameras. The output of this library can be varied due to the number of flags that can be used, for example: include hands / face detection, just represent the key points (no background), save results to images (video frames), save various key points identified in files, etc. Consequently, this library and its features require a computer with large computational and parallel processing capabilities, as well as the installation of specific software. The computer used for the development and test of the proposed approach has the following characteristics:

Software:

- OpenCV (version 3.3.1);
- Caffe (version *custom*);
- CUDA (version 8.0);
- CuDNN (version 5.1).

Hardware:

- Nvidia 1080 TI (11GB *frame buffer*);
- 32Gb RAM;
- Intel i7 with 8 *cores*.

B. *OpenPose Results*

The first step was to build the database of "Confident" postures. For this, several videos were recorded in which the subject showed himself with a positive and strong attitude (see Figure 3). Quickly, and with the naked eye, it was possible to detect some characteristics about the key points that a posture of the type "Confident" returns, for example:

- The level of the shoulders forms a line perpendicular to the line of the spine.
- The subject's head is always with a degree of 90°, or greater, in relation to the spine.
- The arms are slightly further away from the body.

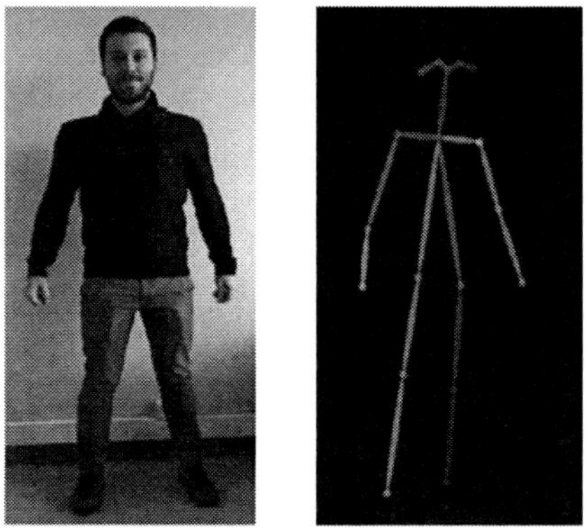

Figure 3. Schematic representation of key points provided by the OpenPose library.

Three individuals participated in the video samples, where each one recorded at least one video enhancing one of the 4 labels. In total, 1002 pictures tagged "Confident" were created. The same steps were repeated for a "Not Confident" posture where 1220 images were generated.

The next step was to construct the "Interested / Not Interested" type database. Several videos were recorded in which the subject enhanced positions that showed interest - like a more advanced posture, arms on the table or the head in the alignment of the body.

In this type of posture, the key points of the face and hands are quite expressive and quite strong indicators of the subject's posture. Hence, with the use of *--hand* and *--head* functionalities, the OpenPose returns the key points of the face and hands. The main goal was to obtain the best accuracy possible in the deep learning algorithm (see Figure 4).

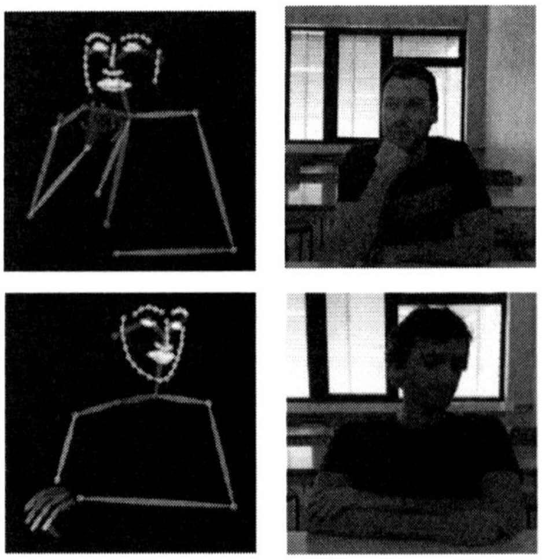

Figure 4. Representation of the key points: "Interested" above, "Not Interested" below.

In many generated frames, the position of the hands was not correctly determined. Therefore, to obtain the best possible precision in TensorFlow, images with only the -- head functionality were also extracted. In addition, it was decided to do another extraction but only with the basic (18) key points. This way, we studied 3 different cases for the type "Interested / Not Interested" posture: basic points, face and hands; basic points and face and only basic points. These results were stored in different databases. The objective was to study which case obtained the better precision values in the classification model. 1270 images labeled "Interested" and 1335 "Not Interested" images were obtained, for each type, one of the three cases that are about to be analyzed.

C. *TensorFlow*

TensorFlow is an open-source library for machine learning, more specifically for deep learning, developed by Google in 2015 [8][9]. This library was chosen because it allows the development of classifiers in an easier way than the other options considered, not compromising the quality of the results. The Keras library [10][11] was also used since it eases the workflow of creating a neural network.

Because our training set are digital images, we decided to use the neural network class, i.e., Convolutional Neural Network (CNN). The great advantage of using CNN is that it does not require pre-processing when compared to other image classification algorithms. Thus, it was possible to train a network without prior knowledge.

The TensorFlow library is available in Python and C++, whereas Keras is only available in Python. We developed our solution in Python programming language to do image classification.

The first step was to develop the classifier training software, obtaining the model that would classify the images. The biggest challenge was to find the most accurate parameters that would lead to good classifier accuracy. Better results were experimentally obtained when using 25 epochs and a batch size of 100 images.

When training the "Confident / Not Confident" model, the precision results obtained were about 93% for validation and 87% for the test phase, which were quite satisfactory. Figure 5 shows the performance of the classifier when trained.

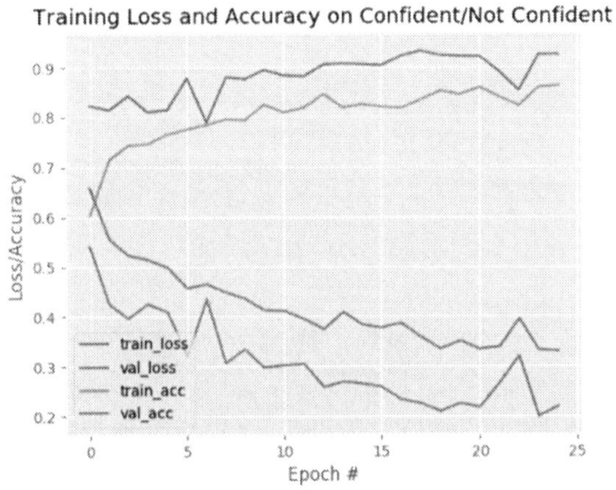

Figure 5. Results obtained when training the "Confident / Not Confident" classifier.

Then, the models of "Interested / Not Interested" were trained, for the three different cases, in search of the best results.

For the case with face and hands, the results are presented in Figure 6.

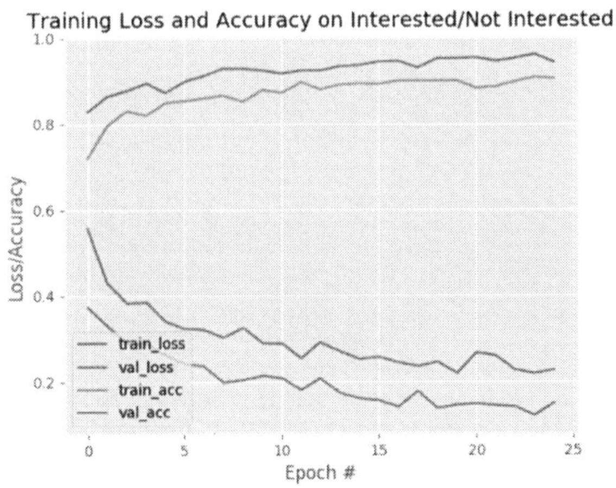

Figure 6. Results obtained when training the "Interested / Not Interested" classifier, for the head and hands case.

As shown in Figure 6, the precision values were steadily increasing, reaching a maximum validation value of 94%.

For the case that only considers the hands, the results obtained are presented in Figure 7.

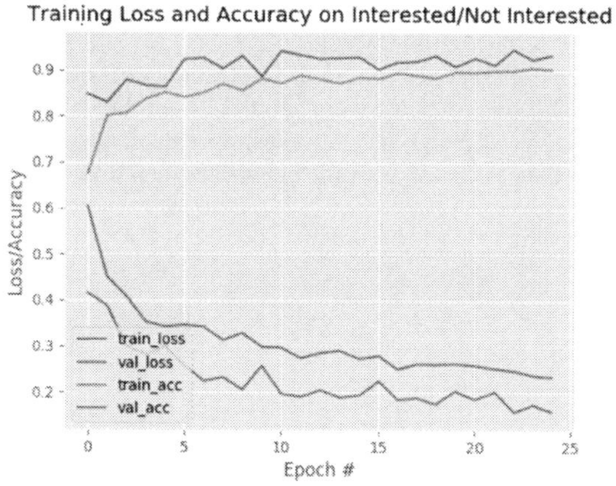

Figure 7. Results obtained when training the "Interested / Not Interested" classifier, for the hands only case.

Finally, for the database of images with only the basic points, the obtained results are presented in Figure 8.

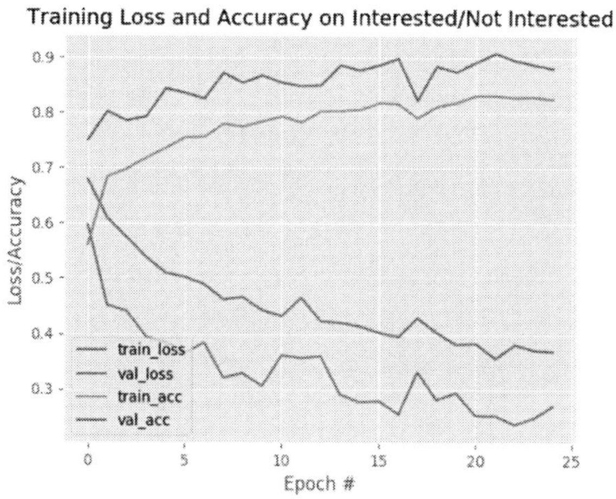

Figure 8. Results obtained when training the "Interested / Not Interested" classifier, for basic key points case.

It is possible to conclude that the model with face and hands obtained a better precision when compared with the others, obtaining a final precision of, approximately, 94%. Thus, this will be the model used for the classification phase.

The next step was to develop the classifier that allows us to obtain a label - "Confident / Not Confident" or "Interested/ Not Interested", with the input of a video and a previously trained model. This program is described in the following subsection.

D. Classifier

The developed classifier loads the classification model and opens the provided video. Then, frame by frame, the program questions the model and gets the posture label for that frame. The program returns the subject's posture classification, not only based on the current frame, but also with the previous frames.

Since the posture of an individual does not change frequently in a short period of time, and to eliminate false positives, we decided to create a filter that rules out false positives. First, we implemented a sliding window that follows the behavior of the subject in the last seconds. For the attribution of the final label, we considered the average of all postures analyzed in this time window. Then, to eliminate cases in which the model does not have a high degree of certainty about the analyzed frame, a threshold was created that only considered frames that contained a reliable degree of certainty. After some tests, we decided that the certainty percentage of a given label should be greater than 65% to be considered.

III. Experimental Results

To verify the effectiveness of the developed classifier for the "Confident / Not Confident" postures, a new video was recorded in which the subject initially presented himself with a more contracted posture. This video was not used during the training phase for the deep learning algorithm. Any assigned ratings were based on already existing databases.

Throughout the video, the subject changed his posture to a more expansive posture, reflecting a more confident attitude. Finally, it changed again to a more contracted posture. It was expected that the label assigned to each change was the correct one.

Observing the obtained output (see Figure 9, 10), we conclude that the developed classifier properly labeled the subject's posture. In the first seconds (2-3s), while the sliding window is not filled - and there are no certainties of about the posture - no label is assigned.

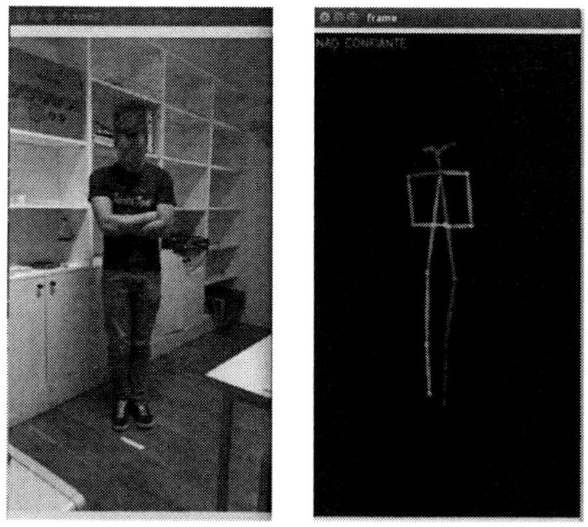

Figure 9. Results obtained for a "Not Confident" posture. In image to the right, the label assigned is at the upper left corner.

Figure 10. Results obtained for a "Confident" posture.

Due to decisions taken to prevent false positives, the classifier became quite robust. It took some testing to adjust the correct size of the sliding window so that the program did not become too strict and did not require a lot of time to obtain the posture confirmation. At the moment of this writing, the sliding window had a size of 25 frames.

To test the detection of sitting postures, i.e., "Interested / Not Interested", the same procedure as the previous classifier were followed. A video was recorded in which the subject enhanced a less interested posture (looks at the sides, up, has the head rested in one hand) (see Figure 11). As the video continued, the subject's posture changed to an "Interested" posture (see Figure 12) and after some time this posture was changed back to "Not Interested". In this test case, the classifier also labeled correctly the posture presented throughout the video.

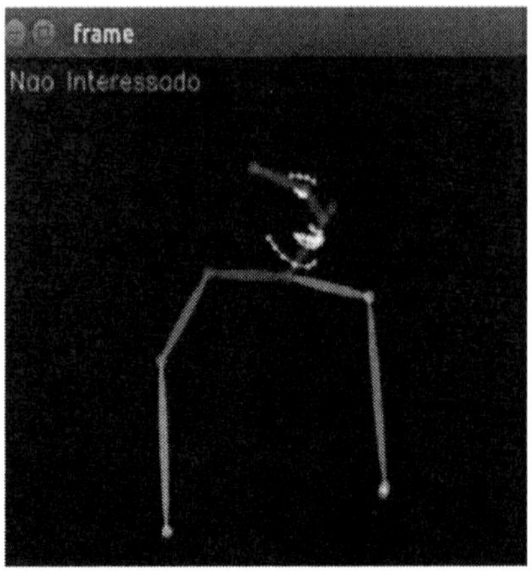

Figure 11. Results obtained for a "Not Interested" posture.

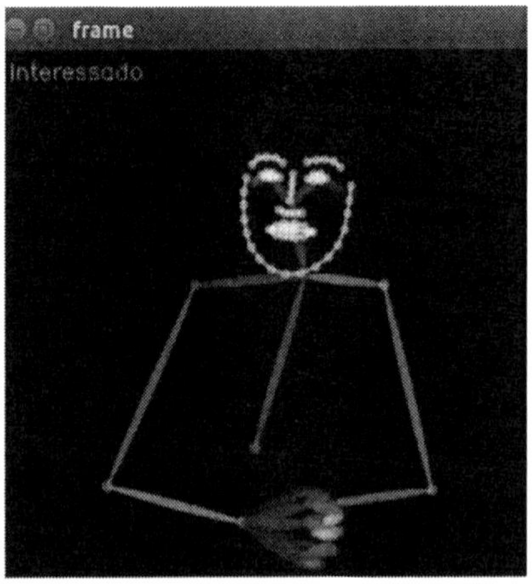

Figure 12. Results obtained for an "Interested" posture.

IV. Conclusion and Future Work

The comprehension of body language is an area that is in great development. However, despite the positive results obtained in this work, this is a very complex research domain, mostly because human emotions and their body language can't be classified in a binary way. It is not certain that a person who is speaking to an audience with a "bad" posture is less confident or less relaxed. There are other indicators that are important to this classification. This work can be used as a small increment to this theme. In future work, this type of posture classification can be used simultaneously with other parameters of a person's behavior (ex: voice placement, movement in space, etc.), in order to provide more effective emotional categorization from postures.

References

[1] N. H. Frijda, "The evolutionary emergence of what we call 'emotions,'" *Cogn. Emot.*, vol. 30, no. 4, pp. 609–620, May 2016.

[2] S. C. Soares, R. S. Maior, L. A. Isbell, C. Tomaz, and H. Nishijo, "Fast Detector/First Responder: Interactions between the Superior Colliculus-Pulvinar Pathway and Stimuli Relevant to Primates," *Front. Neurosci.*, vol. 11, p. 67, Feb. 2017.

[3] B. de Gelder, "Towards the neurobiology of emotional body language," *Nat. Rev. Neurosci.*, vol. 7, no. 3, pp. 242–249, Mar. 2006.

[4] "Body Language (1920×1080)." [Online]. Available: https://www.kcbi.org/wp-content/uploads/2017/07/body-language.jpg. [Retrieved: Apr, 2018].

[5] "Body language | Wondersbook." [Online]. Available: https://wondersbook.wordpress.com/2014/04/29/body-language/. [Retrieved: Apr, 2018].

[6] Z. Cao, T. Simon, S.-E. Wei, and Y. Sheikh, "Realtime Multi-person 2D Pose Estimation Using Part Affinity Fields," in *2017 IEEE Conference on Computer Vision and Pattern Recognition (CVPR)*, 2017, pp. 1302–1310.

[7] "CMU-Perceptual-Computing-Lab:OpenPose."[Online]. Available: https://github.com/CMU-Perceptual-Computing-Lab/openpose. [Retrieved: Apr, 2018].

[8] "TensorFlow." [Online]. Available: https://www.tensorflow.org/. [Retrieved: Apr, 2018].

[9] A. C. Schapiro, T. T. Rogers, N. I. Cordova, N. B. Turk-Browne, and M. M. Botvinick, "Neural representations of events arise from temporal community structure," *Nat. Neurosci.*, vol. 16, no. 4, pp. 486–492, Apr. 2013.

[10] "Keras Documentation." [Online]. Available: https://keras.io/. [Retrieved: Apr, 2018].

[11] "Keras: Deep Learning for humans."[Online]. Available: https://github.com/keras-team/keras. [Retrieved: Apr, 2018].

[12] N. Pittaras, F. Markatopoulou, V. Mezaris, and I. Patras, "Comparison of Fine-Tuning and Extension Strategies for Deep Convolutional Neural Networks," vol. 10132 LNCS, 2017, pp. 102–114.

Face Verification in Uncontrolled Environments for Access Control

Daniel Lopes*, Ricardo Ribeiro*, António J. R. Neves*
*Institute of Electronics and Informatics Engineering of Aveiro
University of Aveiro
3810-193 Aveiro, Portugal
Emails: {lopesdaniel, rfribeiro, an}@ua.pt

***Abstract*—In the past few years, face recognition has received great attention from both research and commercial communities. Areas such as access control using face verification is dominated by solutions developed by both the government and the industry. In this paper, a face verification system is presented using open source algorithms for access control of large scale events under unconstrained environments. From the type of camera calibration to the algorithms used for face detection and recognition, every stage has a proposed solution. Tests using the proposed system in the entrance of a building were made in order to test and compare each solution proposed.**

Keywords–Face Recognition; Face Detection; Access Control; Unconstrained Environment; Camera Calibration.

I. INTRODUCTION

As one of the most successful applications of image analysis and understanding, face recognition has recently received significant attention and many new techniques have been developed, especially during the past few years [1].

Most face recognition techniques have been developed to be implemented in biometric-based systems and appears to offer several advantages over other biometric methods. An important advantage appointed by [2] regarding these type of systems is the lack of interaction of the user. In a fingerprint system, for example, the user needs to place his finger in a designated area while in a face recognition system the face images can be acquired passively.

Areas related with security, surveillance, access control and multimedia management are some of the fields with an increase demand of face recognition systems. However, there are some levels of complexity regarding these systems as there are some stages that are needed to execute in order to achieve a system with a good performance. These stages are presented in Figure 1.

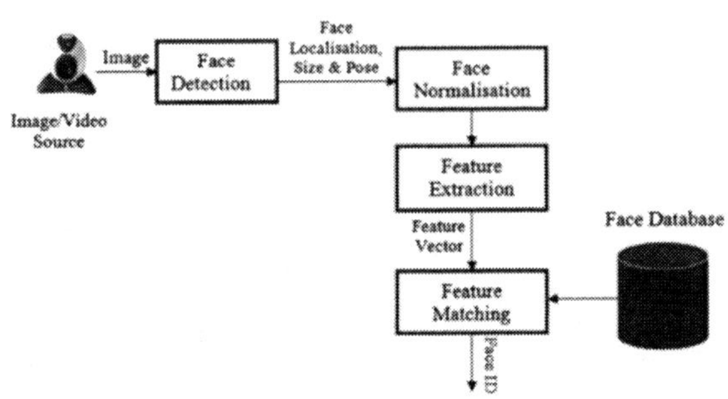

Figure 1. Configuration of a generic face recognition system. [3]

Within each stage, there are specific operations that can be added in order to achieve better performance results. Right on the start, the image acquisition is a crucial step where there is room for improvement. Later, the face detection and recognition can be performed by some specific algorithms, which are presented and studied. Finally, two of the face normalization (also known as preprocessing) algorithms, which are mentioned on state of the art articles are also analyzed for this specific project.

State of the art face recognition systems are dominated by industry and government using large scale datasets. There is a large accuracy gap between todays publicly available face recognition systems and the state of the art private face recognition systems [4]. However, this gap is closing up as it starts to appear better open source algorithms and datasets with more and better images.

Despite the success and high verification or recognition rates, there are still some challenges such as age, illumination and pose variations. Most of these systems work well under constrained conditions (i.e., scenarios in which at least a few of the factors contributing to the variability between face images are controlled), however the performance degrades rapidly when they are exposed to conditions where none of these factors are regulated [2].

In this paper, towards exploring this field, an access control solution for unconstrained environments is proposed using face recognition with open source algorithms. An introductory section is presented that provides a brief introduction to the face recognition system. In Section II, the proposed solution is described. Later in this section, the major problems for a face recognition system for unconstrained environments is explained. These problems are some of the challenges that will achieved and solved in this paper. Section III presents the hardware used in the system. The several implemented algorithms are described in Section IV. In Section V, there are provided experimental results showing the effectiveness of the proposed algorithms and the comparison between them. Finally, a summary of the work done, comparison of the different experiments, concluding remarks and the future work are featured in Section VI.

II. PROPOSED SOLUTION

The project consists in the creation of a face verification (1:1 match comparison) system using open source face recognition and detection algorithms. The main goal is the implementation of this system in large-scale events with access control, such as sport infrastructures. An example of people accessing a sports infrastructure is presented in Figure 2.

Figure 2. People accessing a sports infrastructure through turnstiles with manual security check. [5]

To access this type of events, it is usually through the acquisition of a ticket/ID card. In order to improve the access control, the ticket access/acquisition are complemented with a face verification system. In the project presented, at the time of the acquisition of the ticket, face images of the person are acquired and then sent to the database. When the person attempts to enter the infrastructure through a turnstile, another face images are acquired and compared with the images that were taken previously.

The environment of these places are usually outdoors, therefore the lighting conditions cannot be fully controlled. In the light of this, a camera parameters calibration is proposed for industrial cameras, which do not have a proper calibration for these type of environments. It was also added an artificial light, which helps to compensate the lack or the excess of light in the scene.

The privacy of people using face verification systems is an important factor in their implementation. The proposed system must be optional, only those who wish to participate, or be mandatory by law in the access control areas.

In order to build a face verification system with these characteristics, an important factor is taken into account: the unconstrained environment where the system is going to be implemented. In a recognition point of view, there will appear some problems related with these kind of environments that are mentioned below.

- **Head pose:** At the time of the image acquisition, the viewing direction of the subject may not be towards the camera. These face images may not be the best suitable for the face recognition system.
- **Face Image Resolution:** As the subject approaches the camera, which he/she is still a few meters from the turnstile, his/her face starts to be detected and tracked. However, if the person is still at some distance from the camera, the face images collected may not have enough resolution for the system.
- **Subject Motion:** It is taken into consideration that the subject is in movement and that may cause some blur in the images acquired.
- **Face Tracking:** It is crucial that there will be distinction between different subjects specially at the time of the ticket acquisition as if not done correctly, the face images of different subjects may end up in the same person database.
- **Non-Controlled Illumination:** This may be the most difficult challenge to overcome as the cameras may be installed in an outdoor environments and, therefore, different lightning conditions according to the time of the day and the meteorological circumstances.

All of these challenges are taken into account when choosing all of the hardware and software for this system.

III. HARDWARE

In this work, there are used two cameras: the *UI-1220LE-C* (Industrial Camera) and the *Logitech C310* (Webcam). The purpose of the use of these cameras is to compare the performance between them in this specific system as the Webcam does not allow to change its camera parameters such as exposure or gain. On the other hand, the industrial camera, despite not being the most suitable for this scenario, it provides a Software Development Kit (SDK) that enables the fully control of its different parameters. Additionally, as the industrial camera does not have a lens integrated, an 4,5mm lens with manually adjustable aperture is used.

Finally, an 168 LED illumination with adjustable intensity is used in order to compensate the excess or lack of illumination. It also eliminates any occlusion that may be caused by external lightning. Another major advantage is its use on darker scenarios where the camera will have a substantial exposure time. If the illumination is turned on, the scenario will have more light and the exposure needed will be lower thus, the blur captured by the person motion in the image will be far less than with no illumination.

IV. SOFTWARE

The software developed obeys to some specific steps, which are exposed on Figure 3. The head pose estimation block is not mentioned as it was explained in a previous work [6].

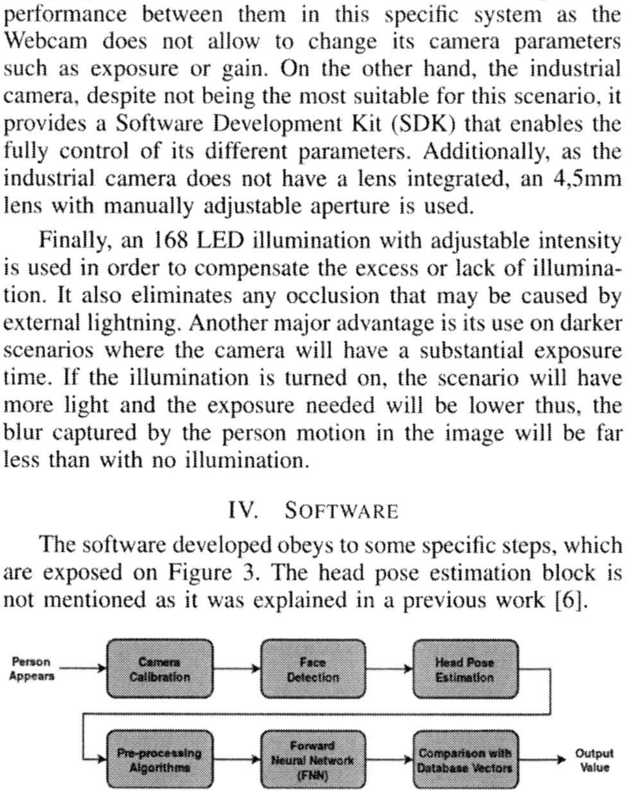

Figure 3. Main steps of the software developed.

A. *Proposed Calibration Method*

In this section, a different type of calibration is proposed in order to acquire the best digital image for the face verification system.

When using the automatic calibration of the parameters provided by the camera, which is done for the whole image, the Region of Interest (ROI) can be affected by the light intensity that there is in the background.

In order to get a ROI (in this case the face) with the best quality, a calibration focused on this ROI is created. The algorithm proposed is a mixture between the calibration of exposure and gain.

Since the system will be installed in an uncontrolled environment, an initial calibration is done using the auto parameters calibration provided by the camera in order to adapt to the light and environment conditions and to detect the first face for the use of the proposed calibration. At this point, a timer is set to wait a few seconds, so that the parameters of the camera have time to be internally changed and established. Exposure time, gain and white balance are the parameters changed automatically by the camera software.

Using the auto parameters calibration provided by the camera, the state of art algorithms used for face detection work well for this type of environment. However, this is not true for face recognition algorithms.

When a face is found, the auto parameter calibration is disabled and it continues to the next steps of the calibration.

1) Mean Sample Value: Introduced by [7] in order to create an autonomous setup of the most important parameters of digital cameras for robotic applications, the Mean Sample Value (MSV) is used to set the exposure and the gain of the camera. In this stage, the MSV is calculated through the gray level histogram of the face region with the equation described next.

$$MSV = \frac{\sum_{j=0}^{4}(j+1)x_j}{\sum_{j=0}^{4} x_j} \quad (1)$$

where x_j is the sum of the gray values in region j of the histogram (in the proposed approach the histogram is divided into five regions). A range of values is set for the MSV. If the calculated MSV is within that range, the camera parameters (gain and exposure) have acquired values.

This method has the main advantage that, if the same person appears on different parts of the day, the face images acquired will have very similar intensity values as the gain is calculated in order to have the same intensity values between a certain range.

2) White Pixel: This method addresses the situations when the face of a subject is partially directly exposed to sunlight, which causes that part of the face too bright. In order to solve this, if a region where the intensity pixels have the maximum intensity is found, the camera parameters values are decreased in order to reduce the brightness of that region of the face.

Figures 4a and 4b show the comparison between parameters calibration provided by the camera and the proposed calibration, respectively.

(a) (b)

Figure 4. Comparison between the automatic calibration and the proposed calibration.

B. Face Detection and Recognition Algorithms

As for algorithms, there were studied and implemented the following ones into the system. These algorithms are state of the art where the use of neural networks is prevalent, which are trying to close the gap between the performance of commercial and open source of face recognition solutions.

- **Face Detection:**
  - **Histogram of Oriented Gradients (HoG):** *Dlib*'s [8] implementation based on the algorithm presented in [9] that it is used for the face detection stage. Specially useful as it provides 68 face landmarks that are further used at the recognition step for pose estimation.
  - **Multi-task Cascaded Convolutional Networks [10]:** Deep cascaded multi-task framework which exploits the inherent correlation between detection and alignment to boost up their performance. It provides 5 major face landmarks instead of the 64 of *Dlib*. It is, however, more immune to light variations and occlusion.
- **Face Recognition**
  - **Deep Metric Learning (DML):** Implementation also provided by *Dlib* library where the network implemented was inspired in [11] that does the face verification. The model trained achieves an 99.38% in the benchmark Label Faces in the Wild (LFW) [12]. The input data of the network model for training were two datasets: the FaceScrub dataset [13] and the VGG dataset [14] with about 3 million faces in total.
  - **OpenFace [4]:** Face recognition with deep neural networks, which achieves an accuracy of about 92% on the LFW [12] benchmark. The training of the neural network was done with the CASIA-WebFace [15] and FaceScrub [13] containing about 500k images.
  - **DeepFace [14]:** Algorithm inspired in [16] and [17]. The CASIA-WebFace is used on training. In LFW benchmark, it achieves 99.2% of accuracy. The implementation used of this algorithm can be found in [18].

Noteworthy to mention that the *OpenCV*[19] library was used in the image processing and transformation.

C. Preprocessing techniques

1) Gamma Correction (GC): Gamma is a very important characteristic in any digital system. In the world of cameras, it defines the relationship between a numerical value of a pixel and its actual luminance. The GC enhances the local dynamic range of the image in dark or shadowed regions while compressing it in bright regions and at highlights [20]. However, this operation is still affected by some level of directional lightning as pointed by [21].

Given a certain gamma (γ), the relation between the gray-level image with gamma correction (I_g) and the original one (I) is given by $I_g = I^\gamma$.

Figure 5 presents three images acquired with different gamma values. As it possible to analyze, the image with a higher gamma is more uniform regarding light. The ambition then is that using an appropriate gamma value, the images acquired will not be as susceptible to lightning variations.

Figure 5. Images acquired with gamma of 1, 1.6 and 2 respectively.

2) Contrast Limited Adaptive Histogram Equalization (CLAHE): CLAHE is an adaption of Adaptive Histogram Equalization (AHE) [22] that was first introduced for contrast enhancement for both natural and non-visual images [23].

Figure 6 shows a face image before and after the application of the CLAHE.

(a) (b)

Figure 6. Face image without and with the application of CLAHE

This variation that introduced the limitation of contrast started began to be used in the face recognition field [24], which improved the contrast in face images.

Later, it began to realize its utility in the facial recognition field and a variation entitled of contrast limited adaptive histogram equalization (CLAHE) was started to be used. In this approach, the face image is divided into small blocks, also called tiles, and in each of these blocks the histogram equalization is applied. However, if any of the histograms calculated is above of the predefined contrast limit, the pixels are clipped and distributed uniformly to other bins before applying histogram equalization.

V. EXPERIMENTS

In order to test both software and hardware for the proposed system, an access control system was simulated with face verification at the entrance of the research unit, Institute of Electronics and Informatics Engineering of Aveiro (IEETA), where this work was developed. In these tests, the participation was optional, where the data retrieved from the people remained private.

The system consisted in both industrial and webcam cameras acquiring images with the artificial light, a laptop processing all the software and showing a interactive message to the people who would agree to try to participate in this study. A NFC card reader was also connected to the laptop that would help to register/compare the face images to the NFC number tag provided by the card that the users presented. Figure 7 presents the system set up.

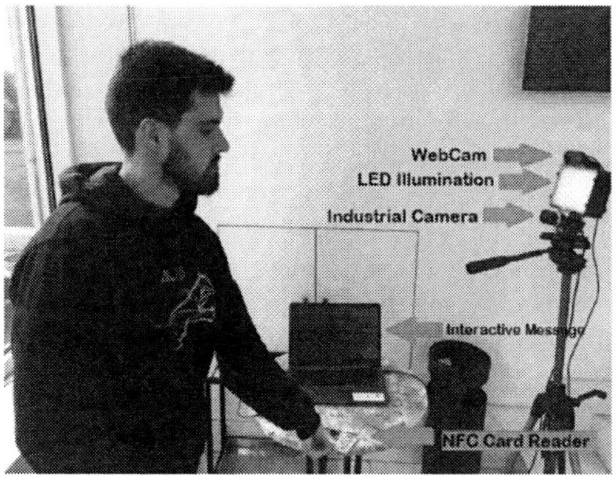

Figure 7. Set up of the system for the experimental results.

The tests were done in three distinct days where the first and the third day were sunny and the second one was cloudy. People who were entering the building were asked if they want to participate this study. If the person agreed, he/she posed himself/herself in front of the camera and the registration was done (if it was the first time that the person presented in front of the camera). As for the next times that the person appeared, the comparison between the face images made on registration and the ones acquired at the time was made. Figure 8 displays some of the face images acquired in the different days.

Figure 8. Example of face images acquired in different days with different meteorological conditions.

About 50 people (a big majority of Caucasians from both sexes) participated and all the participants entered the building at different times of the day, which caused different types of directions of lightning in the face images acquired.

The comparisons between the face images registered in the database and the ones acquired next gave output values, which were used to construct the Receiver Operating Characteristic (ROC) curves. In total, about 2500 comparisons values with both false and true positives were used to construct each curve presented next.

As for the processing times measured, the CPU *Intel Core i7 8550U* was used for the processing of all algorithms.

A. Camera Calibration

The first test analyzes the performance between the webcam with its automatic calibration and the industrial camera with the calibration proposed. Figure 9 presents the ROC curve as well the Area Under Curve (AUC) for this comparison.

The HoG and the Openface algorithms were used with both cameras for detection and recognition respectively.

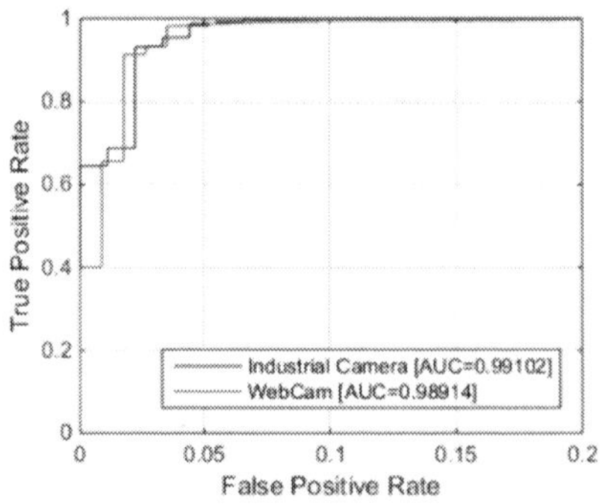

Figure 9. ROC curve comparing the WebCam and the Industrial Camera performance using the same algorithms.

B. Face Detection Performance

In this section, the performance of the HoG and MTCNN face detection algorithms is presented. It was first measured the time that it takes to detect faces in images with dimensions of 752×480 pixels. Posteriorly, the accuracy of each algorithm was tested using a video recorded at the time of the tests. Table I provides the results for both algorithms.

TABLE I. PROCESSING TIMES, TOTAL DETECTIONS AND FALSE POSITIVES FOR EACH FACE DETECTION ALGORITHM.

	HoG	MTCNN
Processing Time (ms)	60	121
Total Detections	592	740
False Positives	1	8

As it can be seen in the table above, both algorithms presented a good performance. The MTCNN algorithm detects more faces, since subjects in profile view are detected.

C. Face Recognition and Preprocessing Algorithms Performance

Results of the performance of the recognition algorithms tested with and without the preprocessing techniques of gamma correction and CLAHE are presented here. As all of the algorithms are based on neural networks it is important to point out that, despite using a specific preprocessing technique, the network was not retrained. The results might improve if the preprocessing technique is applied to the images that are used to train the neural network.

Figures 10, 11 and 12 present the algorithms performance using no preprocessing algorithms and comparing its results with the use of CLAHE and Gamma Correction.

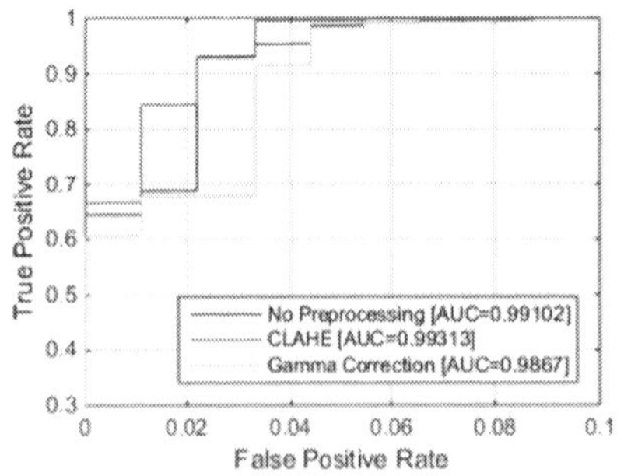

Figure 10. ROC curve presenting the performance of OpenFace using CLAHE, Gamma and no preprocessing technique.

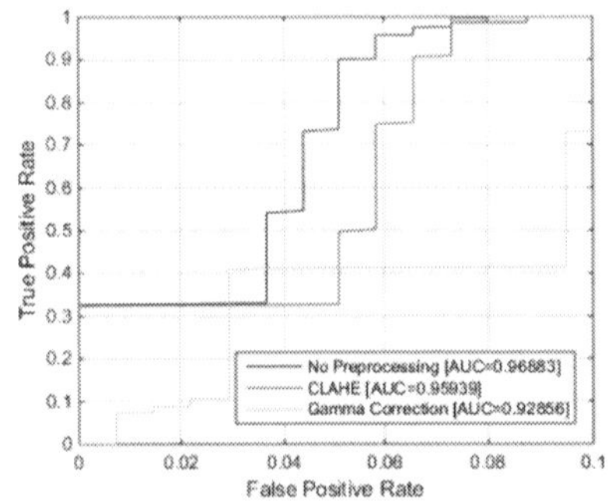

Figure 11. ROC curve presenting the performance of DML using CLAHE, Gamma and no preprocessing technique.

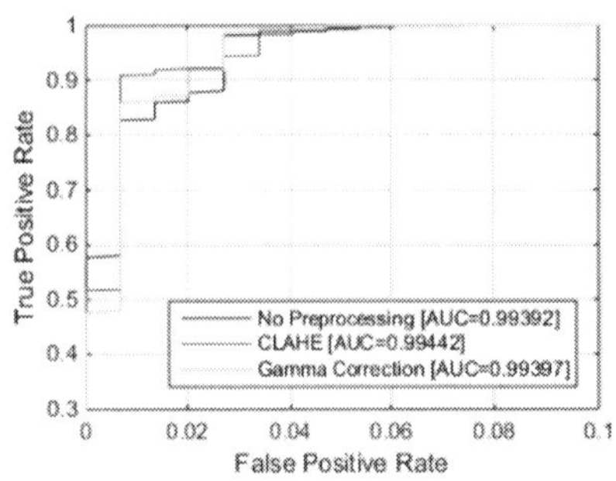

Figure 12. ROC curve presenting the performance of DeepFace using CLAHE, Gamma and no preprocessing technique.

Table II shows the processing time that takes each face image to forward pass the neural network of each algorithm.

TABLE II. PROCESSING TIMES FOR FORWARD PASS IN EACH NETWORK.

	OpenFace	DML	DeepFace
Forward Network Runtime (ms)	236	293	110

The DeepFace is the algorithm with a lower processing time for face recognition.

VI. CONCLUSIONS AND FUTURE WORK

This paper presented a face recognition set up system and studies, which software and hardware is the most appropriate to use under uncontrolled environments. Regarding the camera and its calibration, the industrial camera had a better performance comparing to the webcam as the calibration method presented focus on the best face image that can be acquired. As for software, both detection algorithms presented a good performance. Despite that, MTCNN seems to have the best performance as it detects faces where subject is in the profile view. In relation to the recognition and the preprocessing algorithms, CLAHE algorithm had a positive impact in all of the recognition algorithms as for the gamma correction had a negative impact. It is believed that the results would improve if the preprocessing technique was applied in all of the face images used for the training of the neural network. Unfortunately, the training of these type of neural networks took over a day using powerful GPUs, which are difficult to access. Despite that, the performance overall of the system was satisfactory and, from now on and according to the experiments, the best solution for these type of system is in the use of an industrial camera, MTCNN for face detection, CLAHE for preprocessing and DeepFace for the face verification stage.

The future work goes through the implementation of the system in larger scales where more people would use it. Until then, the train of new neural networks using the preprocessing techniques presented and the study of new alternatives for cameras are on the agenda.

ACKNOWLEDGMENT

This project is partially funded by National Funds through the FCT - Foundation for Science and Technology in the context of the project UID/CEC/00127/2013 and the company ExclusivKey, Lda.

REFERENCES

[1] W. Zhao, R. Chellappa, P. J. Phillips, and A. Rosenfeld, "Face recognition: A literature survey," ACM computing surveys (CSUR), vol. 35, no. 4, 2003, pp. 399–458.

[2] R. Jafri and H. R. Arabnia, "A survey of face recognition techniques." Jips, vol. 5, no. 2, 2009, pp. 41–68.

[3] M. Hassaballah and S. Aly, "Face recognition: challenges, achievements and future directions," IET Computer Vision, vol. 9, no. 4, 2015, pp. 614–626.

[4] B. Amos, B. Ludwiczuk, and M. Satyanarayanan, "Openface: A general-purpose face recognition library with mobile applications," CMU-CS-16-118, CMU School of Computer Science, Tech. Rep., 2016.

[5] P. TURNSTILES, "Wireless Battery-Powered Portable Turnstiles," URL: http://www.turnstile.com/Product/PWBP/portable_turnstiles_01.jpg [retrieved: April,2018].

[6] D. Lopes, "Pre-processing approaches to improve facial verification in unconstrained environments." RecPad - The 23th edition of the Portuguese Conference on Pattern Recognition, 2017.

[7] A. J. Neves, B. Cunha, A. J. Pinho, and I. Pinheiro, "Autonomous configuration of parameters in robotic digital cameras," in Iberian Conference on Pattern Recognition and Image Analysis. Springer, 2009, pp. 80–87.

[8] "Dlib library," http://dlib.net/ [retrieved: April,2018].

[9] N. Dalal and B. Triggs, "Histograms of oriented gradients for human detection," in Computer Vision and Pattern Recognition, 2005. CVPR 2005. IEEE Computer Society Conference on, vol. 1. IEEE, 2005, pp. 886–893.

[10] K. Zhang, Z. Zhang, Z. Li, and Y. Qiao, "Joint face detection and alignment using multitask cascaded convolutional networks," IEEE Signal Processing Letters, vol. 23, no. 10, 2016, pp. 1499–1503.

[11] K. He, X. Zhang, S. Ren, and J. Sun, "Deep residual learning for image recognition," in Proceedings of the IEEE conference on computer vision and pattern recognition, 2016, pp. 770–778.

[12] G. B. Huang, M. Ramesh, T. Berg, and E. Learned-Miller, "Labeled faces in the wild: A database for studying face recognition in unconstrained environments," University of Massachusetts, Amherst, Tech. Rep. 2, 2007.

[13] S. W. H. Ng, "A data-driven approach to cleaning large face datasets," 2014 IEEE International Conference on Image Processing, ICIP, 2014, pp. 343–347.

[14] O. M. Parkhi, A. Vedaldi, A. Zisserman et al., "Deep face recognition." in BMVC, vol. 1, no. 3, 2015, p. 6.

[15] D. Yi, Z. Lei, S. Liao, and S. Z. Li, "Learning face representation from scratch," arXiv preprint arXiv:1411.7923, 2014.

[16] F. Schroff, D. Kalenichenko, and J. Philbin, "Facenet: A unified embedding for face recognition and clustering," in Proceedings of the IEEE conference on computer vision and pattern recognition, 2015, pp. 815–823.

[17] Y. Wen, K. Zhang, Z. Li, and Y. Qiao, "A discriminative feature learning approach for deep face recognition," in European Conference on Computer Vision. Springer, 2016, pp. 499–515.

[18] "Real time deep face recognition," https://github.com/bearsprogrammer/real-time-deep-face-recognition [retrieved: April,2018].

[19] "Opencv (open source computer vision library)," https://opencv.org/ [retrieved: April,2018].

[20] B. Vinothkumar and P. Kumar, "Gamma correction technique based feature extraction for face recognition system," International Journal of Computational Intelligence and Informatics, vol. 3, no. 1, 2013, pp. 20–26.

[21] F. R. Al-Osaimi, M. Bennamoun, and A. Mian, "Illumination normalization for color face images," in International symposium on visual computing. Springer, 2006, pp. 90–101.

[22] K. Zuiderveld, "Contrast limited adaptive histogram equalization," Graphics gems, 1994, pp. 474–485.

[23] S. M. Pizer, E. P. Amburn, J. D. Austin, R. Cromartie, A. Geselowitz, T. Greer, B. ter Haar Romeny, J. B. Zimmerman, and K. Zuiderveld, "Adaptive histogram equalization and its variations," Computer vision, graphics, and image processing, vol. 39, no. 3, 1987, pp. 355–368.

[24] G. Benitez-Garcia, J. Olivares-Mercado, G. Aguilar-Torres, G. Sanchez-Perez, and H. Perez-Meana, "Face identification based on contrast limited adaptive histogram equalization (clahe)," in Proceedings of the International Conference on Image Processing, Computer Vision, and Pattern Recognition (IPCV). The Steering Committee of The World Congress in Computer Science, Computer Engineering and Applied Computing (WorldComp), 2011, p. 1.

International Academy, Research,
and Industry Association (IARIA)
412 Derby Way
Wilmington, DE 19810

ISBN 978-1-5108-6547-1

CURRAN ASSOCIATES INC.
proceedings
.com